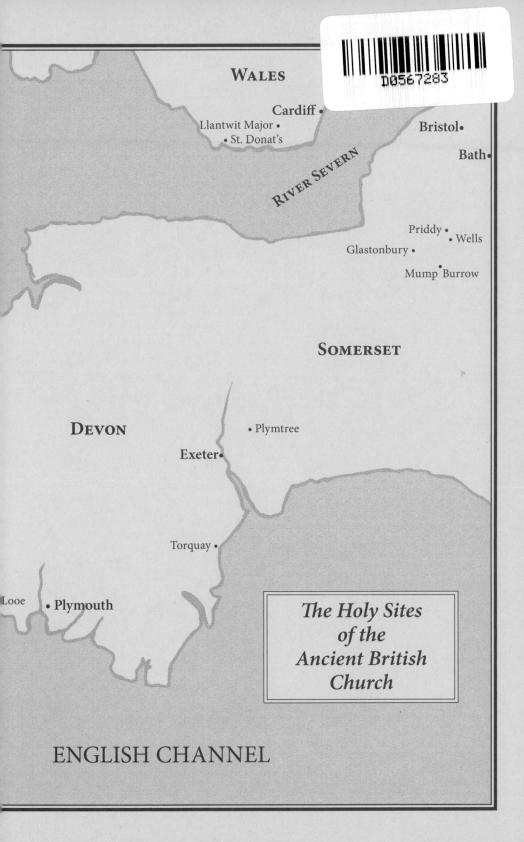

WALES

Cardiff •

Llantwit Major •
• St. Donat's

Bristol•

Bath•

RIVER SEVERN

Priddy •
• Wells

Glastonbury •

Mump • Burrow

SOMERSET

DEVON

• Plymtree

Exeter•

Torquay •

Looe

• Plymouth

*The Holy Sites
of the
Ancient British
Church*

ENGLISH CHANNEL

D0567283

for Mary and Ron Pierson
with fond love,
Bob Harvey
Feb. 9, 2010

TO THE ISLES AFAR OFF

ALSO BY ROBERT C. HARVEY

The Restless Heart:
Breaking the Cycle of Social Identity

TO THE ISLES AFAR OFF

HOLD FAST TILL I COME

Robert C. Harvey

†Robert C. Harvey

FOUR DIRECTIONS PRESS
RHINEBECK NEW YORK

Published in the United States by Four Directions Press,
P. O. Box 417, Rhinebeck, New York, 12572.
Four Directions Press website address: www.fourdirectionspress.com
Telephone: 800-556-6200

ISBN 978-0-9627659-1-9
LIBRARY OF CONGRESS CONTROL NUMBER 2009936798

Printed in the United States of America on acid free paper.
Published October 2009
FIRST EDITION

Title Page Illustration: Coat of Arms of Robert C. Harvey

Book and jacket design by Sean McCarthy

To my wife
Marguerite

ം Contents ം

❧ Chapter 1 ❧

Traditions of the Early British Church

And I will set a sign among them, and I will send those that
escape of them unto the nations, to Tarshish. . . to the isles
afar off, that have not heard my fame, neither have seen my
glory; and they shall declare my glory among the Gentiles.
Isaiah 66:19

If your knowledge of the English Church comes from the standard histories, you may have learned that Christianity reached Britain in AD 597 with St. Augustine of Canterbury and his band of forty monks. The assumption among other historians, at least in the books they write, is that Christianity reached Britain some time in the second or third centuries. They state that the Gospel *probably* crossed the Channel with Roman soldiers or traders from lands where it had already been proclaimed.

Yet the truth may be far different. There is a great mass of tradition that, because it falls short of enabling historians to make unqualified statements, has been altogether ignored. It is quite certain that, far from being one of the last nations to receive the Gospel, Britain was one of the first and that this is, at least in part due to the well known fact that a Celtic Church had already flourished there for many centuries. There is evidence, in fact, that Britain was the first nation in the world to become *officially* Christian; the Venerable Bede declares that this took place in AD 167. [1] during the reign of Good King Lucius, who was a great grandson of the warrior King Caradoc and himself the great grandfather of Constantine the Great. [2]

Whatever the date of Britain's Christian beginnings, and it is the intent of this book to posit that it was the earlier date, it is well known that in the Middle Ages the English bishops were given the first order of seating at every council because of the understanding that Britain had been the first Christian country. (France was second and Spain third; the oldest Christian state in the East was Armenia, dating from AD 309)

Although historians regard there as being little documentary proof, there are ancient traditions that several of the Lord's disciples visited Britain. One was St. Peter, who is said to have preached on the sites of Westminster Abbey and of St. Peter-upon-Cornhill, built a century later by King Lucius as London's oldest church. [3] St. Paul is supposed to have preached at Paul's Woods, west of Portsmouth Harbor, and to have founded the great Abbey at Bangor Iscoed in Wales, whose twentieth abbot in AD 395. was the heresiarch Pelagius.[4] An even earlier visitor was St. Peter's father-in-law, Aristobulus, who was one of the seventy elders referred to in Luke 10, and who is said to have been followed to Britain by his brother Barnabas. [5] Like the others, Barnabas returned, but Aristobulus met a martyr's death in the mountainous heart of Wales. Another martyr was Simon the Zealot who, after evangelizing in north Africa and Spain, is said to have gone to Britain and been crucified by the Romans at the village of Caistor in Lincolnshire.[6]

But what about documentary evidence of the Church itself? Fortunately, there is plenty. The third pope, Clement I, Irenaeus, Tertullian, Origen, Hilary, Athanasius, Chrysostom, Jerome, Augustine of Hippo—scholars and prelates of the early Church [7]—wrote of the Church in Britain. They spoke of it as doctrinally one with their own. For this Church's dating, the most important record is that of Gildas the Wise, a British monk and historian who died in AD 512. To him is attributed this statement, "We certainly know that Christ, the True Sun, afforded his light, the knowledge of His precepts, to our island in the last year of the reign of Tiberius Caesar." [8] That year, AD 37 matches what we are able to piece together of Joseph of Arimathea, Mary's uncle and protector, who was the first missionary and evangelist on the scene.

Our best proof of an early dating lies in first and second century missions *from* the British Church to the Continent which attest to its early foundation. Seven men are associated with those early missions. One was Beatus, [9] who is supposed to have been baptized in Britain by St. Barnabas, and who went to the heart of the Alpine region as Apostle to the Swiss, arriving no later than AD 96. The cavern in which he lived, taught and was buried is on the northeast edge of Lake Thun near Interlaken. Another missionary was Mansuetus,[10] an Irishman baptized in Britain who founded the Church in Lorraine and was martyred about AD 89 in the eastern Adriatic region of Illyria. A third was Marcellus, [11] the first Archbishop of Treves who died a martyr in AD 166. Already martyred there were the first three bishops of that city, Maternus, Eucharius and Valerius. [12] who came from Britain a hundred years earlier and gave their lives before the first century's ending. Maternus, however, died at Tongres in Belgium its first bishop. Ancient tradition is that he was the widow's son at Nain whom Jesus raised from the dead. The seventh was St. Cadwal, [13] who in AD 170 founded the Church at Tarentum in the south of Italy and whose shrine is there today.

With the citation from Gildas, we are able to assign the year AD 37 for the Church's start in Britain. As a body, this Church looks only to Joseph of Arimathea as its Apostle; there is no competing tradition, nor is there record of Joseph's ministering elsewhere. His arrival in AD 37 squares with what we know of the persecutions that took place in the Holy Land that year as well as with the tradition that he, along with Martha, Mary Magdalene, Lazarus and eleven other disciples landed as refugees in the south of France. [14] Some years thereafter, Jesus' disciple Philip is said to have consecrated Joseph as Apostle to the British, and his primacy in that regard has not been contested.[15] From an early date Joseph lived at Glastonbury as an anchorite in community with eleven others including his son. His date of death was AD July 27, 82.[16]

The Bible describes Joseph of Arimathea as a rich and just man, a disciple of Our Lord and a councilor, i.e. a member of the Sanhedrin. St. Jerome, who evidently knew some extra-biblical tradition, describes Joseph in his Latin (Vulgate) translation as "a noble decurion," a courtesy title, perhaps, for what he had been earlier. Joseph is chiefly remembered as an uncle of the Virgin Mary who in later life became her guardian.

As a young man he had been placed in charge of Rome's tin mines in Spain. When the tin lodes and stream tin played out, he became a private dealer in metals. As such he made regular trips to Britain, buying tin in Cornwall as well as lead, copper, silver and gold elsewhere in Britain and Ireland. [17] On one of these trips he is said to have taken Jesus, then a boy. Local tradition speaks of that visit in a dozen places in Cornwall, three places in Somerset and, as I understand it, one each in Gloucestershire and Ireland. I know nothing of the last two but have visited all the other places where these recollections are found. Each has its simple and particular narrative, and each has two things in common with the rest. First, the central character is not Jesus, who was a youthful stranger, but Joseph, who was already known in the places where they went. Second, each of the sites was one where, in the first century, metal was mined or shipped. In Cornwall it was tin. In Somerset it was lead and copper.

It is a matter of record that in the latter years of the first millennium BC most of the tin trade between Cornwall and the three Mediterranean lands was carried on by Jewish traders in Phoenician ships. Long before the Christian era, the outreach of Roman power had made it necessary for merchants and traders to protect their sources. Dealers such as Joseph shipped their ingots from Cornwall to Brittany and thence by pack animals across France to the Mediterranean ports[18] as an alternative to a sea passage through Gibraltar, where every cargo would have been subject to clearance by Roman authorities.

How much assurance can we have about these traditions, especially those concerning Jesus? For one thing, the local recollections are almost too simple to doubt, and there has been no attempt to capitalize upon them or to spin them into elaborate legend. For another, there are far-away traditions that match those held in Britain. Among the Maronite Christians in Galilee, for example, there is a tradition that as a young man Jesus signed on as shipwright with a vessel of Tyre, went to Britain on that ship and spent a winter because of inclement weather. [19] I have been told that similar traditions of Joseph and Jesus and the tin trade exist in France.

I should say that I *had* heard these traditions existed there. But I then wrote to many libraries and museums in that country for confirmation without success. I met a French priest in New York who had gone to seminary at Morlais in Brittany and had never heard of this tradition. This was baffling, since Morlais was the site on the Continent where those trans- shipments began, a record of which was made by the Greek historian Diodorus Siculus in 60 BC.

So I checked my map for alternatives. There is no easy route running across France from Brittany. There are no portages, and the Massif Central in the heart of France rises several thousand feet. But across the southwest of France there is a remarkably easy water route. It begins at the Garonne estuary on the west coast and leads past the modern cities of Bordeaux and Toulouse all the way to Carcassonne. Then comes a portage of fifty-five miles from the Garonne River to the Aude, with passage down the latter to the Mediterranean near Narbonne. At no point would travelers have been more than two hundred feet above sea level.

This, to be sure, was simply speculation, as I could find no documentation to support it. But in the late 1970s, I met Rene Lefebvre, an elderly Frenchman, who, as a Parisian boy in World War I, had been taken by his mother to live with her uncle, a priest in a tiny village not far from Agen on the River Garonne. There he learned of the tradition of Joseph and Jesus and the tin trade. He said it was common knowledge in the region of the Garonne that Joseph and Jesus had come that way.

Local tradition, in settings like these, can hardly be described as myth or legend. Yet our greater interest is in Glastonbury, which had been the heart of pre-Christian Druidism and would later be the heart of Celtic Christianity. Regarding Glastonbury—the famed Isle of

Avalon where King Arthur would one day die—we find a fascinating bit of correspondence between Augustine of Canterbury and Pope Gregory who sent him on his Saxon mission. In his letter to Gregory, Augustine confided, "In the western confines of Britain there is a certain royal island of large extent, surrounded by water, abounding in all the beauties of nature and necessaries of life. In it the first neophytes of Catholic Law, God beforehand acquainting them, found a Church constructed by no human art, but by the hands of Christ himself for the salvation of his people. The Almighty continues to watch over it as sacred to himself, and to Mary, the mother of God." [20]

As I have said, we already have a tradition of Jesus' having been at Glastonbury, but apart from Augustine's letter there is only one hint of his having built there. [21] However, there is such a tradition of Joseph, complete with dates. He is said to have constructed, at the foot of Glastonbury Tor, a rectangular church of wattles and thatch. It was built, moreover, to the same dimensions as the tabernacle in the Temple at Jerusalem. [22] In AD 620 the Bishop of York, St. Paulinus, was invited to visit the Glastonbury community and its Ealde Chirche, as the wattle structure by then was known, Not only did Paulinus come, [23] he brought funds to rebuild it. He had it built of wood, overlaying the wattle church inside and out and making a ceiling of lead. In later centuries that wooden church was overlaid with stone, yet the wattle church remained within—the holiest shrine in Britain. In 1184 all was destroyed by fire.

We now turn to British Christianity in an entirely different part of the world—Rome itself. In AD 51, eight years after Rome invaded Britain, its most dreaded adversary, Caradoc, the king of the Silures in South Wales and Pendragon of the British armies, was captured and brought with his family to the Imperial City. Because he had lived in Rome as a boyhood hostage, he knew many of its leaders and, during a pause in the triumphal procession, was taken to the Senate bound in chains to address the Senators and Emperor Claudius. [24] So flawless and impassioned was the address he gave (according to Tacitus, who records it) that Caradoc and his family were offered the freedom of the city provided two conditions were agreed to. During seven years' captivity as hostages they would make no attempt to escape and upon returning home would never again take up arms against Rome. Both conditions were accepted. The war, of course, would continue for many years beyond the seven. The Romans' clemency resulted from the fact that Caradoc had not been captured in battle but was betrayed into their hands by a relative whose own kingdom, without Caradoc's knowledge, was already in a client relationship with the Romans.

While in Rome, the royal family enjoyed great favor. Caradoc's daughter Gladys, was made an honorary daughter of Claudius Caesar, and henceforth called Claudia. She became known as the most beautiful woman in Rome and its most gracious hostess. In the second year of their exile she was married to a wealthy Roman Senator, Rufus Pudens, who had been military tribune of the occupying forces at Chichester and who, like Claudia and her family, had become Christian. When Caradoc and the others returned home in AD 58, Claudia and Pudens remained behind, as did her brother Linus, who, prior to Peter and Paul's martyrdom, had been consecrated Bishop of the Roman Church. In years to come Linus and Pudens would also die as martyrs as would Pudens' and Claudia's four children. Their palace on Mons Sacris, originally Pudens' family home and later known as the Palace of the Britons, was the first and oldest of Rome's churches. It still bears the name of Pudens' and Claudia's elder daughter, St. Pudentiana.

No one knows how or when the British royal family was converted. It may have been in response to the ministry of Joseph of Arimathea, to whom Caradoc's cousin Arviragus had given a large tract of land at Glastonbury. It may have been due to Aristobulus, whose ministry was chiefly in Wales and who successfully evangelized Caradoc's own people. If, on the other hand, the royals' conversion took place at Rome, it would have been at the hands of St. Paul, who was Pudens' half brother and whose mother lived there with her younger son. Paul's relationship with Pudens is confirmed in Romans 16:13 and with Claudia and Linus in 2 Tim. 4:21.

Whatever the facts of the British royal family's conversion, there can be no question that nearly two hundred years before the Empire became officially Christian there were royal British converts as leaders of the Church in Rome. Nor can there be doubt that as hostages enjoying the Emperor's protection, they and their in-laws would have been a persecuted faith's most resourceful and dependable sponsors. When Paul wrote from Rome to the Philippians 4:22, "All the saints salute you, chiefly they of Caesar's household," he could be referring to none other than the British royal family.

It has been thought by many that one reason for the early conversion of Britain was a similarity of doctrine between Druidism and Christianity. An early bishop of Syria tells us that Druids as well as Christians believed in a Triune God, in a vicarious atonement, and in the immortality of the soul. Moreover, we are told that the third person of the Druid godhead would be an incarnate savior yet to come whose name would be Jesus! If true, the Druid converts could look on their intuited religion as a God-given preparation for the Revealed and True.

It is also likely that the rapid growth of the British Church came about because the country was evangelized from the top down rather than from the bottom up. The influence of the conversion–in captivity (or even earlier)–of the family of Caradoc, the country's greatest hero, would have been enormous. Before long conversion would accelerate still further by the fact that British princes and princesses had been among the national Church's earliest martyrs. Whatever the reasons for its conversion, in little more than a century after Caradoc's return, the whole land was Christian.

What meaning can this have for descendants of these early Celts today–whether English churchmen, Irish Catholics or Bretons, Scottish Presbyterians, Welsh and Cornish Methodists or English-speaking people around the globe? All are descended from these Celtic Christians, whether by blood or culture. In the face of increasing secularity, there is urgent need to learn anew the meaning of right and good and true. These values must be absolute in more than theory as they have always been essential elements in the teaching and understanding of the Church of which we speak. (As they had been to the pre-Christian Druids, for example, whose motto was "The Truth against the world.")

Let us reflect on a few things from that ancient past that are worthy of study and emulation. One is the strategic value of the monastic form of life in converting pagan violence to peaceful pursuits and in transforming hatred, lust, and greed to a righteous life. Although it is generally believed that Christian monasticism began with St. Anthony in fourth century Egypt, it actually began earlier in Britain with the return from Rome of Caradoc's second daughter, Eurgain (or Eigen). Hers was an adaptation of the monasticism that had been practiced among the Druids of Britain and Ireland long before the Christian era. With St. Eurgain as its patroness, the Welsh Church adopted the monastic Druid format for much of its early life and work. It is said that by the second century there were great choirs at the three former centers of Druidic worship: Glastonbury in Somerset, Ambresbury in Wilshire and Caerleon in Gwent. Each center had 1,200 monks who were divided into hourly watches, singing the Divine Office twenty-four hours a day. This monastic offering–the unending chanting of the Psalter–was intended to be the earthly Church's antiphonal echo of the praises offered by the heavenly choir. The Welsh participation in this worship seems to have originated in St. Eurgain's village, later called Llan Illtyd. After her death it was transferred to Caerleon as the center of Welsh Christianity. Today her village, now called Llantwit Major, is twenty-seven miles from Caerleon and two miles from her father Caradoc's seaside home at what is now St. Donat's.

It was because of that piety native to the Celts that early Britain was called the Isle of Saints. The missionary dynamic that also flourished there had been demonstrated in the Continental missions I described as belonging to the British Church's earliest years. This bright light would be dimmed in later years when the Roman legions were withdrawn, for with them went the cream of Britain's stalwart men–unable to help at time of crisis and most of them never to return. Those were the years when Angles, Jutes and Saxons crossed the Channel, pushing Brits and Celts into the crannies of Cornwall and Wales to the West and across the Channel to Brittany in the south. Yet during the century and a half of Saxon invasion, the British continued to preach the Gospel to other Celts. Ireland and Scotland were won to Christ through such men as Ninian, Patrick, David, Finnian, Columba and Aidan. Following the Synod of Whitby, when the monastic piety of the Celtic Church was fused with the pragmatic disciplines of Rome, the light burned so brightly that all of Northern Europe was won to Christ.

Celtic Christianity was and always has been mystical. It identified itself from the start with catholic Christianity on the Continent. Yet its emphasis was more on the mystical than the sacramental element of religion. There were good reasons for this. The Druids had made a point of minimizing the use of human or animal figures, whether in worship or art. Based on artifacts discovered in digs, the only figures ever found in Britain are thought to have been used by legionnaires in the worship of Mithra, Isis or other idol-gods. It may also be that the British Church's emphasis on the mystical was due to an attachment to the Word. Bede himself, a Saxon, clearly singles out the Britons as a "People of the Book." The mystique may also be linked with an individualism that appears to have been innate with the Celts. It is notable that every part of Europe that broke with Rome at the Reformation had first received the Gospel from the British and/or the Irish Church. Among the continental countries the linkage in demarcation extends virtually to county and village lines.

Much of what has been related here as historic hangs on the simplest of local traditions. In Cornwall, for example, the places claiming a visit from Joseph and Jesus describe it in no more than a sentence or two. At St. Just-in-Roseland it is said they arrived in a boat, anchored in St. Just's pool and came ashore. At Falmouth it is recalled that they landed at the Strand, crossed a brook and climbed up Smithick Hill. In Priddy in Somerset it is said only that Jesus came to Priddy and walked across the green. Yet for centuries that event has been held as absolutely true; when one wants to take an oath he says, "As sure as Christ was at Priddy," or "As sure as Jesus walked on Priddy's earth."

Concerning what may be documented from the past, there is no end of possibilities. As stated earlier, the standard histories fail to say more of the British Church than that it was on hand more than half a millennium before the advent of the Saxon (i.e. the English) Church. But there are good reasons for the absence of written information. The

Celts used oral teaching to convey their sacred lore on the theory that to do so in writing invited desecration. Their later history proved the danger to be not only desecration but also near-total loss. Scholarly writings during the later Saxon years–the fifth, sixth and seventh centuries–resulted in the creation of fine and useful libraries. But the years of Danish invasion and Viking raids–the eighth, ninth and tenth centuries–saw not only death and destruction, but also the loss of most of the Church's written knowledge of the past. The one way to preserve their remaining manuscripts seemed to be to send them to Rome for safekeeping. And there they were sent–English writings as well as those in Celtic tongues. And there, in the Vatican Library, they remain today. Very few, if any, have been translated or catalogued.

Some years ago I had a brief correspondence with Margaret Deanesly, a retired professor of history at the University of London and the leading authority on the pre-Norman Church. I had asked Miss Deanesly to give me an appraisal of writings I had gathered on the early Celtic Church, which she did. She then added that the opportunities for research in this field were limited for two almost insurmountable reasons. One was the difficulty of ascertaining what was actually in the Vatican Library, for despite its availability, by far the larger part has never been translated or catalogued. The other reason related to manuscripts that may have originated in Britain or Ireland, or that did at the time of our correspondence thirty years ago. Miss Deanesly pointed out that there were no first class historical scholars familiar with the ancient Celtic tongues, and the same may be true today. Yet we do have a great deal of traditional material on hand, even if it fails to meet the standards by which history is ascertained. I would hope that by making known what we *do* have on those early years, we may delight the layman and stimulate the curiosity and imagination of our scholars.

We may also be hindered by one other factor. Traditional British reserve may well have inhibited the sharing of such knowledge. Those who "know and care" may be few in number but if they care deeply they may, by character, tend to guard their information as a precious secret. While on the north coast of Cornwall, I looked for an ancient well called the Jesus Well. It is near the estuary of the Camel River, which provides one of the few anchorages on that whole rocky coast. I asked directions of several people and was led to the one woman who might know its location. It turned out to be in the middle of a pasture, protected by a small stone springhouse. The spring that may once have served Our Lord, and from which he may have carried water to his nearby vessel, is now used by lowly cattle.

As a more dramatic illustration, when I visited Priddy—a tiny village of no more than a dozen houses—I found behind the hilltop church a parish school whose children were at recess. The schoolmistress, who was standing among them, turned out to be a devout and enthusiastic churchwoman. Yet when asked if she had heard the local tradition, she said she had not, nor, in fact, had she even heard the tradition that Christ had come to Britain. But she quickly volunteered that she had only lived in Priddy five years and offered to ask the other teacher, who had lived there her whole life. She disappeared into the schoolhouse. Presently she returned, bubbling with excitement. "Yes, she knows all about it. And it's true. There's a tradition that has come down from the time of Christ. She says if you'll go down to the village and call at the house next to the store you will find Mr. Bertie Weeks. He can tell you more than anyone in Priddy." And he did.

British reticence is curious. More than anything else, it leads me to think these traditions are probably true. (If, for example, the Jesus Well were in Spain or Italy it could be the site of a cathedral.) And yet, must we light a bonfire under those who know something about Jesus and are not eager to make it known?

Even the national hymn of the English recalls the visit of Jesus I have described. Yet if you ask the average Englishman if he's heard of Christ's visits to Britain, he'll say he has not. Though he knows the national hymn, he will not have made the connection, despite the clear words

That hymn, written by William Blake in 1803, is not above criticism, since it reflects his own ambivalent feelings about the Christian faith. He was deeply attached to the Jesus of Scripture but harbored a keen resentment of God the Father as Lawgiver and Supreme Authority. Blake's contempt for the Industrial Revolution depicts him as a kind of proto-Marxist more than a dozen years before the author of *Das Kapital* was born. Yet Blake's hymn has a quality of patriotism that accepts inequities and may well serve the purpose of the best of national symbols by leading a self-questioning people to a future that, more truly than the present, reflects what was always intrinsic to life and never far from sight. Here is the hymn as Blake wrote it and as the English love to sing it:

> *And did those feet in ancient time*
> *Walk upon England's mountains green?*
> *And was the holy Lamb of God*
> *On England's pleasant pastures seen?*
> *And did the countenance divine*
> *Shine forth upon our clouded hills?*
> *And was Jerusalem builded here*
> *Among those dark Satanic mills?*
>
> *Bring me my bow of burnished gold*
> *Bring me my arrows of desire!*
> *Bring me my spear! O clouds, unfold!*
> *Bring me my chariot of fire!*
> *I shall not cease from mental fight,*
> *Nor shall my sword sleep in my hand*
> *Till we have built Jerusalem*
> *In England's green and pleasant land.*

❧ Chapter 2 ❧

Reflections on the Biblical World

A recent finding of Earth scientists will be of interest to students of Holy Writ, whether Christian, Jew or Muslim; it involves the Earth's climate in the days before the Great Deluge. Between the Ice Ages and the time of Noah's Flood, the Earth displayed a kind of greenhouse effect. It was shrouded in mist with little if any wind and it appears not to have rained during those years. The differences in temperature, whether seasonal or that between poles and equator, were little more than a few degrees. The land areas were semi-tropical and lush. The Sahara for example, now a wasteland, was the Mediterranean area's garden spot, and remained that until early in the Christian era.

When the Bible speaks of the Flood as having been caused by the sins of men, scientists have little to say; it is beyond their disciplines' capacities to prove or be concerned with. As indicated, they do confirm the Bible's reference to the antediluvian world (Genesis 2:5,6), "The Lord God had not caused it to rain upon the earth.... But there went up a mist from the earth and watered the whole face of the ground." We can only speculate as to how the writer of that passage of Scripture obtained that information.

Earth science is also in agreement with Scripture as to the historic fact and physical origins of the Great Deluge. On every continent evidence of a Flood is so enormous that high mountains give indications of having been inundated. Sedimentary deposits in the lowlands show not only a one-year deposit of epic depth, but of animals and fish that were vital and active at the moment of their demise; their fossils are reminiscent of racehorses in a photo finish. It may also be that on the Deluge's first day whole species came to an end for having missed the Ark. In what is now Siberia one of several mammoths found in recent decades stood in a flowering meadow feeding on succulent shoots. With no warning came a fall of snow and hail so dense that the animal's hip snapped under the shock. Yet it could not fall; it was already buried and, in a few moments, quick-frozen in what, from that day to this, has been permafrost. When the mammoth's body was discovered and examined its flesh was still edible. In its stomach were buttercups, in bloom and undigested.

Our present weather patterns are presumed to have been initiated on that day. Yet no discomfort we could experience comes close to what happened at that time. Where did the waters come from that caused the Deluge? A flood that could leave an Ark stranded near the top of Mount Ararat was far beyond the capacity of Earth's surface waters and oceans to provide. A global-wide flood as this was, more than three miles deep and covering mountains as high as Ararat, would require more than twice as much water as Earth's oceans have held before or since.

It is likely that a fault in the ocean's bottom tore open along what we call the Mid-Atlantic Ridge. Along this area the Americas had, for eons, been floating away from the land-mass of Africa and Eurasia. The rift thus opened may have been thousands of miles in length, for the Ridge extends from the Antarctic to Iceland. Whatever and wherever the fracture, billions of tons of steam burst into the world's upper atmosphere and surrounding space. Depending upon latitude and distance of propulsion, it could have fallen as water, snow or ice. The Bible says that on that day (Genesis 7:11) "all the *fountains of the great deep* were broken up and the windows of the heaven were opened."

The Deluge continued for forty days. Another eleven months were required for the waters to drain back beneath the Earth's crust from whence it came—allowing the oceans to return to their former levels. Because Ararat's summit is nearly 17,000 feet above sea level, and because the Ark was not beached till nearly four months after the Flood had begun abating, it's likely that the Deluge had crested some 19,000 feet above sea level. If the flooding that followed the break had come entirely from rainfall—with no condensation of steam to water while issuing from Earth's core, the average rainfall during those forty days would have been nearly twenty feet per hour!* With such force of rainfall and runoff, there could only have been one way in which—apart from the Ark itself—men and beasts could have survived. They could have been saved if, before the Deluge began, they had taken shelter in caves near the summits of mountains having an elevation in excess of nineteen thousand feet. There are one such mountain in Africa, three in North America and none in Europe; there are, however, dozens in South America and Asia. While Noah may have been the only man to whom God gave time to prepare an Ark, it is possible that there were men in other continents who, whether by intuition or forethought, had taken the necessary steps to survive. Being aware of how sensitive the higher animals are to portents of seismic danger, we can accept that the beasts may have been better equipped than humans to do the right thing and perhaps to have demonstrated to man their fright and the direction of their flight. While Genesis 7:23 seems to contradict the possibility of others' survival, it has to be the reason why indigenous peoples worldwide have similar traditions of that Flood. Even as legend, such diverse witnesses point more acceptably to historic fact than to myth.

Another case may be made for this possibility. The length of time it would have taken for descendants of Noah's sons, Shem, Ham and Japheth to become, respectively, Semitic, black and Eurasian, seems

*This is an outside figure. It assumes that all the steam bursting through the fault reached the stratosphere, condensed and fell as water. Initially this may have been largely true. But as the pressure from beneath was reduced, increasing amounts would have condensed directly to sea water. Meanwhile a boiling Atlantic would give off steam, thus adding to the rainfall. After the rain ceased the flooding also ceased, and the waters began their withdrawal.

far too brief for Genesis' claim (10:32) to be valid. Consider that in Solomon's time the differences in coloration of blacks, whites and orientals were virtually the same as today. Since Solomon lived 3,000 years ago it is hard to believe such transformation could have taken place during the 1,350 years between Noah and Solomon. Accordingly we may not only suppose, but fully accept, that the Flood traditions among other peoples are genuinely historic. What is also suggested is that, though these others may have had no supernatural revelation from God, the Almighty may have revealed the danger they were in by such natural means as imagination, intuition and the animals' example, with the result that others besides Noah's family are likely to have survived the Flood.

What about the Ark? This much can be said: Regardless of what one may believe about the Deluge or about God himself, the structure near the top of Mount Ararat is unquestionably Noah's Ark. It has always been known to Armenian Christians and Kurdish Muslims who live within sight of the mountain. We have record of people climbing Ararat in search of the Ark in almost every century of the past three millenia. It has been seen, approached, photographed, climbed over and poked through by many people in the century just past; all have been in agreement as to facts. The vessel's interior contains the three decks, pens and cages installed in response to God's specifications. Its gopherwood has a strength and durability like no other ever known. The carbon dating of fragments taken from the vessel are fairly uniform, averaging 2529 BC. Since the Ark was built well in advance of the Deluge, its carbon datings compare favorably with the Flood's biblical dating of 2350 BC published in 1660 by Archbishop Usshur, and with the dating of 2344 BC, found by 20th Century scholars when the Great Pyramid's inner sanctum revealed its secrets.

Is it possible the vessel on Mount Ararat is a hoax? Not only has it been visited over thousands of years and by many people, its dimensions, measured on several occasions, appear to jibe with those of Scripture. The Ark's underwater design is not that of a vessel meant to be propelled. It is box–shaped: 450 feet long, 75 feet wide and 45 feet high. In Genesis 7:20 there is an easily misconstrued figure of fifteen cubits. Its purpose is not to tell us the measure of rainfall or how high the mountains were over which the Ark floated, but how much water it displaced while afloat. That displacement measured 22 ½ feet. If we multiply the Ark's length by its width and again by the depth of water thus displaced we arrive at the cubic content from which we derive its weight: more than 24,000 tons with passengers and provisions on board! The Ark, when finally afloat, was four times heavier than the 19th century's largest wooden ship, the Great Western. Considering that its weight was more than two thirds that of the World War II battleship North Carolina, we can be sure it was not built upon, or hoisted up to, the 14,000 foot level of Mount Ararat. Except for a hundred foot section that broke off as a result of a violent earthquake in June, 1840, sliding 2,000 feet lower and lodging at the edge of a deep chasm formed at that time, the Ark remains where it grounded so long ago.

What can such information mean to people of today? The message is the same as always—a proclamation of important and ever-relevant facts. With God as Architect, the Ark as Artifact and Noah as key man to the world's survival, we can be convinced that the God who made us is as essential to our lives as we are to the fulfilling of his purpose and design. The story of Noah's Ark is more than quaint narrative; it is solid history. It reminds us that in all times, places and circumstances, God is attentive to our needs, responding to the prayers of those who seek to do his will and who entrust themselves to his merciful and loving care.

Noah's achievement must place him among the first rank of history's great figures. Who among us has had the time, talent, wealth and courage to tackle such a hard and dangerous job? Who the patience and dedication to do it by himself? Who took on the job of saving the human race from extinction? Except for Jesus Christ for the larger and eternal life, the answer must be Noah.

Still, there are the animals to consider. Noah had no wranglers, no one to summon the animals or convey to them the danger they were in. Yet they came, and in such good order as to fulfill in advance the prophecy of Isaiah 11:6–9. We cannot ignore the promise God made when, as a concluding act, He set his rainbow in the cloud as a sign of his pledge (Genesis 9:7–17) never again to cut off all flesh by the waters of a flood. His promise was unconditional, made not only to Noah and his seed, but to the animals aboard the Ark and their seed as well. Why the latter, one may ask? Because, like Noah and the righteous who were to follow, the animals also walked by faith. They came by twos, not knowing where they were going or why they came. Some had walked thousands of miles with a guidance that was unerring. Noah needed only to open the twenty foot door that still provides an access.

All over the world in those climactic days there could have been other creatures, walking, flying or crawling by twos, following the same instinct, in accord with their Creator's purpose. Only one Ark was available, yet with animals searching in all directions one pair of most species could be counted on to find it. Those that succeeded were given the privilege of entering the Ark without hindrance. They could discover for themselves the deck and pens designated for their care. In the quiet of their souls (or whatever) they made their entry, found their designated quarters and settled in. A fortunate few may also have settled into a hibernation that lasted till their departure 12 1/2 months later.

New Name for God Associated with New Dimension of His Being

Whatever the name by which God was known to Noah, it would not be till Moses' time, more than a thousand years later, that the Lord could be regarded by many as acting providentially in man's behalf. In Abraham's time God's most evident attribute would have been a *transcendence* that placed him beyond the reach of those he had made in his image and for himself. That left only the possibility of his revealing more about himself to a few later to be known as patriarchs and prophets. Noah could not fail to have a sense of God's nearness, for the Lord had spoken to him directly, revealing his purposes and choosing Noah as the agent of his will. But not till God revealed himself to Moses–giving a new Name by which to know him and entering a Covenant with one People–could the Lord be widely understood to be near-at-hand as well as at-a-distance. The historical context would disclose God as ordering, directing, helping, providing, protecting, punishing—all with the intent of forming a seasoned and resourceful people dedicated to his service.

In terms of man's understanding, Abraham's God had been much the same as Noah's. He was One whose promises would be fulfilled in time to come—but not immediately. By contrast Moses' God would be a present provider as well as One to promise future benefits. In thinking of God not only as distant but as ever-present, one could perceive in Him feminine as well as masculine attributes. His Most Holy Name from that point would be Yahweh, I AM—to be further understood as Yahweh-'aser-yihweh, "I Who Bring Into Being What Comes Into Being." In this more intimate relationship with man, the concept of God as Divinely Provident could be compared with the pagans' "earth mother"—near at hand if not yet indwelling. It would not, for another fifteen hundred years, occur to any but the prophets that Israel's God could be Personally Three as well as Corporally One.

The Miraculous and the Holy

Throughout the history of the New Israel and the Old we find evidence of miracles. This comes not only as proof of God's providential goodness, but of man's inability to meet his needs without God's help. With this in mind, we look back to God's miraculous intervention in two of history's most important events. One was the miracle already described—enabling man and beast to survive the Deluge and the Flood. The other was the release of the Israelites after long years of bondage in Egypt—with the opening of a path across the Red Sea. That path was denied to Pharaoh's army, who were overwhelmed in the returning waters, enabling the Israelites to continue on their way to their longed-for Promised Land.

It may help our grasp of the miraculous if it is understood that the Latin term *miraculum* suggests no more than "a little thing to be wondered at." We need not think of a miracle as "something that couldn't happen but did." Nor need we think of it as accomplished by a setting-aside of natural law. Apart from God's telling Noah and Moses what he was about to do and asking for their assistance, the chief factor in the Miracle of the Flood and in the Miracle of the Red Sea Crossing appears to have been the certainty and regularity of natural events. One of these was the undersea cataclysm that caused the Flood–along with the evidence that God gave Noah (without his knowing it) 100 years' advance notice in which to build the Ark. As it happened, when it was completed Noah was given seven additional days to get his passengers on board! The other natural event referred to (as I shall try to demonstrate) was an undersea cataclysm that had the effect of raising the bottom of the Red Sea high enough above sea level so that the Israelites as a body could safely cross it. What made this possible appears to have been a *subterranean seismic shockwave that crested under the continents and isles with a trough and lesser waves to follow–sweeping 'round the world.*

Like the tidal wave (or *tsunami*) that does such damage to the shores against which it strikes, a similar wave is now said to pass– though seismologists have only learned of this in the past few years– through molten magma under the earth's crust at much the same speed and with even greater force. (This is hard to visualize and may never actually have been seen, but the subterranean shock-wave can raise–and likewise lower–the continents by several hundred feet with a gradually diminishing effect as it moves around the world.)

What made the Exodus possible was the greatest undersea eruption in human history. The year was 1486 B.C. The site was the island of Thera (known to Latins as Santorini) in the Aegean Sea some seventy miles north of Crete. Even though the eruption itself was at the edge of prehistory, we know of the devastation it wrought, where and when it happened. The miracle itself was one of timing. Only God could know exactly what would come to pass, though scholars have sought ever since to ask and answer questions. Ian Wilson, for one, has shown how the warning signs of Thera's eruption* could have caused the ten plagues that Moses prophesied against the Egyptians. While it is almost certain that such a thing as the Red Sea Crossing never

*EXODUS: The True Story Behind the Biblical Account, Harper & Row, 1985

happened before nor has it happened since,* the miracle was that it occurred at the exact moment the Israelites needed it and for which many must desperately and fervently have been praying.

We can be sure that God had long known when, how and where that eruption would happen. He saw to it that when it did take place the Israelites would already be at the Red Sea and taken by surprise when Pharaoh's forces came out of the wilderness they had just passed through. He further saw to it that when the background was in order—with the tidal wave already engulfing the delta of the Nile and the Israelites filled with terror at the certain prospect of destruction, a pillar of cloud would come between the two forces. Unable to make a decisive strike, the Egyptian were forced to hold their attack until the morning's light. Meanwhile, a pillar of fire lighted the Israelites' path to seaward, enabling them to cross the Sea and climb high enough on the far side to avoid the returning waters.

When Moses took up his rod and raised his hand over the sea—signaling for the waters to be divided—he could not have known that several cubic miles of granite had blown to smithereens at Thera an hour or so before. Because of that ignorance we can confidently hold that Moses' raising of his hand did not "trigger the event." He raised it because God told him to. An hour or two later—on the far side of the Red Sea—Moses raised his hand again and the waters returned. Now the Exodus would have been completed and the forces of the Egyptians totally destroyed. The miracle lay in the preciseness of its timing and the fact that the Israelites had not had to strike a blow in their own defense. They had been given a total victory through a Providential Act of God. For the remainder of their lives on earth, Jews and Christians could be reminded from their Psalter (Ps. 118) as they recited or chanted it, "This is the Lord's doing, and it is marvelous in our eyes."

As we shall later see, the eruption of Thera did far more damage in the Mediterranean basin than in the destruction of Pharaoh's army. The early Minoan culture in Greece and on the island of Crete was

---

* It *may* have happened with the eruption of Java's Mt. Krakatoa in 1858, which darkened the sun for two years and whose tidal waves raced around the earth killing great numbers of people. But if a seismic wave passed under the continents it seems to have left no record. Those near the seashore would have lost their lives. Others at a distance would very likely have noticed nothing.

almost totally wiped out. Hundreds of thousands would have been drowned. Virtually all who were involved in maritime activities would have been lost along with their vessels, building materials, tools and skills. For perhaps a century after the same would have been true of the Mediterranean peoples' capacity for defense against aggression.

For those who have depended on what the Bible says, that "a strong east wind all that night...made the sea dry land," it may be disconcerting to add what is here described. Yet even a seismic wave as unique as this does not change our belief that the cause was "of nature" yet divinely given. Rather than devote further time to this shock-wave, let it be enough that as historic fact, it gives support to two additional theories that have taken traditionalist scholars by surprise. Both hold, to begin with, that the traditional theory of the Red Sea Crossing as having taken place at the north end of the Gulf of Suez through or near the "Sea of Reeds" is no longer tenable. For one thing, the Bitter Lakes area—with its Sea of Reeds—is a part of Egypt. One would not leave Pharaoh's jurisdiction by crossing to the other side. Moreover, if this were the site of the Crossing, Moses would have been disobeying God's instructions to take an escape route that involved a 200 mile journey south and east from the Israelites' home in Goshen to the point where God intended to act providentially in their behalf. The proof is in Exodus 13:17–18 & 21–22 and in Chapter 14:1–14. This requires a journey of many days south and east of the Bitter Lakes, with the Lord providing a pillar of fire by night and cloud by day to show the way.

The new theory—advanced from the mid-1990s—is that the Israelites crossed the Red Sea's Gulf of Aqaba rather than the Gulf of Suez or shallow extensions of that sea. (The implication is that the Crossing brought them into Arabia rather than the Sinai Peninsula and that the forty wilderness years were spent in Arabia. It also presumes that the Mount Sinai or Mount Horeb before which the Israelites encamped and on which the Law was delivered to Moses was actually a mountain in Arabia.) The proponent of both these theses is an American writer and novelist, Howard Blum, whose semi-fictional work, *The Gold of Exodus*,* makes and fairly well validates that proposal. In checking the Old Testament record of the numbers assigned to each tribe—which

---

*Book and audio, Simon & Schuster, N.Y.C., 2001

added up roughly to two million men, women and children, Blum was convinced that no such number could have camped at the foot of a Mt. Sinai/Horeb in Sinai; there simply was no room. However, by following the route through the Sinai Mountains described elsewhere in the Torah, he and an English partner, checking charts of the Aqaba waters–and diving for the purpose of finding an underwater land–bridge–found it at exactly the place where God's instructions to Moses would have the Israelites' encamped in order for God's honor to be redeemed. The Gulf of Aqaba is thirteen kilometers (7.8 miles) wide at this point and some 80 feet deep.

The other discoverer of the Red Sea Crossing–in exactly the same place–is a man named Ron Wyatt, whose long-time hobby has been diving in Egyptian waters with the purpose of finding remains of the Pharaoh's army. In that spot Wyatt and two sons found a great many artifacts dating from the Egyptians' engulfment by the returning waters. The site is shown on modern maps as Nuweiba on the eastern coast of the Sinai Peninsula and about a hundred miles south of Ezion Geber. Here–in eighty feet of water in a gulf that elsewhere is a thousand feet deep–Wyatt and two sons found dozens of chariots, wheels, axles, human skulls, horses' hooves and bones scattered over several miles of bottom. The chariot wheels included four-, six- and eight-spoke varieties, including one having a gold veneer that shone brightly for the reason that the coral covering other artifacts could not grow on the gold. On showing his findings to the Cairo Government's Director of Antiquities, Wyatt was informed that all three wheels were in use only in the time of Egypt's 18th Dynasty when the Exodus occurred. As to Blum's belief that the number of Israelites had to be close to the two–million estimate, we have it from Josephus that following the Exodus the Egyptian army lost 600 chariots and 251,000 men. Though the location of the Mt.Sinai/Mt. Horeb of history is of lesser importance than the fact of the Crossing, we cannot let it stand at that. To Christian, Jew and Muslim alike, the place where God gave the Law has got to be treated as holy ground. Only time will tell whether Blum's claim is a true one; that the real place where God gave the Ten Commandments is a mountain in the north of Saudi

Arabia called Jabal al Lawz. Meanwhile, on the strength of these discoveries, a new edition of the *Atlas of the Holy Land* was published in 1997, offering these two possibilities–that the Law was given, and the Wilderness years lived out either a) in the Sinai Peninsula or b) on a larger mountain with a far broader expanse at its base in which a post–Exodus population of two million could live and travel in orderly formations.

The author must opt for the Israelites' forty years of training in Arabia. St. Paul seems to have believed this, for in Galatians 4:24, 25 he refers to "Mount Sinai which is in Arabia." And God's instructions to Moses, quoted above, quite literally seem to prove it.

Returning to what has been introduced here as the natural event necessary to the Red Sea's Crossing on dry land, it was, most likely a once-only event; highly unlikely to have happened before or since. For such an escape route to be available to fleeing people only once in 3,500 years–at the exact time needed–is almost beyond belief. The occasion was natural; the timing miraculous. Even to the agnostic it would seem sufficient proof that a Creator God–having perfect foreknowledge– was at hand and watching over his own. All the more reason for the Israelites' awe and wonder to be spiced with grateful thanks in every generation for what, liturgically, they have never allowed their children to forget.

Chapter 3

Burgeoning Skills, Natural Religion

It may be more than coincidence that the Industrial Revolution had its origin in the same land where the Christian Church was first established. Comfortably distanced from the continent where the world's greatest achievements have been wrought–and to whose culture Britain has made its own unique contributions–Britain has been remarkably free from the need to maintain large standing armies. Given the opportunity, the temperament and the leisure to attend to peaceful pursuits, she and many other peoples have been the beneficiary.

The aggressor nations of the century past have had no such goals or rationale, nor will their like in years ahead. Taking into consideration the attainments of Christian Europe in science, technology, literature and the arts, it can be held that Britain's own unique concepts–government as servant to the electorate, the rule of law rather than of men, equal justice under the law–have been the most beneficial gifts of all. Along with these has been the sufferance of a market economy, allowing citizens to earn their living in whatever way they will, provided it be within the law and harmful to none.

This chapter has two purposes. One is to outline a few of the factors in pre-Christian Britain and elsewhere that had to do with natural religion. The second is to present the skills and endeavors by which we may appreciate the entrepreneurial spirit of the ancient world. We err if we regard the ancients as inferior to ourselves. No one who has studied Latin, Greek or Hebrew can fail to appreciate how superior those languages are in allowing clarity of thought and expression. No one whose education has ignored the ancient world can appreciate our debt to those who went before us and our need to remember what they teach us.

Those who think of Columbus as overcoming a "flat earth" mentality and of Copernicus as discovering the dynamics of the solar system would do well to look again. Two hundred years before the time of Christ there was a Greek who, as head of Alexandria's Library, already knew what Copernicus would later learn about sun and earth and planets. That scholar, Eratosthenes, had already calculated the earth's circumference to within a few miles of what it proved to be. There was, among the Old Testament writers as well, knowledge of the physical creation. The Psalmist (98:8) wrote of God's praise ascending from "the round world, and they that dwell therein." A thousand years earlier the author of the Book of Job (26:7) had already said of God "He hangeth the earth upon nothing."

A great deal of archeological evidence points to the acuity of design and skills in ancient times. We have record, for example, of the hull and cargo of a Bronze Age merchant ship sunk off the coast of Turkey around 1,400 BC. [1] It was a fifty foot vessel, wide and spacious. Its keel and planking were of fir, the planking two inches thick, butted together and to the keel with mortise and tenon joints secured by hardwood pegs. Though the vessel's range may have been limited to the Eastern Mediterranean, much of its cargo came from far distant points: six tons of copper ingots from Sardinia and Cyprus; a half ton of tin thought to have come from Afghanistan; ostrich eggshells, ebony and elephant tusks from Africa; glass ingots and pottery from Syria; amber from lands along the Baltic; glass and amber beads from Phoenicia; swords from Canaan and Mycenaea, bronze spearheads from Greece, gold tableware from Greece and Egypt; fishing nets, stone mace heads, carved ivory, gold bracelets and pendants, wines and aromatic woods from diverse places; and from Egypt, a gold scarab containing Nefertiti's seal. The most valuable consignment would have been the hundred or so amphorae containing yellow terebinth resins used in making perfumes and cosmetics, often found at sites of ornate and costly burials.

In the process of researching this book, several of my own questions concerning shipping and navigation have been resolved along the way. Some writers have held that mariners of ancient times rarely ventured out of sight of land and sailed only during daylight hours—beaching or anchoring their ships by nightfall. The impression is also given that Mediterranean ships rarely entered the Atlantic because of risks that included a limited ability to work their way upwind. I have come to the conclusion that these scholars have been overly cautious. The earliest of wooden vessels—the lateen-rigged dhows of Arabian waters and feluccas of the Mediterranean—had a remarkably high capacity to sail upwind. As time went on and as larger vessels were commissioned—with seas made safe from piracy by navies built to that end—the earlier precautions were no longer necessary. As divers have learned from a trail of artifacts at the bottom of the Channel, the Veneti of Brittany carried their freight to Cornwall and back in a direct line. At the time of Rome's greatest power and size, the grain fleet from Egypt, carrying 150,000 tons per year, came directly across the sea—and often under full sail—to relieve anticipated starvation. In support of that there were those who chose to sail out of sight of land, we have evidence of magnetic compasses and astrolabes early in the Iron Age. An astrolabe, intricately wrought in brass and almost in working condition, has been recovered from a Mediterranean vessel sunk in ancient times.

Of all risks and achievements in ancient times, none can surpass those of Irish monks who, while 1,500 years behind the Phoenicians in reaching the New World, were four centuries in advance of the Norwegians. The work of Tim Severin in duplicating the voyage of Saint Brendan the Navigator to Iceland, Greenland and Newfoundland leaves little doubt as to the historicity of the ancient legend. [2] While Severin did not undertake his work as a "true believer" but as an adventurer sparked by curiosity, his imagination and patience in experimenting and duplicating the leathers, woods, metals and hemps needed for icy salt-water shipping were a tribute to the historian's interest in probability as well as certitude.

The Hold of Natural Religion on Men's Minds

Normally we think of *natural* as being distinguished from *supernatural*. However, since supernatural can carry the connotation of the demonic as well as the divine, let us accept the term *natural* as differing from *revealed*. Alongside the Hebrew and Christian faiths and the Judeo-Christian moral order—the two bestowed, the third required and all three by divine revelation—the Druids' religion may well have been the truest and most ethical that humanity, unassisted by special revelation that is documented, has yet provided. Even here, however, there may be an element of the supernatural or revealed that we cannot escape. For example, if the Druids' was a natural theology given by intuition, may it not be held that God's grace was present in that intuition and that the Druid doctrine, even without direct revelation, must have been a gift of grace?

I have posited this question in order to point out two other possibilities, both of them "of nature" and derived from the most ancient of times which continue to draw a great deal of attention. Neither is divinely revealed in the sense that Judaism and Christianity are revealed, nor do they involve man in relationship with God in the sense found in Holy Scripture. One is the knowledge of a Zodiac that appears to have been picked up almost simultaneously throughout the ancient world. [3] The other example is a mini-science based on discoveries within the Great Pyramid at Gizeh in Egypt. [4]

The major difference between revelation given in Sacred Scripture and the Zodiac would be this: far from being concerned with human behavior and the God—man relationship, the Zodiac is, in effect, a mythology based on the pictorial arrangement of stars and planets.

It appears to have been imaginatively configured by people not yet in touch with one another, with the result that a consensus was unwittingly adopted in which the Zodiac itself became the data. What followed was that the changing relationship of stars and planets and the changing possibilities of relationship between the figures became the science. It can be called a natural science in that neither the names of the constellations nor the stories about them were divinely given. By contrast, the Great Pyramid appears to have required, for its planning, mathematical formulae identified with numeric studies that would be unknown to any for thousands of years to come. (Specifically, we have in mind the use of infinitesimal calculus, a branch of mathematics unknown till its *discovery* by Sir Isaac Newton and Gottfried Leibniz.) There were, as well, two mysteries involved in the Pyramid's location. One: it was considered to have been built at the exact weighted center of the land surfaces of the earth. The other: that it was at the radial center of a ninety degree arc comprising the delta of the Nile with forty–five degrees on either side of north. [5]

Yet for all this evidence–in the design and building of the Pyramid– of divine intervention in the natural order, the question would have to remain "on hold" through all the millennia until early in the century just past. Only when its interior was completely explored, cleaned out and made available for study could its major mysteries even be discovered.

One indication that the Pyramid may have been divinely revealed had been the fact that each of its four surfaces was designed and built with just enough concavity to focus the sun's rays into four perfect beams, each visible for a very long distance. With its original surface of highly polished white stone, the Pyramid served purposes not unlike that presumed by Stonehenge in Britain–as an astronomical observatory, as a calendar of celestial events and an almanac of times of planting and of harvest. On the first day of summer, the sun's rays at noon on the Great Pyramid's southern face would be deflected through a right angle towards the south. At the same time its rays on the eastern and western faces would be reflected in two beams extending horizontally along the ground to the northeast and northwest, with the 90 degree angle so formed embracing the whole of the Nile delta.

I shall say no more of the Pyramid from this point on other than to mention that a young science has sprung up concerning this lone survivor of the Ancient World's Seven Wonders. [6] A part of it deals with prophesies concerning the Israelites. It must be emphasized, however, that the Pyramid's prophecies, unlike those of Scripture, are revealed numerically rather than in words. Using a time-relation of inches to years and notable scorings in otherwise evenly-cut passageways, a Pyramid Time line described in the Egyptian Book of the Dead and decoded in 1909 appears to have prophesied many significant biblical dates, a few of which are shown here:

> 2622 BC .... Completion of Great Pyramid
> 2344 BC. .... The Biblical Deluge
> 1486 BC......... The Exodus
> 1000 BC. ...... Dedication of Solomon's Temple
> 520 BC......... Foundation of the Second Temple
> 4 BC .... Nativity of Jesus Christ
> AD 30............ Crucifixion, Resurrection and Ascension of
> Christ
> AD 1918......... Recovery of Holy Land from Ottoman rule
> AD 1948. .... Israel restored as sovereign State

In respect to this time line, it must be acknowledged that because it is numeric rather than verbal, it can be prophetic only in a retroactive sense. Yet despite the limitation, its accuracy is astonishing. In his first book on the subject, written and published in 1909 by David Davidson (the man who deciphered the code) he noted a critical period a few years in the future. Using a second time line measured in months rather than years, he described that period as dating from August 8, 1914 to November 11, 1918. As it turned out, those were the opening day* and the final day of World War I. So the time line, though marvelously prophetic in pointed to the "whens," was dependent on its interpreters to discern what notable events may have been signified by the dates.

*Actually this was the special date of Britain's entry into the war.

The Mystery of Ley Lines

In the early 1920s Alfred Watkins, a 65 year old man was riding across the hills near Bredwardine in south Wales. Coming to a spectacular view, he pulled up his horse to look over the landscape below. "At that moment he became aware of a network of lines, standing out like glowing wires all over the surface of the country, intersecting at the sites of churches, old stones and other spots of traditional sanctity."* What Watkins had recovered, at the age of 65, was the capacity to see what primitive men and perhaps higher animals may well have perceived as a matter of everyday experience. [7] Fortunately Mr. Watkins had the gift of curiosity and, joined by others, did extensive research into what in earlier times (but nearly forgotten) had been called *ley lines*. His own theory was that the leys were traces of terrestrial power crisscrossing the countryside. He believed further that ancient men, having psychic capabilities that in today's world are all but lost, may have regarded ley lines as track ways to be held to for vigor and health.

One of the discoveries made by Watkins and others is that where ley lines intersect were regarded as especially holy places. Chartres Cathedral, for example, stands at the intersection of two ley lines extending for many miles. In Britain these lines can be traced on ordnance maps where cathedrals, parish churches, abbeys, stone circles, standing stones, barrows, mottes and baileys, hillforts and earthworks are still shown. Buoyed up by the experience and by the widespread interest that attends such discoveries, Mr. Watkins wrote a book that continues to be widely read in updated versions. The supposition is that ley lines are manifestations of terrestrial magnetism, related perhaps to such phenomena as St. Elmo's fire on spars of sailing ships, and likewise to auras surrounding human beings–manifesting (according to extent) their state of health and (according to color) their feelings and state of mind. There was, for some years, the supposition that unidentified flying objects (UFO's) from outer space might be alternatively powered by such magnetic currents, and in the 1960s a book was published linking reported UFO sightings on the European continent along known ley lines. Although the purposes the ley lines serve can only be

*John Mitchell in "Note on Alfred Watkins" in new edition of *The Old Straight Track* by Alfred Watkins.

supposed, it is evident that along those traces, for thousands of years, men have been led to dedicate holy sites for the sanctifying of time and space.

Among the most remarkable of such lines is one that begins at St. Michael's Mount and passes through the Cheesewring on Bodmin Moor, St. Michael's Brentnor in Dartmoor, Burrow Mump in Somerset, then through Glastonbury and Avebury. It continues eastward, following the line of Icknield Way through Bury St. Edmunds and crosses the coast just north of Lowestoft. Along its route are ancient edifices, stones, markers, earthworks and sighting notches to confirm it. Another and shorter ley line begins at Clearbury Rings south of Salisbury, traces through the cathedral, continuing through Old Sarum and on to Stonehenge.

The question seems never to have been asked whether these ley lines were created as a result of the sanctifying of places that merely happened to be in line—as a kind of aura attending holy things standing in relationship to one another. What seems to be accepted is that ancient peoples, seeing these lines and holding them in awe, built their holy places along them, using the lines as paths and roads for whatever travel might be undertaken. If these ley lines are among the "permanent things" found in nature, it is likely that along these same track ways were built the wooden churches of the ancient Britons, long since disappeared and replaced by those of stone built by Saxons, Danes and Normans. In addition, from ancient times there had been holy springs, wells and rivers. They were often associated with healing, and bore the names of holy men and women who had lived nearby as penitents, teachers, confessors and recluses.

Temple of the Stars

It is said that when Alexander the Great was besieging Tyre and entertaining plans for war against Carthage, he was visited by envoys from the Celts. Whatever their mission may have been, at its conclusion they are quoted as saying, "We fear no man; there is but one thing that we fear, namely, that the sky should fall on us." [8] The same concern is found in the 12th century *Book of Leinster*, "Heaven is above, and earth beneath us, and the sea is round about us. Unless the sky shall fall with its showers of stars on the ground where we are camped . . . we shall not give ground." [9]

Such apprehensions may well have led ancient man to build temples honoring the stars in addition to those like Stonehenge, raised in honor of the sun. In Britain there are at least three places where the Celts are said to have built temples to the stars—at Kingston upon Thames, at Nuthampstead and at Pumpsaint in Wales. In the French foothills of the Pyrenees, is a gigantic stone circle whose circumference is seventeen miles and whose "stones" are whole mountain-tops trimmed and refashioned in ancient times. Spread within and around it is a series of grids and track ways not unlike Alfred Watkins' ley lines. Within the circle are geometric grids including parish churches and other holy places dating back a thousand years or more. But their relationship as a Temple had been long forgotten and was only brought to light when Henry Lincoln, a coauthor of *Holy Blood, Holy Grail*, learned of an encrypted parchment found hidden inside an altar at Rennes-le-Chateau. The deciphering of its code took several years and the discovery of mysterious track ways and geometric figures more years still. The result was a fascinating narrative of topographical detective work.* But no movies have been made inspired by the book; Neither Lincoln nor archaeologists could suggest a script. There remain no clues as to who built this Temple of the Stars or why.

The Glastonbury Zodiac

An even larger Temple of the Stars seems to have been built at Glastonbury far earlier. Like that in France, its very existence had been forgotten. Nevertheless there were farmers working the land and other who had known of patterns demanding lifelong attention as part of some great design but none had any idea what these things meant. In 1947, before the Zodiac's rediscovery was widely known, a local farmer was asked if he could explain why certain strips of his land were so awkwardly shaped and why they were bounded by hedges that

*Henry Lincoln, *The Holy Place*, Little, Brown, New Yor, 1991.

emphasized those shapes. His response was, "It is all beyond memory but will never be altered."

The ancient design came to light after an artist, Katherine Maltwood, was asked to draw a map illustrating the Grail-quest for an Everyman edition of *The High History of the Holy Grail*. After her own quest shortly before World War II, she announced that she had discovered elements of a vast terrestrial Zodiac hidden in the Glastonbury landscape and that it followed the structure of the 13th century Arthurian text. Her book, *Glastonbury's Temple of the Stars* caused a sensation. As a consequence there has been a deluge of studies by archaeologists, historians, Arthurian scholars and those in quest of the occult and arcane. [10]

We know something of the Zodiac's antiquity. It is akin to the earliest in Sumer, Babylon and Egypt, dating no later than 2700 BC, a date that in curious ways has corroboration. One involves a reference made time and again by Welsh bards of a mysterious unnamed work as being "the first mighty labor of the land of Britain." Stonehenge was second. Other support comes from Sargon, the ancient monarch of Sumer and Akkad, who boasted of his ships as bringing tin from Britain. Sargon set on his royal standard the four creatures featured in the Sumerian Zodiac at the quarterings of the year: the Bull, the Lion, Man (Sagittarius) and Bird (Phoenix). Glastonbury also uses the Phoenix, though in place of the Aquarius used elsewhere. This raises the question as to whether Sumerians may have come on one of Sargon's vessels. If so, and if they helped those on hand to pattern the Glastonbury Zodiac after the Sumerian model, this may explain the origins of the name Somerset (a.k.a. Summerland).

As the Glastonbury Zodiac has been reconstructed, other features are unique. Its Sagittarius is no archer, but rather a king who is being drawn from his horse after receiving a fatal wound from Scorpio. In addition there is a ship in place of Cancer the Crab. Considering the ancient age of the Zodiac—and its strikingly different figures given at the very inception of astrology as a science—we may consider the differences not as discrepancies but as perhaps divinely given and replacing signs already considered sacrosanct. For instance, the dying king's betrayal and death at the hands of one of his own, we can see as illustrative in prophecy both of Arthur and of Jesus as the Divine One. To be sure, Christ needs no such tribute–and in Scripture his birth is of necessity kept hidden. Yet like Arthur's it is mythically ascribed. For the historic event the Magi will be the first to find and worship the Infant Messiah, and their science will find sufficient sanctity in the Church's eyes for all three Magi to be enshrined as saints in Cologne's Cathedral. Yet in acknowledging the Zodiac's prophecy of Christ to have been given two millennia before Isaiah's, it cannot fail that some who go to Glastonbury looking for Aquarius will discover Jesus and accept him as their Redeemer. Meanwhile, the figure of Arthur as a type of Christ may draw attention to the way in which a matchless King can almost single-handedly deliver a defenseless people from their foes.

The final difference in the Glastonbury Zodiac is the use of the Phoenix in place of the Archer. Here is the mythical bird that rises from the ashes of death to life anew, symbolizing the Atoning Death, the Harrowing of Hell and the Resurrection of Christ the King. So we find in Britain's ancient and newly recovered Zodiac a unique place for the historical Jesus. For Arthur we have had a useful but historically hopeless myth in place of legend. Hopefully–and perhaps with the Zodiac's help–we can look forward to the historic recovery of Arthur's place as the mightiest of Princes and Champion of his people.

Yet, as contrasted with the fact of Glastonbury and its historic witness to a long-dead Arthur, evidence of so ancient a Zodiac as Glastonbury's is frail indeed. Yet the evidence of those startling differences from the ancient "norms" may provide all the proof that some people need. If Katherine Maltwood, among others, in looking for a conventional Zodiac, have found one so curiously different, how much more likely would it be to influence a response than the garden variety they expected to recover? Whatever the case, it must be said that if this Zodiac is truly what the Welsh bards were speaking of–"the first mighty labor of the land of Britain"–it could well be the most enormous monument ever made at men's hands. [11] A circle ten miles in diameter would enclose more than 78 square miles, which is to say 50,265 acres. My own guess is that this Zodiac's figures occupy about one sixth of the actual space, which would be 8,377 acres or thirteen square miles. All of that acreage–rearranged by picks and shovels, strong backs and bushel baskets into roads and hills, fields and forest, rivers and dams, lakes and pools, stone walls and hedges–had to be integrated into whatever else would continue to be there.

And how perfectly would that Zodiac–already there at the time of the Celts' first arrival in the time of Hu Gadarn–endear, sanctify and make holy for time to come the great Tor and its life–giving ever–abundant Spring. The worst thing they had feared had happened! The sky had fallen before they got there, and in a Paradise beyond belief. No wonder they loved it. It was a joyful mystery–with nothing left to fear.

The Hidden Years of Jesus

Who among the curious has not given thought to the years in Jesus' life following his family's visit to Jerusalem when he was twelve? For five days he was lost. Mary and Joseph searched frantically in every corner of the city, at last finding him at study in the Temple and conversing with the doctors of the Law. Luke concludes the incident by telling us that Jesus returned with his parents to Nazareth; that he was "subject unto them" and "increased in wisdom and stature, and in favor with God and man." But does this imply that he remained there, learning the carpenter's trade and awaiting the time when he must turn to his eternal calling? There are many who hold to that view and Luke at least allows it.

Yet the Gospels of Matthew and Mark point implicitly to anther path. So, quite explicitly, do traditions of the Early Church. Mark and Matthew make clear that Jesus' hearers in the synagogue at Nazareth were offended by him on the occasion of his initial preaching. They knew that elsewhere he had a reputation as a teacher, preacher and worker of miracles. But they could not understand why one whose background was the same as theirs could perform the mighty works ascribed to him. On the other hand, Mark and Matthew also describe the townspeople as puzzled about Jesus' identity. Was he not the same man they earlier had known, the son of Mary and cousin to several who were still living there? That they should be puzzled over his identity implies that Jesus had been away from Nazareth for some time. Given *any* absence, their uncertainty would seem more appropriate to an absence of eight, ten or twelve years rather than two or three.

John's Gospel bears this out. When Jesus came to be baptized of John, the Baptist failed to recognize him even though they were second cousins. There may have been a twenty-five year difference in Elizabeth's and Mary's ages, yet these two were very dear to one another. There was only a six months' difference in the ages of their sons and the boys would have been inseparable from childhood—the more because John's father had been murdered by Herod's soldiers during the Slaughter of the Innocents for refusing to tell where John was. [12] Why did John not recognize Jesus when he saw the Holy Spirit light upon him? It would suggest that Jesus had been away from Palestine, perhaps for many years, while John was preparing for his ministry in the desert.

There is, in John's Gospel, a further suggestion of Jesus' absence. It is implied in the remark made by Nathanael of Cana when Philip asked him to meet Jesus of Nazareth, whom he and others believed to be the Messiah. Jesus and several disciples were already in Cana for a wedding, and Nazareth was only five miles away. Nathanael had never heard of Jesus and his query was, "Can there anything good come out of Nazareth?" Yet within minutes of their introduction, Nathanael would be saying, "Rabbi, thou art the Son of God; thou art the King of Israel."

The case appears to be a good one for Jesus' being out of Palestine for many of the eighteen years between his boyhood visit to Jerusalem and his baptism at the age of thirty. Three of the Gospels seem to confirm such absence, and old tradition speaks of several places outside the Holy Land where there is record of Jesus' presence.

Anecdotally, some years ago I received a phone call from a travel agent near Fort Worth, Texas asking whether I might be interested in a guided tour for clergy in the Holy Land. I told her I would be, but that if I had the time and money I'd prefer to go to Britain. When asked why, I told her of my interest in the Early British Church, of my plans to write on the subject and mentioned Jesus' visits. "Oh," she said, "I know all about that. I was born and grew up in Jerusalem. When I finished high school I decided to be a travel agent. So I joined one of the agencies and was given their training. The very first thing I learned was that Jesus had gone to Britain." She added for emphasis, "Every travel agent in Jerusalem knows that."

Let me speak of other traditions of Jesus during the years for which Scripture gives no accounting. Mainly they exist along the old trade routes leading from the Holy Land through Syria, Iraq, Iran and Afghanistan into Pakistan, India, Nepal, Tibet and Ladakh. Many travelers have, since the mid-nineteenth century, traced out Jesus' travels through this region. They have sought, either in local tradition or in written documents, to learn of Jesus' presence during the so-called hidden years. [13] The answer appears to be that there is such tradition although it is hard to come by, especially in the mountainous areas of Tibet, where the numerous hardships of travel are hindrances. In India there exists the understanding that Jesus spent several years traveling through the land, becoming acquainted with people and studying their beliefs. It is broadly acknowledged that "Issus" was revered for his teaching, his holiness and miracles he performed. He is remembered as causing anger among some of the Brahmans because of his compassion for outcasts that would later anger certain of the Jews. In India there is oral tradition that there were those who added Saint Issus to their pantheon of gods. In Tibet and Ladakh, by contrast, several of the old Buddhist monasteries proved to have records of Jesus' visits, but they showed these to very few and none was able to borrow the records or have copies made.

I mention these indications of Jesus' presence because of his interest in native religion in those lands where knowledge of God could only been guessed at since he had not, in the East, made himself known. Unlike the case with the Druids, whose theology was already trinitarian, and which Jesus confirmed rather than borrowed from, he appears to have adopted or adapted no doctrine or practice from the East. It may be added that, though Thomas, Bartholomew and Matthias are believed to have preached the Gospel in India, and Thomas to have died there as a martyr, the Christian faith did not subsequently grow as in the West. In India's multicultural society, the Church could survive only by becoming a caste—which it did—and until the twentieth century its numbers were few and its influence small. Today it appears to be taking lessons from the Western churches. It holds to its old concern for holiness and humility, but manifests an increasing readiness to proclaim Christ to those outside the fold in obedience to his Great Commission.

᎒Ꮕ   Chapter 4   ᎒Ꮕ

The Readying of the Soil

When St. Paul wrote of Christ's having come "in the fullness of time," he was inviting comment from every generation. A corroborating opinion on God's timing came from the Anglican Benedictine, Dom Gregory Dix in his book, *Jew and Greek*. The timing's appropriateness, he held, lay in the readiness of three peoples for the event—the Jews, the Greeks and the Romans. By that point the three were providing, as he said, "the truest religion, the highest attainments of science and the arts, and the most just system of governing" [1]yet known to man.

We can agree as to what Dom Gregory says of Jew and Greek. Jesus said (John 4:22), "Salvation is of the Jews," and we accept it without further thought. As to the intellectual and artistic attainments of the Greeks, the Church both East and West has shown its indebtedness and gratitude. What weakness exists in Dom Gregory's hypothesis must lie with the city referred to in John's Apocalypse as "Babylon."

Actually, Imperial Rome provided little more than sure highways and protected sea lanes for communication of God's Word. But it went to the greatest lengths to assure the Law would not be obeyed and the Gospel not be heard. Rome's responsible civic life had come to an end during the final years of the Republic. The imperial era was one of aggression and world conquest. At home there had come to be such degeneracy and love of luxury as invited rule by generals drawn from the conquered peoples—men who had the ambition and nerve to elbow their way to the top. The single way in which Rome gave help to Christ's religion was to use every means to destroy the new religion and erase the name of Jesus Christ from human memory. What we have from Tertullian may be the final word, "The blood of the martyrs is the seed of the Church."

A dramatic example of Christian witness at the heart of the Roman scene was found in the Theban Legion, which had been called from the Eastern provinces to deal with civil turbulence in Gaul. Upon arriving at a way-station in the Swiss Alps, its soldiers were directed to make the necessary sacrifice to the Emperor—each man in turn casting a few grains of incense upon a perpetual fire burning before a statue of the Emperor. They all refused. For their disobedience, every tenth man was executed and the order renewed. Again they refused and again the Legion was decimated. To those in charge, the Legion's commander—himself a Christian—explained that they would obey any order consistent with their duty to the State, but that this thing they could not do. Other troops were called in to carry out the executions, and the whole Legion laid down its arms, suffering martyrdom for Jesus' sake. It may be noted that there was no resistance. With arms and armor on the ground before them, the men stood silent, waiting for the executioner's sword.

Instead of considering Rome as providing a spiritual matrix, let us consider three peoples whose religion was hardly truer than the Greeks' and Romans', but who contributed to the concept of Law and allowed the Gospel to be preached without hindrance. One was the Phoenicians, whose awareness of the Law goes back to Solomon's time. Another was the Brythons or Britons, the first of whom came to the British Isles in the time of the Hebrew Patriarchs. The third was the Celts, who arrived in Britain no earlier than 800 BC and who adopted their precursors' customs and faith. The latter two seem not only to have been familiar with Divine Law, but riper for conversion than any of the other peoples to whom the Gospel came. While the origins of their customs and beliefs go back to ancient times, the proof of Britons' and Celts' readiness for the Gospel lies in the fact that in Great Britain, Brittany and Ireland their conversion seems to have taken place rapidly and virtually without bloodshed. If true, it has to be one of history's most astonishing events.

The Phoenicians

The Phoenicians were a Semitic people who migrated from Arabia to Canaan, and who became the finest mariners of the ancient world. While in Arabia they may have honed their skills in the use of the dhow, whose lateen sails allowed it to tack smartly into the wind. Once settled in Palestine they could enlarge their skills, for while the dhow and its counterpart the felucca were river and harbor boats, the Mediterranean and Black Seas would become *the* seas of commerce till the Americas were discovered.

Like the Greeks, the Phoenicians were forced into commerce because of the erosion of their land through ignorance of agricultural husbandry—with added removal of soil during the floods caused by Thera's eruption. Unlike the Minoans and Myceneans, whose early seafaring appears to have ended with that catastrophe, the Phoenicians' survival hinged on the one valuable asset remaining to them. It was Lebanon's forest, much of whose remaining fir and cedar would go to the building of Solomon's Palace, Temple and Red Sea Fleet. The early demand for timber came from Egypt, a powerful neighbor with no timber of its own. The wealth that would in time build Phoenicia's ships began with the felling of these trees, dragging the logs to the beaches and through the surf, then hauling them through the coastal waters three hundred miles or more to the mouths of the Nile.

The Phoenicians' maritime life seems to have included centuries of prehistory, for they were the principal shippers of tin, which was alloyed with copper in the making of bronze. While the Early Bronze Age began in Egypt prior to 3,500 BC, the Bronze Age as such extended from 1,500 to 800 BC. Our earliest written record from the Phoenicians shows one Himilco of Carthage, Phoenicia's western colony, sailing c. 450 BC to Brittany and Cornwall in search of tin. A few years later another Carthaginian, Hanno, took a party of traders south from Gibraltar as far as Guinea and possibly to the Bight of Benin. The first date is deceptive, however, for Himilco's journey took place after the Bronze Age–as now defined–had ended. Nor can that date be tied to the Phoenicians' early trade; it is merely our oldest written confirmation of what had already been going on for a thousand years or more.

The oral record points to a far earlier date than Himilco's. Ancient tradition at Cadiz holds that the port was the Atlantic base for Tyre and Sidon by 1100 BC, more than three hundred years before Carthage was founded. The accuracy of the oral dating is confirmed by other facts. As will be seen later, we have clear proof that c.3500 BC there was mining and shipping of Cornish tin. Supporting this is the evidence that throughout the Bronze Age two of the three main sources of tin for the Mediterranean and Near East trade were near to the Atlantic and available to Phoenician ships. One was that in Britain and the other near Compostela in northwest Spain, from both of which they carried ingots to Tyre by way of Cadiz. Other than these, Europe's only important tin source was in Bohemia, some miles west of Prague. Most of its output went to smelters in the Balkans, but some would have been shipped down the Elbe to the North Sea where Phoenicians came regularly to obtain amber originating in the Baltic basin.

Several things can be said about the Phoenicians to distinguish them from other peoples. They were merchants as well as seamen; their voyages of exploration were not for curiosity's sake but for trade. Their products were designed for marketing to primitive buyers as well as sophisticates, to processors as well as users. One of their first and most popular items was the purple dye obtained from mollusks found in their homeland's shallow waters. Purple fabrics made with this dye became their hallmark throughout the world. If they happened to carry cosmetics, perfumes, silks, spices, fish paste, wines, it was as transshippers of what they had bought or received in exchange for other goods. The manufacture and sale of inexpensive trade-goods was the principal activity of Phoenicia's cottage industry.

The Phoenicians seem to have been the first to possess a work ethic, the first to be motivated by a puritanism concerned not so much with moral behavior as with an awareness of the "deferred good" so necessary to economic expansion. They were the first to give evidence of a desire peaceably to outdo the competition, winning markets by mannerly approach and attentive service rather than by restraint of trade and force of arms. Though they were the first to use an alphabet, they left no artistic or literary output at all. The artifacts found in vast numbers at their ancient worksites are all of a kind. They are clay tablets recording details of business transacted, contracts for purchase and delivery, records of loans, debts, transactions and payments—all inscribed on tablets for future record.

There is a revealing narrative by the Greek historian Herodotus, who died in 425 BC after having traveled through most of the then known world. Though the Phoenicians had already been trading widely for a thousand years, what he describes may have been their standard procedure for opening new markets. He tells how traders from Carthage introduced their goods to tribesmen on Africa's Atlantic coast:

"They lay out their goods in a row on the beach, return to their ship and raise a smoke signal; the natives see the signal, go to the beach, put down an amount of gold and move away from the goods; the Carthaginians disembark, take a look, and if the gold seems enough for the goods take it and go off, and if not they go back to the boats and wait, and the natives come out and add to the gold till the sellers are satisfied."

In a sense Phoenicia served the purposes of commerce as did Holland in later years. Its fighting ships could not compete with the Greeks' as was proven at Salamis, and its home base was under constant pressure from far larger continental powers—Assyria, Babylon and Persia. On the whole its use of armed force was limited to defense of its bases and its commerce rather than for conquest or aggression.

Phoenicia's free-market policy was, for many centuries, followed profitably and with service to those allied with it in trade. It continued until the Greeks' most powerful warrior, Alexander, besieged its island fortress and capital. With Tyre's destruction, Phoenicia's days of glory came to an end.

Carthage in turn would similarly leave the scene. During its years of competition with Greek city-states there was little warfare. What occurred was chiefly jockeying for position. But as Greece's power and importance declined and Rome's increased, the picture changed to active, and finally to fanatical, warfare. Rome had earlier shown no interest in naval power. Though it had equal access to land and sea, Rome had limited itself to supremacy on the continent. Now it focused on building warships, principally triremes. From this point Carthage was doomed. Africa had no population or economy sufficient for war with Rome. Nevertheless three losing Punic Wars were fought–the second on Italian soil by one of history's bravest and most brilliant generals. The net effect was to make Rome a military power superior to any seen before, transformed from a republic to an empire bent on conquest, enslaving as many tributary lands and people as it could. Touching on Rome's economic rivalry with Carthage, we have a first century BC narrative from Strabo describing a much earlier attempt by the Romans to track down their competitors' sources. A Roman ship at Cadiz seems to have been instructed to follow a Carthaginian vessel engaged in the tin trade, with the intent of learning where the tin came from. When the Carthaginian captain learned he was being followed, he led the other through a series of tortuous straits until both were wrecked. That captain then made his way back to Carthage by land, where the senate reimbursed him for his loss and gave extra compensation for loss of profits.

We cannot leave the Phoenicians without noting some remarkable feats of seamanship. One involved a Phoenician circumnavigation of Africa c. 600 BC, reported by Herodotus:[1]

"[Necho, pharaoh of Egypt,] sent out a naval expedition manned by Phoenicians, instructing them to come home by way of the Straits of Gibraltar into the Mediterranean and in that fashion get back to Egypt. So, setting out from the Red Sea, the Phoenicians sailed into the Indian Ocean. Each autumn they put into whatever point of Africa they happened to be sailing by, sowed the soil, stayed there till harvest time, reaped the grain, and sailed on; so that two years went by and in the third they doubled the Pillars of Hercules and made it back to Egypt."

Surprisingly, what Herodotus describes as having taken place around 600 BC seems to have occurred hundreds of years earlier. When Solomon had completed the Temple at Jerusalem, he arranged with Hiram, King of Tyre, to build and man a fleet of ships at Ezion-Geber whose chief purpose was to sail clockwise around Africa. Once in commission, these were known as ships of Tarshish, the southern part of Spain extending to Cadiz. The ships departed from Solomon's Red Sea base every three years. They arrived at Tyre in the third year out—carrying gold, silver, ivory, apes and peacocks from Tyre to Jerusalem—or traded as the king demanded.

Why, we may ask, should there be boasting of the Phoenicians' achievement in 600 BC when precisely the same thing seems to have taken place in what Ussher dates at 992 BC? (The Scriptural narrative is cited in 1 Kings 9:26 & 10:22 and in 2 Chronicles 9:21.) It may be because the Phoenicians accomplished in 600 what was not possible in Solomon's time, namely the *complete* circumnavigation of Africa. This became possible when under one of Egypt's pharaohs—during the ninth or eighth century—a canal was dug between the Mediterranean and the Red Sea in the same location as that later chosen for the Suez Canal opened in 1910. The ancient canal had been abandoned after some centuries of use and for 2,000 years lay covered with sand.

What the ancients knew in the time of Solomon—and confirmed in that of Pharaoh Necho—would not be known again until the fifteenth century AD. This was that the African continent can be sailed around far more easily in a clockwise than in a counter-clockwise direction. The adverse winds and currents during long seasons of the year make a west-to-east passage of the Cape of Good Hope virtually impossible for vessels under sail. Not only Hanno of Carthage would fail to sail in that direction. With the sponsorship of Prince Henry the Navigator, a number of fifteenth century Portugese captains tried and failed. Sailing south from Lisbon, they reached the Cape of Good Hope but could go no further. Vasco da Gama, in 1497, was the first to sail round it heading east, continuing on to India.

The Britons

According to ancient tradition, Britain's earliest ancestors were remnents of three related tribes who together left the Black Sea basin because of the flooding of ancestral lands. These were Brython, Kymri and Lloegrwys, of common ancestry and speech. They were journeying to an island they knew of in the western ocean called the White Island or Albion. When they passed the Alps, however, most of the third clan turned south into Italy and Gaul, where they became known as Ligurians. Further along, many of the Brythons paused at Armorica, later to be known as Lesser Britain or Brittany. The Kymri continued to Greater Britain, where their descendants in the south of Wales continued to be known as Kymri or Cymbry and those to the north as Cambrians. Finding themselves in a land of temperate climate, bountiful resources and (apparently) little native population, they sent word to their erstwhile companions and were joined by most of the Brython and a goodly number of the Lloegrwys. These are remembered in the Welsh Triads as the Three Pacific Tribes of Britain.

Their ruler was Hu Gadarn Isaakson, described in Welsh folklore as Hu the Mighty. Among other things, he is remembered for requiring that poetic triads be the vehicle of memory and recitation, which is to say oral tradition. He is credited with introducing glass-making and the use of Ogham writing inscribed in stone, as well as with creating many of the Triads. He instituted the custom of outdoor convocations for monarchs and people—the annual Gorsedd held at sacred mounds or stone circles during times of equinox or solstice. From the first, the polity of Britain treated the island as one people under one crown.

Yet the Crown was subject to the "Voice of the Country." Hence the maxim, "The Country is higher than the King." which has reflected fundamental Law from ancient times. It is the obverse of the feudal, medieval State, where land and people were in all respects subject to the King.

The greatest of Hu Gadarn's legacies appears to have been giving form and initial substance to what would become the Druid philosophy or religion. But it was not until a second migration of Kymri six hundred years later that Druidism attained the dimensions of what today could be called a world-class faith.

The Second Migration of the Kimri

Those Kymri and the Ligurians who had turned south to Italy during the initial migration, had grown sufficiently numerous by the 16th or 15th centuries BC for some to find reasons to migrate elsewhere. A large faction sailed to Troy, whose people were their kindred, located not far from their ancestral home. Troy had been founded more than a thousand years earlier and was widely envied for its location and wealth. The new arrivals were welcome. Whatever the date, there was time to strengthen and fortify the city. In 1194 BC the Trojan War commenced, involving eighteen pitched battles, a great deal of single combat and a ten year siege. Siege and war ended with the city's complete destruction and the return to Italy of 88,000 Trojans under Aeneas, the son-in-law of King Priam. From Aeneas' second son would come the family of Julius Caesar. A descendant of his third son would be Romulus, the founder of Rome. To Aeneas' oldest son Ascanius was born Brutus, the future king of Britain, who at the age of fifteen accidentally killed his father. Required to live in exile, he persuaded 3,000 others to join him in relocating to the land of their British kindred. It would be a long and risky voyage, but their Greek enemies now commanded all the north shore of the Mediterranean except for the Etrurian and Legurian coasts. A life in Britain, therefore, must have offered promise. Brutus was of Hu Gadarn's own line and as high-ranking a prince as any in that land.

Embarking with their families in 332 vessels, the emigrants added a surprising number of passengers while en route. The first were Kymri from Epirus–now Albania–a lone enclave among Greek ports in the Adriatic. Other Kymri were found in two ports on the southern coast of Spain. On the Atlantic side of Iberia they picked up several Greeks who had been stranded when their ship–bound from Crete for Calabria in Italy–had been storm-driven and wrecked.

After a winter's interlude which saw the migrants involved in three battles with Kymric-speaking men who called themselves Gaels (as they explained it, Gael meant "forest dweller"), they rounded the horn of Armorica for the final leg of their journey. That winter, however, had its own achievement and its price. They had won the battles, and the Gael king had sued for peace. But Brutus' nephew had died in the second engagement and been buried under a large tumulus 160 miles up the River Loire. The young man's name was Tyrrhi, and the terms of peace gave his name to that place. In time to come Tours would be one of the most fruitful centers of the Celtic Church. In AD 732 it would be the site of the Western world's most decisive battle–checking the westward and northward thrust of Islam.

In the spring of 1203 BC the Kymric vessels arrived in Tor Bay in Devon and disembarked at Totnes. The Three Pacific Tribes received the immigrants from the East as brethren. Since Hu Gadarn's time Britain had been governed by patriarchal custom and consensus. Brutus now proposed–and the people ratified–the Constitution and Laws of Troy, under which (in addition to ancient custom) they would live in the future. At a convocation Brutus was elected King. The throne and crown of Hu Gadarn became his both by descent and by popular suffrage. Following the arrival in Britain, three sons were born to Brutus and his queen, Imogene; they were named Locrinus, Camber and Alban after the three Pacific Tribes. Meanwhile, in the third year of his reign, Brutus founded New Troy (later Lud's town or London). After a memorable twenty four year reign, he was buried alongside Queen Imogene at Bryn Gwyn the White Mount on which now stands the Tower.

We may review a few of the Usages of Britain derived from Trojan

Law. First is the Law of Royal Primogeniture, by which succession to the Throne is vested in the King's eldest son. Another allowed the Scepter of the Island to be swayed by a Queen as well as a King. In this the Trojan and British Law and Custom were unique, for among the continental nations no woman was permitted to reign. Aside from what were known as *cyfreithiau* "Common Rights," there were no other laws, and except for times of national emergency each subject was as free as the King. The military leadership was vested in the eldest tribe, the Kymry. From this tribe would also be elected the Pendragon or Military Dictator, to hold absolute power in time of foreign invasion or national danger.

A few of the Usages of Britain are cited below. They were considered to be inalienable rights–not to be altered by edict of Crown or National Convocation. Some came from the time of Hu Gadarn, some from Brutus. Most others date from the time of Molmutius the Lawgiver, who was King in the fifth century BC.

"There are three things belonging to a man, from whom no law can separate him–his wife, his children, and the instruments of his calling; for no law can unman a man, or uncall a calling."

"There are three tests of Civil Liberty–equality of rights, equality of taxation, freedom to come and go."

"There are three things that require the unanimous vote of the nation to effect–deposition of the sovereign, introduction of novelties in religion, suspension of law."

"There are three things which are private and sacred property in every man, Briton or foreigner–his wife, his children, his domestic chattels."

"Three things are indispensable to a true union of Nations–sameness of laws, rights, and language."

"There are three causes which ruin a State–inordinate privileges, corruption of justice, national apathy."

"There are three persons in a family exempted from all manual or menial work–the little child, the old man or woman, and the family instructor."

"There are three things free to all Britons–the forest, the unworked mine, the right of hunting wild creatures."

"There are three of private rank, against whom no weapon can be bared,– a woman, a child under fifteen, and an unarmed man."

"There are three things which every Briton may legally be compelled to attend,– the worship of God, military service, the courts of law."

"There are three things free to every man, Briton or foreigner, the refusal of which no law will justify,– water from spring, river or well; firing from a decayed tree; a block of stone not in use."

"There are three ends of law,– prevention of wrong, punishment for wrong inflicted, insurance of just retribution."

"There are three civil birthrights of every Briton,– the right to go wherever he pleases; the right, wherever he is, to protection from his land and sovereign; the right of equal privileges and equal restrictions."

"There are three persons who have a right to public maintenance,– the old, the babe, the foreigner who cannot speak the British tongue."

"There are three thieves who shall not suffer punishment,– a woman compelled by her husband, a child, a necessitous person who has gone through three towns and to nine houses in each town without being able to obtain charity though he asked for it."

"There are three things the safety of which depends upon the others,– the sovereignty, national courage, just administration of the laws."

"There are three orders that are exempt from bearing arms,– the bard, the judge, the graduate in law or religion. These represent God and his peace, and no weapon must ever be found in their hand."

"There are three whose power is kingly in law,–the sovereign paramount of Britain over all Britain and its isles, the princes palatine in their princedoms, the heads of the clans in their clans."

"There are three sacred things by which the conscience binds itself to truth,– the name of God, the rod of him who offers up prayers to God, the joined right hand."

Concerning the age and merit of these Usages, we have the testimony of great British jurists. In the Preface to Vol. iii of his *Reports*,

Lord Chief Justice Coke affirms, "... the Original Laws of this land were composed of such elements as Brutus first selected from the Ancient Greek and Trojan Institutions." Lord Chancellor Fortescue, in his work, *On the Laws of England*, writes, " ... concerning the different powers which Kings claim over their subjects, I am firmly of opinion that it arises solely from the different nature of the original institutions. So the Kingdom of Britain had its origin from Brutus and the Trojans who attended him in Italy and Greece, and were a mixed government compounded of the regal and democratic."

Considering what has happened to the Brittanic peoples in the years since these beginnings, we cannot overlook a prophecy given the exiled prince at the start of that lengthy voyage. Shortly after leaving Epirus, the vessels stopped at Malta where Brutus visited the Temple of Diana. The prophecy given by the Oracle was engraved in Archaic Greek on the altar of Diana built in later years at New Troy on the River Thames. During the third century it was translated into Latin by Nennius, a British prince in the court of Constantine's uncle, and later into English by Alexander Pope. It is among the oldest on record, and, while issued by a pagan goddess in very ancient times, has proven true to date—while still in process of fulfillment:

Diana:
"Brutus! There lies beyond the Gallic bounds
An island which the Western Sea surrounds,
By Ancient Giants held—now few remain
To bar thy entrance or obstruct thy reign;
To reach that happy shore thy sails employ,
There fate decrees to raise a second Troy,
And found an Empire in thy royal line
Which time shall ne'er destroy nor bounds confine."

The Celts

It is likely that when most of us think of the fall of Rome, we recall what happened in AD 410, when Alaric's Visigoths stormed the gates and sacked the city. We further recall Rome's humiliation in AD 452, when Pope Leo saved the city from rape and pillage by Attila and his Huns, offering a considerable payment in gold with promise of more to come.

What we may never have known is that Rome was put to the sword nearly eight hundred years earlier, 387 BC when Rome still a young Republic, by a band of Celts who, though they had no thought for empire-building or for ruling other peoples, loved a good fight and the challenge of an army-in-waiting. Their leader was Brennus a man they respected and followed. So terrified were the Romans as the Celts drew near that they emptied the city, forgetting to close the gates. When the Celts entered they found only a few old men, sitting as motionless as statues. These were Rome's eldest patricians, who had already decided not to go up to the fortified Capitoline Hill, where their presence during a siege could only mean more mouths to feed and less assurance of survival. So they sat in calm dignity, prepared for and expecting death.

The sight took the Celts aback. As Livy described it, "They gazed up at the old men as if they were idols." Finally one Celt got up his nerve and tweaked the beard of an elder to see if he was awake. The man struck the Celt's head with his staff. This broke the spell and the patrician blood flowed in short order. It also broke whatever spell hung over the empty houses; the city was soon in flames.

The victory was not complete, though, and the Celts surrounded the Capitol but were unable to take it. Late one night they tried to do so under cover of darkness. But the sacred geese aroused the defenders with their honking, and the first man to top the barricade was knocked off by a consular shield. His weight, as he tumbled caused those behind and beneath him to fall like tenpins struck by a bowling ball. The attempt was a failure and so, finally, was the siege.

Actually, the Celts were unprepared for such warfare. They knew nothing of logistics or resupply, and when food ran short, the besiegers had more difficulty in obtaining it than those within. With unburied dead littering streets and highway–and epidemic setting in–the Celts left off siege and campaign. They headed north while still able, carrying what treasure lay to hand.

Some years later–in 279 BC, still under the leadership of Brennus–the Celts broke an agreement with Greek city states and those in power in Macedonia following the death of Alexander the Great. Their involvement in Balkan politics was not new, for Philip of Macedon's own life had been ended by a Celtic dagger. Now the Celts were attempting what earlier they had done at Rome. The Greeks had already been assured by Pytheia's oracle that the Celts could be dealt with; the god Apollo and "the white virgins" (presumably Athena and Artemis) would protect them. What the "white virgins" actually turned out to be was a raging blizzard that caught Brennus under attack in the mountain passes when his van was too far ahead to summon. The frozen and the wounded, including Brennus, numbered several thousand. They were put to death while baggage was burned so that others could survive. Of these few thousand who escaped, but only briefly, none ever returned to their homes along the Danube. The sole survivors seem to have been the men of Brennus' van who fought their way to the Dardanelles, crossed into Asia Minor, and by AD 276 had established the kingdom of Galatia known to St. Paul.

With such an introduction to the Greeks and Romans, it is hard to believe the Celts could be given such bad press by later scholars and raconteurs, Julius Caesar included. One might expect that with the losses each had taken and lessons all had learned, the opponents would be better known to one another. Perhaps, however, those who were on the scene in Caesar's time were simply repeating what had been said of the Celts three hundred years before which was that the Celts fought naked, their bodies adorned with bright colors and outlandish designs. It was said further that they cut off their victims' heads, using them to adorn their public places, and that they practiced human sacrifice.

What was commonly understood from the beginning is what we can be most sure of. The Celts were far bigger than the Greeks and Romans. They were light-skinned, blond and blue-eyed. They gave evidence of fierce delight in fighting and were unafraid of death. Julius Caesar, from whom other historians and raconteurs took their lead, may have been right on two of the above counts; I cannot believe he was even close on the others. The Celts were unafraid of death for the same reason they would be so when under Druid teachers–their belief in an afterlife. The nudity was unimportant since so also, at an earlier time, were the Greeks while at war. It seems more than likely that the head-hunters were not Celts but Scythians, a fierce Asiatic people who introduced the horse to warfare and earlier occupied sites where displays of skulls had been attributed to the Celts. As to the Celts' practice of human sacrifice, the complaint itself shows ignorance of the principles on which such worship was always based. To have any efficacy at all, a sacrifice to a god must have sufficient value to make recompense for the injury done to the god by the offender's misdeeds–the same offender who was offering propitiatory gifts. Those gifts must exceed in value what harm has been done, and must be flawless, perfect, satisfactory in every way. To claim, as Caesar did, that the Celts, in sacrificing to their gods offered as gifts the lives of *criminals,* is utterly eccentric. If the Celts bound their criminals in wicker cages and set fire to them, it would not be sacrifice to a deity but an execution of those who merited capital punishment because of their misdeeds. To offer a gift that cost the giver nothing–in this case a criminal deserving death–would be an unbelievably grave offense which could hardly fail to bring down the wrath of the heavens on the head of him who offered it.

Celts' Shortcomings in Warfare, Discovered by the Romans

We have referred to the Celts' lack of professionalism in combat, the shortcoming of every army ever formed from citizen-soldiers. But Rome's own legions had themselves shown no professionalism in 105 BC when at Aurasio (now Orange) in Provence, several met with such resounding losses at the hands of Cimbri and Teutons as to threaten Rome's expectations for all of Gaul. As a result of that defeat Rome made provisions for highly trained and motivated citizen-soldiers to be a full-time lifelong career. Three years after this decision an army of Teutons, many of whom had fought earlier at Aurausio, were decisively defeated by the new Roman army under Marius. One hundred thousand men, women and children were killed on that occasion, another hundred thousand sold as slaves.

While the army destroyed at that scene was German rather than Celtic, a weakness of the Celts in combat had already been described by the Greek Polybius. The Celts were fighting with inferior swords and ineffective shields. The swords seem to have been Bronze Age weapons, or modeled after those of the Bronze Age and tipped with iron. But their tips were curved and had no sharp points; they could be used to strike a foe but not effectively to stab him. In addition, their swords' blades, when coming in contact with a foe's arms or armor, were likely not only to be dulled, but to bend. Such a blade had to be straightened before further use, which in battle might require jumping on its blade. Furthermore, the Celt's shield was inferior as well. Wearing no armor saving a helmet on his head and a torq around his neck, the Celt could not get much protection from this small shield. The Roman's, by comparison, would protect its possessor from helmeted head and neck to knee. The legionnaire carried a throwing spear whose head would bend or break on contact with the ground and thus not be picked up and thrown back. He likewise carried a thrusting spear to be used once at the clashing of line with line, then dropped. He carried a sharp and wieldy two foot, double bladed sword for hand-to-hand combat with a dagger in addition. There was enough curve in his shield to allow a chariot to wheel over his body should he be on the ground—enough width for him and others, side by side, to be shielded from spears and arrows as well as from rocks and hot oil dropped from the walls of a defended city as they drew near to breach them.

The Celtic Background

But what of these Celts and of their background? Like the British, they originated on the European side of the Black Sea basin. While the Cimmerians or Kymri claimed to have come from the area around Crimea, the Celts' homeland was that watered by the Danube—between Bucharest and the sea. The Celtic migrations came later and on a much larger scale than the Kymri's. Except for that portion of the Gauls who, late in the second century BC, crossed into Asia Minor and founded Little Galatia, the mass of Celts began crossing Europe around 1000 BC. They began settling into northern Italy, Switzerland, upper Germany, France, northern Spain, Britain and Ireland between the ninth and fourth centuries BC. Their traces in Britain show the Celts'* earliest arrivals as taking place during the eighth century and as having settlements there by the fourth.

Of all the peoples of antiquity, they seem to have been the most gifted as artists and workers in bronze, pewter, gold, silver, and enamelware as well as in small items for bodily ornamentation and dress. Because they were in quest of a land of their own, only a few of their sites were settled long enough to give evidence of their skills as artists and craftsmen; one such site is La Tene in Switzerland. The Celts' skills with metals may have developed during their passage through the Balkans, for this took place when the Bronze Age was at its zenith. But it is enough to say that their art involved small-scale, easily transportable work, finely detailed and bursting with vitality–as compared with the formal, picture-perfect work of the Greeks and Egyptians whoe handiwork was intended to remain in place.

There seems to be no record of conflict between the Britons and Celts while the latter were settling in. Though both made superb warriors, their peoples were not as uncultured as most of those thronging from the East twelve to fifteen centuries later. The Celts' earlier wars were fought for adventure's sake, the later in defense of new homelands against aggression. So far as religion was concerned, Cimri and Celt alike seem to have looked to the invisible world rather than the visible for the sources of knowledge, of life and power. We see this in the Celts' fear, not of man but of the heavens falling. This is evidenced by a recollection of the younger Brennus having laughed derisively at the report of Pytheia's oracle and at the Greeks' belief in a clan of gods having human form.

From the beginning, the British seem to have been familiar with Old Testament concepts of God and Law. We have already seen evidence of this in their triads, even though it was in the age of the Biblical Patriarchs that their original migration took place. There are

*It can be held that the Kimri *were* Celts, and the point is here conceded. But in this presentation it will not normatively suggest that meaning. *Britain* and *British,* as terms, date back a thousand years before the Celts' arrival.

evidences of a similar understanding of God and man and of Law and grace, which may have been acquired during the Celts' own years of migration. If so, this would have come in the final stages of their move, for the evidence is beyond dispute that during many of their centuries on the move they were both a feared and a fearsome people.

A few wholesome customs of the Celts are to be noted. One was the freedom of choice given to individuals in the normal social setting. This is radically different than the universal view in tribal cultures (whether ancient or modern) in which the majority of members are subordinate in rank and function and have little or no voice in community decisions. One noteworthy element among the Celts was freedom given to women to own and dispose of property, to be entitled to education and the creative use of leisure, to give one's self in marriage and to endow that marriage with one's own wealth, and finally the freedom to fight if need be alongside men in the community's defense. This individualism appears to have been characteristic of the Celts throughout their history of contact with indigenous tribes already on the scene.

Two things come uniquely to mind as featuring the westward migration of the Celts. One is that, unlike the Saxons, Franks, Vandals, Lombards, Goths, Huns, Alans, Suebi and Slavs whose migrations began twelve to fifteen hundred years later than the Celts' (and became the causal factor of the Dark Ages), the Celts were not forced out of their homelands by encroaching neighbors. Theirs was a leisurely and largely a pastoral migration. They appear not to have displaced other peoples as they made their way. Some Celts remained in each of the lands they crossed, and what peoples earlier occupied those lands must have allowed them to settle in among them.

One cannot but see the Celts' five hundred year journey across Europe as paralleling the Hebrews' forty years in the Wilderness—on a larger scale and giving evidence of God's larger purpose for the participants and their descendants. Except for those who regard the Wilderness years as a training ground for a called and dedicated people, neither journey makes much sense. When the Israelites crossed the Red Sea as a free people under God, the point where they would cross the

Jordan into their Promised Land was barely two hundred miles away. Yet it took them forty years to make that journey.

In contrast, the distance from the Black Sea, say to Tor Bay in Devon, is sixteen hundred miles. We can only guess how long it took the mass of Celts to cross Europe from the time of departure from their homeland to that of their arrival at what would be their new and permanent homes. Let us guess five hundred years. But why so long? There were not that many people in the way; it was not until more than a thousand years later that the Dark Ages descended, with millions seeming to pour in from the East and civilization itself to disappear. We may do well to accept that those years between their departure from the home in the Danube basin and their settling in Western Europe were years of preparation.

For the moment we shall leave the Celts still in transition across the transalpine north of Europe. The coming chapter will offer speculation–as this has not–of the forces, factors and peoples that may have played a part in the Celts' acceptance of a Druidic matrix that seems quite miraculously to have furthered, in tranquillity and peace, their readiness for Christ.

❧ Chapter 5 ❧

The Firming of the Celts

It is many years since my sabbatical year at Canterbury's College of Clergy where I learned of a British Church long neglected by historians and resolved to find out and make known whatever I could. Yet till writing the preceding chapter concerning the Celts, it never occurred to me that what they went through during that migration might have had God's hand in it–as with the Hebrews during their Wilderness Years. It seems evident that during those centuries the Celts underwent a substantial transformation of character and outlook. But how and in what circumstances? Who may have joined with them on their journey? What events may have influenced their self-image and manner of life?

One obvious possibility is that while crossing Europe, the Celts were joined by some of the 27,290 Israelites who in 721 BC. were deported from the Kingdom of Israel into Assyria, or much later of the 50,000 Jews who between 598 BC and 587 BC were removed from the Kingdom of Judah to Babylon. The time-periods would square quite well. However the facts at hand do not seem to point in that direction. When in 612 BC Assyria fell and Ninevah was laid waste, the surviving Hebrews were moved to Persia. Although most of these exiles had come from the kingdom of Israel rather than that of Judah, those at Persia did include both Israelites and Jews, and they are on record as part of the Diaspora (Dispersion) in the years that followed. As for the Jews in Babylon, when by Cyrus' edict in 538 BC they were given leave to return to Palestine, comparatively few did so. In 359 BC and again in 338 BC many who remained in Babylon would rebel against Persian rule and migrate to India. Of these a number would go to China. These Indian Jews and Chinese Jews have remained in the Jewish faith until today.

By contrast, those who were transferred from Ninevah to Persia would in a distant future be invited to help convert to Judaism a large nomadic people from central Asia who had settled north of the Black and Caspian Seas. These were the Khazars whose monarch, after becoming a Jew, had extended the invitation. From AD 700 to AD 1016 the two peoples—by now one people and officially a Jewish kingdom—co-existed with Christians and unbelievers, allowing citizenship to all. However, at the latter end, the Khazar kingdom was destroyed by a joint Russian-Byzantine army. Its Jews were dispersed throughout Russia, Poland, Germany and the Mediterranean seaports.[1] As with those in India and China, intermarriage with Gentiles and the passage of time had left them racially non-Semitic. Yet by religion they were Jews. So while it is quite possible that a few or even many of the exiles in Assyria and Babylon escaped and joined the migrant Celts, the proportions may have had little significance.

What next comes to mind has to do with unsolved mysteries of the ancient world. One involves the Israelites who remained in Palestine, known to us as the "Ten Lost Tribes." Another is Atlantis—a legendary land that would be classed as mythic had not Plato written about it at length. A third involves the mysterious invaders who in the 14th century B.C. came seemingly from nowhere and for two hundred years dominated the Eastern Mediterranean lands before their overthrow and disappearance. Could any of these have thrown in their lot with the Celts during that journey, either to go with them or to help some on their way? We can also speculate about a link between Celts and the Jews—a people about whom much is known, yet who continue to be a folk of mystery because of differences between the Gentile and the Judaic mind and psyche.

Atlantians as Movers and Shapers

Let us, of these, consider first the Lost Atlantis. It must be thought of as "prehistoric" in relation to the world we know. That is a mere technicality however; the Deluge and Flood wiped away all record save ancient legend and Plato's slender thread of witness and tradition. His knowledge of Atlantis, though considerable, was hearsay; it was derived from an official in Egypt and from old archives seen there by that official. Yet the historic evidence of an Atlantis is now supported by discoveries in two sciences, one of carbon dating and the other of archaeology.[2]

Charles F. Libby, an American chemist in 1949 discovered a method for dating the age of organic materials. He did so by testing, in organic tissues, the ratio of natural carbon (C-12) to the residue of radioactive carbon (C-14) received from cosmic rays in earth's atmosphere. Following an organism's demise the C-14 diminishes at a steady rate, the half-life being 5,600 years.

An error in Libby's assumptions was found when another American, Charles W. Ferguson, in date-testing identifiable tree-rings in 4,000 year old trees, discovered that the earth's atmosphere had considerably less radioactive carbon prior to 1500 BC than subsequently. What this did was to add 750 years (by way of correction) to the age of items shown by Libby's method to date from 1500 BC or earlier.

A British archaeologist, Colin Renfrew, was thus enabled to announce in 1971 what many scientists already believed—that ancient monuments in the north of Europe, such as Stonehenge and the megaliths at Carnac in France, predate by many centuries the oldest monuments of Egypt and the Middle East. A conclusion based on many carbon datings demonstrates that assumptions held in the West for centuries have been false. The Northern European world did not derive its civilization from the Mid-Eastern world, nor did its start come at a later date. Actually it may have been the reverse, though for the moment it seems reasonable to hold that our Western civilization had two cultural and civilizing sources—one in the Mid-Eastern world and the other in the Atlantic north.

What the carbon datings in Northern Europe have seemed to prove is borne out by archeological discoveries by Renfrew and others. Bronze Age artifacts in one whole band of latitudes in Northern Europe have been given significantly earlier datings than those of a comparable level of development in Egypt or Sumer. Artifacts with those early dates have been in found in the south of Britain, northern France and Germany, the Low Countries, Denmark and southern Sweden.

Not surprisingly, this locality is exactly where scientists, following the lead of theologian/historian Jurgen Spanuth, claim to have found the Atlantis described by Plato. They believe it included the areas referred to above, centering in Denmark and in much of what is now the North Sea, with Helgoland as the sole surviving bit of land. Whether Atlantis' disappearance was sudden and entire or partial and by degrees is not available either in legend or in what Plato wrote. I am proposing that Atlantis' submergence came in several stages and without critical loss of populations. I do so because of what seems to be a related sequence of events.

In support of Spanuth's proposal has been the discovery that the earth's climate was considerably warmer between 5000 and 2500 BC than in any period since the Ice Ages. Some time before 1500 BC there came great changes in weather and climate in addition to cataclysmic earth-shocks and flooding. To begin with, there had been a span of years with such widespread drought that water tables lowered greatly and wells dried up; so also did the rivers. Ovid, writing of this period in his *Metamorphoses,* names some of those waterways gone dry—the Rhine, Danube, Rhone, Nile, Euphrates, Don and Ganges. Herodotus, in speaking of the same era, says that the severity of the famine led King Attys of Lydia in Turkey to send half his people to the land of the Umbricians in Italy. To those years can also be traced the beginnings of desertification in the Sahara. Libya seems to have been the first among many lands to be transformed from grassland to arid desert.

If we were to choose a date of 1700 BC for the beginning of a drought, that would be followed by centuries of calamity from changes in the earth's crust, weather and climate. For Atlantis, the drought would be the beginning of the end. The Platonic years had been years of commerce, prosperity and peaceful interaction with other peoples. As Plato describes Atlantis' sports events, the chariots were larger and more ornate–and their horses' gear and trappings more elaborate–than at any time to come. This may be of interest considering that when Rome invaded Britain in AD 43–as it had done also in 55 and 54 BC–the Britons' use of chariots was conceded to be the most skilled and daring ever seen in warfare. I speak of it because a half mile north of Stonehenge is an ancient cursus or race-track having the same dimensions as that where, according to Plato, the Atlantians' horse and chariot races were regularly held.

Gerhard Herm, in his 1975 book, *The Celts*, draws a convincing picture of Atlantis as on this site.[3] He cites the thousands of years of warm, moist weather that brought climatic advantage to Nordic people–along with the wealth and leisure to provide what amounted to an ongoing Olympiad. He points to the ironic fact that the epoch now described as Northern Europe's High Bronze Age had, for several centuries, been described as its Middle Stone Age. It would not be long, in any case, till terrible calamities came throughout the world. This began with the years of drought already mentioned, followed by a century and more of violent storms, earthquakes and severely cold weather. If these calamities–ending with a severe change in climate–did not mark the end of Atlantis as a place where people existed, it did mark for budding science what appeared to be a Stone Age and no more than that. With the loss of much of their land, many of their people and virtually all their wealth, the people of Atlantis may have thought of themselves as living in a Twilight of the Gods. Britain would henceforth be at a distance from the remainder and perhaps depopulated. The North Sea waters between would doubtless be held as haunted and forever cursed.

The Relocation of Atlantians

We can hazard a guess that the Atlantian survivors' interests would henceforth lie along the southern seas rather than the western. Many would migrate southward, returning to the climate that had so long been theirs. Those who remained in what later was Denmark, Norway and Sweden might turn to piracy rather than commerce. This, of course, would be limited to their brief and frenetic summer seasons. The remaining months would find them huddling round village fires while the sun edged over the horizon late in the morning only to drop beneath it in early afternoon.

However, the Viking life for which Atlantis' descendants would later be feared, might not come till the final years of tribulation. The continued drought in the 17th century BC gave cause for migration to a warm and distant land. In the Atlantians' now-unused fleet were a great many longboats for their water travel. They had the horses, equipage and wagons or carts to use by land. There was enough wealth in precious metals to provide for them during months of migration, especially when behind that wealth lay intelligence, organization, mobility and force of arms.

Where could they have gone? History provides one possibility. In the 17th Century BC an Indo-European people known as Aryans came out of the northwest in great numbers, settling in India's Indus Valley.[4] Their coming was not meant for war or conquest, though accompanied here and there with armed conflict. The newcomers were Indo-European and light skinned. Their language, customs and religion were so admired that these Aryans became and continued to be the most influential of India's many castes.

If our supposition is correct, these migrants can be removed from the focus of our attention. Yet since the supposition is highly speculative, we may explain how simply such an extraordinary migration could have been undertaken. To begin with, we offer a reminder of how easily the Viking descendants of those remaining in Scandinavia slipped into the Black Sea as pirates during the Middle Ages. Their shallow-draft longboats were ideal for river travel. They could ascend the Rhine to a point beyond Basel in Switzerland where an easy 40 mile portage put them on the Danube headed for the Black Sea. A more hidden route could take them up the Elbe to a point near Prague where a similar portage might be accomplished. If Ovid was wrong about the Euphrates it would have been possible to go by sea to Antioch in Syria, where a portage along valley roads would lead migrants to that river with access to the Persian Gulf. Except for the need to wheel their boats across the isthmus at Suez, they could have made the entire trip by sea. Given this relatively easy travel, and having a horse-drawn alternative to water transportation, the miles from the Mediterranean to the Indus River would pose no great difficulty to an adventuresome people seeking a warmer place to live.

Builders of Henges, Circles, Zodiacs and Monuments

Since no one has yet found an answer to the question of who built Glastonbury's Zodiac, Stonehenge, Carnac and other circles, let us suggest they may have been built by the Atlantians during their own Stone Age. We already know that the great monuments of Britain and France were on the scene when British and Celtic peoples first arrived. We have evidence that when Stonehenge was built, it was by the active cooperation of neighboring tribes, and quite possibly part of the Atlantis culture. It might then follow that when Hu Gadarn and his Cymbri arrived in Britain they may have found a remnant of Stonehenge's Atlantian builders still on the scene and thankful to be joined by peaceful, accomplished and industrious newcomers.

Such a proposal may in fact find support in a few already-mentioned facts. One is Sargon of Akkad's boast of friendship and commerce with this distant people.[5] His claim is backed up by our knowledge of a heavy traffic in Cornish tin two thousand years before the Phoenicians were on the scene. Another is the seeming certitude on the part of Hu Gadarn's people that Albion, the White Island, was meant to be their homeland. If we can accept their awareness of a Britain associated with Atlantis, we can appreciate these hopeful expectations. Most convincing is the high probability that whoever built Stonehenge had occupied the site for a great many years before it was built.

Rodney Castleden, in his 1987 book *The Stonehenge People*, informs us that, though the henge's design as a computer anticipated its completion by 3,000 BC (which may not have happened), the initial planning for that use goes back infinitely further. Posthole A, the first in a sequence of trial sites lining up the position of the summer solstice's sunrise, is assigned by carbon testing to a date of *8100 BC*[6] The second in that series of tests (Posthole B) is found to have been put in place a thousand years later. Thus, while we have no proof of who the builders were, it can be said of them that they were an advanced culture, people who, from the start, possessed an infinite patience and a concern for getting things right. This guess has got to be given some credence, for without it we are still in the dark. A few other items described in Castleden's book make clear that, whoever these people were, they gave attention to things mundane as well as celestial. A roadway thought to be the oldest in Europe has been found near Glastonbury, dating back to 4,000 BC[7] A footwalk one meter in width and 2.7 kilometers in length crossing the bog between the island of Westhay in Meare and the hamlet of Shapwick in the Polden Hills, was begun with two underlying sets of rails being placed end to end upon the marshy ground. The rails consisted of coppiced lime, resting in parallel and eighteen inches apart, each segment having the thickness of a telephone pole and upon which were placed split oak planks (totaling five kilometers), cut to size. These were secured to the underlying peat through holes and notches made in the planks by 10,000 sharpened birch pegs. This road, upon which turves could be laid to assure safe and dry passage in all seasons, was the first of at least a dozen built nearby during the next thousand years. All were used for the convenience of those crossing the bog to small islands for the purpose of gardening or fishing. Most of the later roadways, put in place around 3000 BC give the appearance of having been prefabricated in workshops to simplify their installation.

The Sea Peoples

If the Aryans who settled in the Indus Valley in the 17th Century BC came from a drought-stricken Atlantis, those who made the move may well have included folk from what is now Britain as well as from the Continent. If the drought was the only calamity thus far to have occurred, the migrants could also have included Atlantians from areas later to be submerged.

However, the next migrants are likely to have had other reasons for their move, for the drought would long since have ended. The later calamities may have been violent weather, earthquakes and tidal floods attending the submergence of those parts of Atlantis' towns and countryside lost beneath the sea. If the calamities were followed the eruption of Thira, an additional reason for migrating could be a permanent change in climate. We are aware that following the 1883 eruption of Krakatoa the sky was darkened and the climate chilled for four years while the dust settled to the ground. In the case of Atlantis, as already stated, the change in climate became a permanent one. Those suffering most from such a change would have lived in the Baltic lands and Scandinavia. Britain, France and the Low Countries would have been less affected because of the benign influence of the Gulf Stream.

Let us suppose that Atlantians seeking warmer climes may on their own have migrated to the Mediterranean coast. Following Thira's devastation of that coast, a final wave of migrants–chiefly men–appears to have hurried south, perhaps to serve in repair parties, perhaps to take part in the appropriation of stricken ports and shores, perhaps in search of adventure. Those moved by the last of these motives may well have become the extraordinary adventurers of whom we speak.

Judging by appearance and manner of combat, it seems probable that the invaders who dominated the Eastern Mediterranean from the fourteenth to the twelfth centuries BC either were–or were led by–men from Atlantis.[8] (It is only in recent years that these have been described as Sea Peoples.) Their earliest appearance came with the overthrow of the Hittites in Asia Minor. From there they swept over Syria and Palestine, working their way into the many mouths of the Nile. Their first appearance in Egypt was as migrant workers, laying the groundwork for confrontation and attack. When they came in armed force, it was in longboats sporting carved eagle heads on their high stems fore and aft. It seems very likely that they were equipped with the remains of what Plato had described as Atlantis' great fleet. They had upon their heads horned helmets, in design like those of the later Vikings and they bore as well their flame-shaped lances. They carried what Diodorus of Sicily (himself a Dorian) called the "Germanic hilted sword," one of the finest weapons ever made. Though he ascribed these weapons to the Celts, we must remember that the Sea People would have been using the Atlantians' boats and weapons six hundred years before the Celts began their westward trek. What seems likely is that a sizable force of men from Atlantis had succeeded in moving the remains of Atlantis' armory and fleet from Jutland to the Black Sea where, with whatever Mediterranean kindred or allies were available, they began their years of conquest.

Till recently almost nothing was known about these men, where they came from, or where they went. A king of Ugarit in Syria had written to a colleague in Cyprus, "Enemy ships have been sighted on the sea; be prepared." But the tablet was never dispatched. It was found by archaeologists in Ugarit's ruins.[9] All the Egyptians knew about the enemy was that they were Indo-European rather than Semitic like themselves. The name "Sea Peoples" was assigned following the discovery early in the 20th Century of a victory inscription in Pharaoh Mernepta's Temple at Carnack. It described them as "all northern peoples ... coming from all sorts of countries and remarkable for their blond hair and blue eyes."

An earlier and more detailed record says the marauders were thought to be a confederation including Danaeans from Greece, Tyrrhenians from Liguria, Shakalsha from Sicily, Lyceans from Turkey, and Philistines who as a tribe had left Crete and settled on the Palestinian coast. What seems quite possible is that such men had been associated as pirates and perhaps were kin to the Atlantians.[10] Now, however, they were profiting by the use of longboats, helmets, shields, lances, swords and daggers unlike anything seen before. In their garb, their appearance, the boats they came in, the weapons they used and the manner of their attack, they were virtually identical with the Vikings who preyed on the English, Scottish and Irish coasts two thousand years later. What part did the men of Atlantis play in this endeavor? They may have organized and led the conquest. They may, as mercenaries or in partnership, have supplied boats and weapons, relying on the others to provide the manpower and logistics.

Our reference to these Atlantians and their associates has one purpose—to point to a people whose descendants might have reason to join the Celts in later years as they made their way westward. In 1191 BC the power of the Sea Peoples was broken by the Egyptian armies under Pharaoh Ramses III. After great loss of life the Sea Peoples withdrew, and within a few years their dominance had ended. Our concern would lie with those veterans who during their years of conquest had married and formed families in Palestine—to whom they could and did return. They lived along the Mediterranean in what now includes the Gaza Strip, with the Canaanites in the hills east of them and the Jews in the mountains beyond. Like the Phoenicians to the north, these Philistines were a seafaring people. There the likeness ended, for the Phoenicians were Semitic merchants and traders while the Philistines were Gentile warriors. Their coming to Palestine would have been roughly during those years when the Hebrews, in crossing the Jordan, were completing a forty year training course fitting them to become a bride to Yahweh and a husband to the land.

The Ten Lost Tribes

By the time of Jesus' ministry it had been nearly a thousand years since David's Kingdom split in two. Each kingdom had gone its way. Each had its own line of kingly succession. At times they stood together as one people against a common enemy. At other times they differed as to who their friends might be and who their foes. During their first century as separates they fought each other in a bitter Civil War. The northern kingdom, Israel, came to an end in 721 BC. From that time its people were treated as a conquered race in their own land, enslaved to whichever of the great powers was in the ascendancy. The southern Kingdom, Judah, lost its Davidic line in 598 BC and though its Temple was subsequently rebuilt along with a puppet kingly rule, both came to an end in AD 70. In AD 90, after further rebellion against the Romans,

Jerusalem was leveled to the ground and its occupants dispersed. On its ruins would be built a Roman Gentile city as a ongoing insult to the Jews.

Yet even in Jesus' time there had been hope for reconciliation of the whole House of Israel and a restoration of the Davidic Kingdom. In telling King Agrippa of God's promise to the Patriarchs, Paul said, "Unto which promise our twelve tribes, [presently] serving God day and night, hope to come." (Acts 26:7). Jesus, in sending the Twelve on a preaching mission, said, "Go not into the way of the Gentiles, and into any city of the Samaritans enter ye not. But go rather to the lost sheep of the house of Israel." (Matthew 10: 5, 6).

What can we say of the Ten Lost Tribes? What can we say of their lost sheep? Unlike the Jews, who are the oldest people on the face of the earth, the Israelites are members of a Diaspora known only to God. They cannot have been lost to genocide; there is no record of any power of the time having such a thing in mind. Moreover, genocide is virtually impossible to accomplish, and on a large and total scale has never been completed. We know what happened to the Armenians after World War I, to the Jews before and during World War II, to Christians in Nigeria a few years ago and to Christians in the Sudan today. It has never been completed even to the most desperate people's satisfaction. There are always those who have lived to tell the tale, and always ongoing witnesses to the tale.

What seems to have occurred is that the people of Israel, spontaneously and without consultation with others, gave up their identity. Singly and in small groups, families and villagers left Palestine on their own. There was no direction to go—whether by land or sea—but west. Israel had become a No Man's Land where larger nations fought their battles and where for the residents there was no survival. So they vanished in order to retain their lives in whatever way it could be done.

Fortunately we have confirmation of the Israelites' presence in the western world. The Tribe of Asher's lands were geographically congruent with the Phoenicians' and we learn of traffic and ties between this people and the clients of Tyre and Sidon—including Britain. The Tribe of Dan had lands both in the south and in the north. The one was between Judea and Philistia, allowing the southern Danites to seek business with both as well as develop their own maritime connections. Dan's lands in the northern kingdom were athwart a river that ran through the Lebanese mountain range to Tyre, with whom there was also maritime partnership and rivalry. There are many in Scandinavia who cite old tradition that Danmark (Denmark) was founded by people of Dan; it is a claim made also by the Irish. The prophetess Deborah, in her victory paean following the bloody battle on the River Kishon (Judges 5:17) speaks of Dan as being absent in his ships and of Asher as having missed the battle because of traffic at the seaside. Zebulon is another whose lands were near to the sea; his tribe is remembered from ancient times as the patron of the Dutch. It may be noted that when Jacob blessed his sons prior to his death, he made this prediction concerning the fifth (Genesis 49:13), "Zebulon shall dwell at the haven of the sea; and he shall be for a haven of ships; and his border shall be unto Sidon."

It is a far remove from biblical prophecy to children's nonsense rhymes. Yet while awareness of history and relationship tend to be forgotten when roots develop laterally rather than vertically, we find our taproots confirmed in strange and curious ways. One may be the way in which a nonsense rhyme used by generations of Scottish girls while jumping rope turns out to be a Hebrew recital of an arithmetic table—and another the record of a fabled event. A recitation of unknown gibberish phrased in rhyme and repeated by countless Cornish generations, is found to be Hebrew, and in translation,

> "Lift up your heads, O ye gates;
> and be ye lift up,
> ye everlasting doors;
> and the King of glory shall come in.
> Who is this King of glory?
> Even the Lord of hosts,
> He is the King of glory."

The Wilderness Years of the Celts

As we reflect on the possibilities and the evidence before us, we must conclude that whoever the persons or whatever the events or ideas that influenced the Celts during their passage across Europe may have to remain unknown. All we can be sure of is that by the time the Celts arrived at their destination they had become a people ready and able to learn and follow the precepts of a religion that by intuition was so perfectly adapted to Christianity that when they first heard the about Christianity they turned to it almost immediately and apparently without the shedding of a drop of blood. This was true both of Britain and of Ireland–though the Gospel reached Britain in the first century and Ireland in the fourth or the fifth. Britain, indeed, was the first to become officially Christian, dated by the Venerable Bede at AD 156.

Little is known even now as to how and when the various Celtic peoples arrived at their destination–or even of how other peoples may have preceded them. Both Spain and Ireland are thought to have been frequented by people of Eber or Heber (i.e. Hebrews) whence the names Iberia for Spain and Hibernia for Ireland. There is as persistent a strain of Judaism in their distant past as of Israelite influence in Celtic France and Britain.

One clue to varieties of Celtic lineage and thought may be observed in language differences, i.e., the Goidelic and Brythonic Celtic tongues. The Goidelic or Gaelic tongue was that of Ireland, Scotland and the Isle of Man, whereas the Brythonic Celt was found among the Bretons (of Brittany), Britons, Cornish and Welsh. It seems to be generally accepted that the Goidelic Celts went from Spain to Ireland and from there to Scotland and the Isle of Man. The Brythonic Celts came to Brittany and Britain by way of Gaul.

Though we are unable to point to specific Israelites or Jews who journeyed with the Celts, we are told of a household that escaped from Judea at the time of the Babylonian Captivity. The family head was Jeremiah, the Prophet and author of the Bible's longest book. He was in his home village of Anathoth when Jerusalem was sacked. With him in his journey came Baruch the scribe. Besides household servants who came as carriers were two young girls, his great-granddaughters and the only surviving daughters of King Zedekiah, the last ruler in David's line.

Their escape took place in 587 BC. When Nebuchadnezzar's men took the king, they blinded him after forcing him to see most of his sons beheaded.* They then took Zedekiah to Babylon where he remained till his death. Unbeknownst to others, Zedekiah's two daughters had been rescued and taken to Jeremiah, whose daughter had been the great King Josiah's queen. The two young girls, Tamar (Tea, pron. Taya) Tephi and Scota went to Egypt with Jeremiah in addition to Baruch, the household servants and a large quantity of gear including a precious relic of ancient times. After several years in Egypt they went to Spain and from there to Ireland. While in Spain, Jeremiah gave the younger great-grandchild, Scota, in marriage to Heber Bruc, a prince of Zaragossa in Spain. Later, in Ireland, he gave the older princess, Tea Tephi, in marriage to Eochaidh the Heremon, the son of the High King of Ireland. Tea and the Heremon became forebears to the central line of Irish monarchs as well as the Scottish and English kings and queens. Beginning with the Heremon, the kings of Ireland–and later those of Scotland and still later those of England–were consecrated upon the Stone of Scone, the relic brought by Jeremiah from Palestine and Egypt. This stone was the Hebrews' most sacred stone, called Jacob's "pillow" actually a pillar he consecrated with oil after his vision of angels descending from heaven and ascending on the ladder seen there. Jacob placed it atop a cairn he built, saying, "How holy is this place ...This is none other but the house of God, and this is the gate of heaven."

After arrival in Ireland, Jeremiah became known as Ollam Fodhla, *Wise Governor*, and Collawyn, *The Long Suffering*. During his last years, he is said to have founded a Hebrew University and to have written and codified the Book of Royal Irish Laws.[11] Tea Tephi's stone tomb can be seen at Tara in County Meath. Jeremiah lies buried under a large tumuls on Devenish Island in Lower Loch Erne.[12]

Both Jeremiah and Tea, along with Heremon and the Irish-Scottish line, are shown in the lineage of the English monarchy as well

---

*A few escaped. Some may have escaped as well to Egypt.

as that restored in Spain and those of European monarchies no longer established or enthroned. The British monarchy, as time has passed, has maintained its descent from King David in such monarchs as Caradoc, Constantine the Great and King Arthur. It has included such Irish monarchs as Ugaine the Great, such Scots as Fergus I, such Saxons as Alfred the Great and such great Normans as Edward III, whose son, the victorious and esteemed Black Prince, died before his father. From the first that stone has, by the Hebrews' intent, been for all generations a witness to God's promises to Jacob. Since its arrival in the Isles, it has borne witness to God's promise to his Covenant People (Jeremiah 33:17), "David shall never want a man to sit upon the throne of the House of Israel."

One may ask whether there is point to having monarchs of the Davidic line to serve Christian nations unless their people can accept themselves responsibly and unashamedly as the Israel of God. Today there are only two such peoples, the British and the Spanish. Fortunately, almost coincident with the ending of this chapter, there have been published several scholarly works that tell how those whom the Celtic Churches converted to Christ were themselves descended from those whom Jesus described as "the lost sheep of the house of Israel."

We shall devote the next chapter to who those peoples tribesmen were and are—giving thought to our calling as One Body under One Head to be ready for the Lord Jesus at his Coming.

cs Chapter 6 cs

Druidic Learning and Religion

While the previous chapter may shed new light on nations of the ancient world, more remains to be said. We cannot point to any peoples whose association with the Celts may have enabled them to grow in the artistry and zest for life that they contributed to Europe's classic best. There is the possibility, however, that during the years when they arrived in western Europe, sizable numbers of Israelites were going there as well –and probably by sea. We have already mentioned Hebrew tribes who were involved in shipping. Their men could have carried thousands of their own to Spain, France, Britain and Ireland, for these people, as refugees, had a dire need to go wherever they could be landed. Others, such as the Phoenicians or the surviving remnant of Sea Peoples would surely have transported Israelites in exchange for the homes and lands they could not take with them. Such emigrants would have held the same desperate hopes and anticipation as steerage passengers in a much later age. Finding an opportunity to settle among men already dedicated to liberty and equity –and living under an ancient and just regime –they would make it their highest priority to be obedient subjects and good neighbors. So also would the Celts.

I am well aware that "anything Celtic" goes today, that store shelves overflow with books on the Celts and their beloved Saints Patrick and Brigid. I am equally aware that there are those in England who ridicule the concept of a British Israel —as well as those in France who would override or suppress the ancient Breton character and tongue. Yet we have no more reason to overemphasize the one than to underplay the other. It is a matter not only of surprise but of vast annoyance to be told that Patrick, in converting the Irish, had to persuade them to give up human sacrifice. Likewise, is it embarrassing to find carvings crude enough to have been made by eight year olds declared to have been Celtic gods or goddesses? It is laughable to read of a bronze helmet "cast into the River Thames as a votive offering in the first century BC." Would it not be reasonable to assume its owner was killed at the river's edge fighting Caesar's crossing of the Thames in 54 BC?

We have already noted the presence in the British Isles of two different strains of Celt. The Goidelic Celts, who became native to Ireland, Scotland and the Isle of Man, appear to have come to the Isles by way of Spain. The Brythonic Celts came to Britain by way of Gaul. In later times —much later —the two would manifest distinct differences in social character. The British and the Gallican peoples, almost from the beginning seem to have been so individualistic as, in the course of time, to become key factors in the Protestant Reformation. By contrast, the Goidelic Celts in Spain and Ireland were, and would continue to be, as devout as could be found in the Roman Catholic Church. While to say so at this point is to paint with a large brush, the character of those Goidelic Celts remains one of the great treasures of the Roman Church. In the closing years of the Twentieth Century, following the liberating influences of Vatican II, the Spanish and Irish Churches' surplus of professions made up for critical shortages of priestly and religious vocations in the U.S.A.

The Record of Pre-Christian Druidism

The evidence seems to be that pre-Christian Druidism was as much a culture as a faith. We have record of Druidic presence and practice for hundreds of years extending into Asia and Africa, though centered in Gaul and Britain –especially the latter. The respect accorded Druids is described by Strabo following a long-remembered visit to Athens of the British Druid and astronomer Abaris,[1]

> "He was easy in his address, agreeable in his conversation, active in his dispatch and secret in his management of great affairs, quick in judgment of present accuracies, and ready to take his part in any sudden emergency, provident withal in guarding against futurity; diligent in the quest of wisdom; fond of friendship; trusting very little to fortune, yet having the entire confidence of others, and trusted with everything for his prudence. He spoke Greek with a fluency that you would have thought that he had been bred up in the Lyceum, and conversed all his life with the Academy at Athens."

It was said of Abaris that Greek fancy transformed the magnetized needle by which he guided his goings into an arrow of Apollo that would transport him wherever he pleased.

Certain distinctions between the Irish and the British Druids may be due to difference in training of initiates and the subject matter of their learning, due to cultural differences between the Goidelic and the Brythonic, to geographical differences, or because Ireland's people were more isolated and therefore more homogeneous than those of Britain. Ireland, not only in ancient times but till the modern era, was a land of villages, pasture lands and farms. Its earliest and for long its only town, Dublin, was established by the Vikings. Yet these Irish, like the British, were steeped in the Druidic training and precepts, with Druids as their leaders and exemplars. Britain Druidism differed in one very noticeable way; it was necessarily involved in towns. Every tribe had its central town and every such town a university.[2] In later Christian times those towns became cities with cathedrals, for under Theodore of Tarsus the whole of Britain was laid out in diocesan structures congruent with county lines based on the old tribal bounds.

The strength of Druidism can be attributed to its system of

education. Britain had forty tribes and forty universities. All followed the same procedures. All taught the same subjects: natural philosophy, jurisprudence, astronomy, arithmetic, geometry, medicine, oratory and poetry.[3] In the years before Rome's invasion in AD 43, it was customary to have as many as 65,000 enrollees from noble families in Britain and Gaul, each youth engaged in a twenty-year course of study in these subjects. For those who would in addition receive ecclesiastical training —as bards, seers or Druids —their training would require a total of thirty years. None could be a Druid who could not prove descent from nine successive generations of free forebears. No slave could be a Druid. If a Druid were forced into slavery or sold himself into servitude, his Order and his privileges were forfeit.[4]

This in itself was enough to assure that British resistance to Rome's invasion would last indefinitely. The war ended in AD 86 by sheer exhaustion, though it was not until AD 120, following a peace treaty, that Rome would be allowed to return[5] only then with the assurance that Britain would retain its kings, its lands, its laws and privileges. In return the Britons would raise and support three legions to be led by officers appointed by the Emperor for the defense of Britain *and* the Empire.

As we look back, we must appreciate why personal as well as patriotic reasons undergirded the British resistance. The Druids had to be holdouts. Their enslavement would, in effect, be the nation's, for they were the governors of the entire civil and ecclesiastical realm. They were its statesmen, legislators, priests, physicians, lawyers, teachers, poets; the depositaries of all human and divine knowledge. The Druids constituted Britain's Church and parliaments, its colleges of physicians and surgeons, its magistrates, clergy and bishops.[6]

All of the forty Druidic universities were south of the Clyde and the Forth, though nine have disappeared from the record. The seats of the three Arch-Druids would at their conversion become those of the British Church's Archbishops —London, Caerleon and York.[7] The chief tribal Druids became the bishops —with an order of precedence that carried over to the dioceses. Given the arrival in AD 668 of Theodore as Archbishop of Canterbury and given the authority of the Roman Church from that point till the Reformation, bishops and dioceses stood in the following relation to one another: Canterbury, Winchester, Verulam (St.Albans), Old Sarum (Salisbury), Cambridge, Carlisle, Manchester, Palmcaster, Colchester, Worcester, Chester, Porchester, Doncaster, Warwick, Meivod, Bristol, Leicester, Uroxeter, Lincoln, Gloucester, Chichester, Cirencester, Dorchester, Caermarthon, Caernarvon, Exeter, Silchester and Bath.

There were several beliefs held by the Druids that were central to the religion revealed in Christ. One was belief in God as Triune, having Three Persons in One Godhead. As the Druids understood and taught it, the First Person was, from time past a Divine Creator known to them as Bel, whose main attribute was transcendence. The Second Person was Taran, creation's Provider and Protector for the continuing present, whose chief attribute was immanence. The Third Person was a Divine Redeemer and Savior yet to come, whose name would be Jesu, and who at the time of coming would be incarnate in human flesh. The corporate name of this Druid Godhead was Thau, in which the Three Divine Persons were not three Gods but One.[8] We may note that Thau was similar in sound to the Greek Theou and to the Latin Deo —a sound not unlike that of roaring wind and flaming fire.

Druidism, the Acme of Natural Religion

It can be seen why the Druidic cult converted so speedily to the Christian faith, for it already understood God's Triunity. Moreover, its anticipated Savior bore the same name as the Christian God's incarnate Son. Having their central doctrines in common, we may pass by such features as Druidic mysticism and worship, of which little is known. What may be important for our consideration is the question of why Druidism, as a natural faith, was far more elevated than the others.

Consider this statement from the eighteenth century's David Hume, "No religion ever swayed the minds of men like the Druidic."[9] This philosopher was supremely the rationalist; how did he arrive at that judgment? Perhaps because Druidism was a supremely rational and ethical religion. While the Stoic and Epicurean faiths had focused on ethics and had been popular with the Romans, they lost influence, however, when constant exposure to dissolute leaders led the populace into moral and spiritual indifference. It was an era worthy of our attention, for the sense of public failure and guilt that permeated the dying Republic and early Empire was very like that found in our own time and summed up by William Butler Yeats,[10]

> "Things fall apart; the center cannot hold;
> Mere anarchy is loosed upon the world."

At that point for the ancient world it was the mystery religions –like those of Cybele, Isis and Mithra–that arrived to fill the gap. They appealed to hidden depths of mind and heart that the ethical religions had never tried to fathom or deal with. What ended the crisis of the ancient world (though it took centuries to bring this about) was a mystery religion given by God himself. That faith would be described by Eusebius of Caesarea, the Father of Church History as, "of all religions the truest and most suited to the needs of men."[11]

The Celts had had no part in Rome's spiritual and psychic failure, having been buoyed up by a Druidic faith that was not only an ethical religion, but a mystery religion as well. What the Druids taught included a doctrine of Atonement almost identical with that prophesied in the Hebrew Scriptures and fulfilled in the Crucifixion of Jesus Christ. It was a feature noted by Julius Caesar in his *Gallic Wars*, as a factor in the Celts' capacity for morale and motivation,[12] "The Druids teach that by no other way than the ransoming of man's life by the life of man, is reconciliation with the divine justice of the immortal gods possible." What Caesar had described would, in Christian doctrine, be the Sacrifice of a Man whose life was of sufficient value to redeem every sinner because he himself was True God and truly man. The Druid faith already possessed that understanding. It needed only know its Jesu as "the Lamb slain from the foundation of the world" to appreciate the power of that one, full, perfect and sufficient Sacrifice to forgive all penitent sinners –wiping from the record every sin of a penitent, contrite and confessing man.

The Druid as Renaissance Man

One of our contemporary wise men has said that a Renaissance Man is one who, if civilization were to vanish, could take the lead in reconstructing it. It would seem that the Druidic system of education had exactly that in mind. It fostered an educated, trained elite as guarantee that the long, patiently contrived work of creating a culture would not be undone by war, pestilence, earthquake, moral rot, national betrayal –or a falling sky.

We may note that the curriculum shown above –that of the Druidic university –is the equivalent of our own liberal arts' education on the broadest scale. It contained no element of vocational training. The martial arts were omitted from it entirely. It was not "practical" in the sense that carpentry, masonry and surveying are that. The curriculum as given here might seem needlessly abstract and theoretical for a people whose wants were simple and whose physical needs, such as food and shelter, did not depend on it. Admittedly the British, Gauls and Irish had little need for architects, engineers, public buildings, aqueducts, military roads and amphitheaters. Their twenty years of training for civil servants and thirty years for Druids, seers and bards were a simple society's provision that its best men would know virtually all that could be known. To instill in each member of a society's elite the capacity to be a law-giver, a judge, a scientist, a physician, an apothecary, an historian, a teacher, a leader in worship, is to put men in touch with one another in a way that an age of specialists cannot do. The one feature here that commands immediate attention is this: it was the pattern for a society devoted to peaceful pursuits, good will, liberty and justice for all. There was no provision for wars of aggression or for stratagems leading to such war. We know only that the Druid was forbidden to carry weapons at any time and that, should he interpose himself between two armies drawn up for battle, every spear would be dropped upon the ground and every sword be sheathed.

In *The Genteel Tradition at Bay*, George Santayana writes, "The mind of the Renaissance was not a pilgrim mind, but a sedentary city mind, like that of the ancients." It is a thought we can understand, since the Renaissance followed the recovery of what, centuries earlier, had disappeared. Once the lost and forgotten had been recovered and made available to all, the Rebirth and New Learning could take place. For the original world, however, the training of society's brightest young men in the basics of all systematic knowledge would provide the highest assurance that the society would blossom, flower and be fruitful. And that was what Druidic religion accomplished till Jesus Christ made himself known as the author and finisher of their faith.

The Druidic Mind: A Parallel for Comparison

Allow me to speak from personal experience. In 1940, with the German invasion of the low countries, I volunteered for training that would lead to a commission in the U.S. Naval Reserve. After a month as a boot seaman on a cruiser later sunk at Guadalcanal, I was given the training that entitled me, as a "ninety day wonder," to be assigned to the Pacific Fleet for "engineering duty only." Five years on destroyers allowed me to qualify for deck duties as well, and I spent the war's final year as executive officer and navigator of a 2,100 ton destroyer.

There was one odd way in which the picture was like that of the Druid schema. The ship's social format was monastic –in a way echoing that of the Celtic Church. Our naval service was carried out in the absence of women. Like it or not, celibacy was the norm. Our pay checks went to our wives while we –like monks –were fed, clothed, sheltered and stood watch; (We may disregard long hours at general quarters and combative action.). This life included the form at least of poverty, and we were under a common and strict obedience. While destroyers carried no chaplains, we had a lot to pray about and though from time to time we were "afeared," the morale was normally high. We felt certain we were fighting God's cause and hoped to be among the survivors.

What was more unequivocal was the way in which the Navy's training paralleled that provided for the Druids. The Reserve program was patterned after that at Annapolis for officers of the Regular Navy. Aside from the distinction between deck and engineering, reserves were on a par with the officers of the regular Naval service. While that parity was unfair to regulars and uncomfortable for reservists, the first bomb at Pearl Harbor saw ranks firmly closed till the war was over.

The parallel with Druidism was this. The Navy was an elite corps in the same sense as the Druid. Every midshipman was given the same training. Once commissioned and given his orders, each officer had his own specialized and well-defined work. Yet that specialization could not compartmentalize his mind, for a fighting ship is a unity in itself. Every man aboard was aware of how necessary to wholeness was the proper functioning of each department. The same was true of task force and fleet. Regardless of what ship one might be assigned to, things would be done in exactly the same way fleet-wide.

Advancement in rank and responsibility did not change the picture. Promotion depended upon an officer's ability to hold in unity all the functions at which he and others worked. It only added to the comprehensiveness of his tasks but gave no additional privileges or comforts. A ship's commanding officer, not only by experience but by the nature of his responsibilities, had to know –better than anyone else on board –the ship as a unit and the tasks of all those who served on it. Yet the higher his rank and responsibility, the more lonely was his lot. The captain was accountable not only for himself and his ship, but for every action of those under him. He could not be "buddies" with anyone. His duty was to God and country, not to those who looked to him as their leader. The same was as true for the fleet admiral as for the captain.

Two things may be added –each a "slant" that makes more realistic the parallel with Druidic studies. For Santayana's "sedentary city mind of the ancients" what was needed was not an *education* in the sense of a liberal arts curriculum. The Druid Curriculum, like that of Annapolis or any naval college, was for the purpose of *training*. If a culture or a fleet was to be rebuilt, it was exactly along the lines of the previous one. So "liberal arts" as we think of it, goes with Santayana's "pilgrim mind." The object of that mind is not training, but *education*.

The remaining thing to point out is why the comparison made above relates to the navy but would not be appropriate for leadership in our Army. An Army general, while trained in a similar, "replacement" setting, cannot have the same mentality as an admiral. He must be a generalist as well as a general. He must be prepared to be military governor of a conquered people or a politician acting on behalf of those under his country's protection. He has to be prepared –as MacArthur was to perfection –to be stand-in for an emperor. While this is a fleeting thought, it cannot be ignored. It explains why ten Americans came to the presidency after wartime service as generals. No admiral except for George Dewey has ever been seriously considered for the American presidency, and his was "the exception that proves the rule." The war (Spanish-American) in which he served was an inglorious one and his consideration did not result even in his nomination for election.

Additional Considerations of Oral Tradition

We have already referred to the discovery, in the field of linguistics, of the capacity of illiterate people to memorize the Iliad and the Odyssey in an unbroken oral tradition of perhaps 3,000 years. We have indicated why, prior to the advent of printing, the oral transmission of texts is considered to have been more accurate than the transcription of copies by hand. We have shown that the legend of St. Brendan the Navigator can be treated as historic fact, though it may yet turn out that St. Barrfoin, a monk of Brendan's monastery, was more the seaman than his Abbot. It would have been he who had founded daughter houses in Iceland, Greenland, Newfoundland and perhaps the North American continent. These would have been the mission stations to which Brendan made a visitation before his death in AD 577.

We could continue with instances of visual and auditory memory by which dependable transmission not only from person to person may be made, but from one generation, one century, one era to another. A photographic memory can involve pictorial scenes or pages in a book. An auditory memory can be the recollections of words in sequence or of passages of music. An unusual conductor can lead a symphony through an entire concert without glancing at the musical score before him. A skilled actor can recite whole plays. A Bible student can recite chapter after chapter, and there are many who have memorized the whole of Scripture. I have been told of memory demonstrations practiced by students of the Quran. You are invited to open the Sacred Book to any page at random and to point to any letter on the page. With little hesitation the scholar will quote the line on the exact reverse of the line pointed to, and tell the letter on the exact reverse of the figure touched. It must be appreciated that not many people in our time are motivated to learn anything that well, but it can be done. The mind's capacity for memory work is aided by a sense of the importance of what is to be memorized. It is also aided by sheltering the hearer or reader from the distractions our eyes and ears are exposed to by an unrelenting bombardment from the media and by our world's fleeting interests and concerns.

A Hebrew Counterpart: Psalmody in the Remote Balkans

Some time ago I read in a forgotten issue of a journal of musicology that, in the years before World War II, two villages were discovered in a remote part of the Balkans made up of Jews whose ancestors settled there following release from the Babylonian Captivity. They were said to have had no contact with or knowledge of a Jewish Diaspora. Of special interest was the fact that through the centuries their worship had included the chanting of the Hebrew Psalter using the tonalities of Gregorian Plainsong.

The latter fact need not be considered as any great feat of memory; in coming pages I shall speak of saints, including Patrick who recited or sang the entire Psalter every day. What is of interest is that Gregorian tonalities seem to have been in common use a thousand years before Gregory the Great was born. We have to conclude that, if this so, Gregorian Chant must have been given that name when someone in Rome −perhaps at Gregory's request −devised a way to annotate these tonalities for the inscribed −and later the printed page.

I wish I could confirm this as fact, but I have been unable to locate the source, and the villages referred to may have vanished due to the War. What can be said is that modern scholars are almost unanimous in their belief that Gregorian Chant dates from well before the Christian era. Dr. Mary Berry, an Augustinian nun who is a Professor of Music at Cambridge University and described as the outstanding living scholar of Gregorian Chant, has confirmed this to me.

A Wry Downside to Tradition

In his book, *Churches and Royal Patronage*, Col. W.A. Salmon recalls an odd situation in a small united benefice on the east coast of England:[13]

> "There, one village now borders the sea which has been eroding the coast line for centuries and is now endangering the church-yard wall. The second village lies about a mile and a half inland and to the west of it. The village on the seacoast was trying to raise funds to put up a sea wall to protect its church-yard, but the sister parish with which it had been amalgamated for over forty years was refusing to help. When the church-wardens of the inland village were asked why they would not help, they replied, 'Because yon folk had never warned us when Danes were coming!'"

Incredible Evidence of Prehistory at a Legendary Isle

The most striking monument of the ancient British tin trade is the granite outcropping known as St. Michael's Mount, just off the shore of Mount's Bay at Marazion in Cornwall. It has an identical twin in Normandy, bearing the same name, Mont St. Michel. Each is a tidal island, capped by a Benedictine monastery built in ancient times. The British mount was so named in AD 495 when Cornish fishermen claimed to have seen St. Michael the Archangel standing atop a cliff on its western side high above the sea. Its earlier name had been Carreg Lowse in Cowse, which in the now-lost Cornish tongue meant "The Grey Rock in the Forest." This was confirmed in 1478 by William of Worcester, who in a visit to the Mount, found the local people still calling it by that name. The legend accompanying the ancient name's usage confirmed that the rock had not only been surrounded by forest, but located five miles from the sea.

How old is that legend? It may be suggested by the fact that in 325 BC, the Greek geographer Pythias, sailing around Britain on a voyage of exploration, discovered the Mount and described it in the terms that have described it ever since. Even then it was a tidal island to which a causeway, exposed at low tide, enabled cargo to be carried from shore to facilitate the unloading and lading of ships docked at high tide along the island's wharves.

A more detailed narrative comes from the historian Diodorus Siculus. He describes how the inhabitants of Belerion (Land's End) ground up, smelted and purified the tin. They gave their ingots the shape of astralgi, *knuckle bones*, with exaggerated H-shaped handles so they could be slung from horses' backs as well as stowed in ships' holds. Having said this, he adds, "(They) carry (the ingots) off to a certain island off Britain called Ictis. During the ebb of the tide the intervening space is left dry, and they carry over to the island the tin in abundance in their wagons." While Ictis is a name used by Diodorus and no other, it is without a doubt the island earlier described by Pytheas and later known as St. Michael's Mount, We can say this, knowing that in recorded history there has been no other such island in Britain[14] –certainly not in connection with the tin trade so central to its history.

One proof of that ancient trade is the extent of Cornwall's moorlands. In ancient times they were forested, but their timber was cut for charcoal to supply the foundries, and the trees were never replanted. Another proof is that on the rare occasion of extreme low tides, the bottom of Mount's Bay is lined as far as the eye can see with stumps from that ancient forest, having also been cut to supply the smelters. In 1962 a former Director of England's Natural History Museum, Sir Gavin de Beer, in his book, *Reflections of a Darwinian*, told of residual carbon tests done on these stumps. Having been preserved in sea water, they bear a combined witness: that the tin trade had gone on before the land was submerged, that the submergence took place after their cutting was completed, and that these things happened at least 1,500 years before Pytheas' visit, that is to say no later than 1825 BC, nearly four thousand years ago.

What significance can we make from the early date? To begin with, it tells us that Britain played an active part in Bronze Age mining and commerce. But with whom was Britain trading? While that date would be at least 600 years before we have any record of Phoenicians in trade, Egypt's Bronze Age had begun a thousand years earlier. There is also the possibility of trade with Akkad, whose King Sargon has already been noted as boasting of his ties with Albion the White Island. Other than these, we can think of no others except the merchants and artisans of Atlantis, whom Jurgen Spanuth and supporters of his theory have held were nearby. If their proposals are correct and Atlantis is historic in time and place, the disappearance of Atlantis and of five miles of freshly-timbered land between the Grey Rock and the sea could have taken place at roughly the same time. The submergence at Mount's Bay could have accompanied that of lands extending to the Scilly Isles, the Severn Estuary and along the coast of Wales to and beyond the long-lost portions of Aberdovey. All have been suggested as belonging to "the lost land of Lyonesse" –itself identified with Atlantis. Regardless of what happened with these "places," what went on between Jew-Market (Marazion) and St. Michael's Mount is manifestly historic. It is no myth. But it continues to mystify us, with much of its past far earlier than legend.

ᏩᏋ   Chapter 7   ᏩᏋ

The Jerusalem Church in Gaul

A n event of great importance in the life of the Church occurred in the early months of AD 37 in Caesarea in Palestine, the capital that Herod the Great had completed fifty years earlier.

Jesus' Apostles had already gone underground to avoid the persecution that followed Stephen's death. For Christ's other followers there was no forewarning awakening them to the need for caution such as the Twelve had been given. Like Stephen, many had let their ardency pass the bounds of discretion and "were all scattered abroad throughout the regions of Judaea and Samaria (Acts 8:1)"

What came next −a voyage of the greatest import −could only have been initiated at Caesarea, the Holy Land's only seaport. Its timing may have been connected with a conversion that took place around then, though this connection is a speculation. The convert was Gamaliel, whose pupil had been Saul of Tarsus. Gamaliel was not only the most respected of the Pharisees and the son of Hillel, but so admired by the Jews that, conversion or no, his offspring followed him as Presidents of the Sanhedrin for the next four generations.[1] He had already saved the

Apostles' lives by his advice to the high priests and Sadducees when at the council meeting these officials had made clear their intent to slay them (Acts 5:33,34).

A Conspiracy Against a Fledgling Church

Gamaliel's conversion, which apparently came before St. Paul's, could have triggered the conspiracy –to do away with fifteen of Jesus' disciples –leading certain Sadducees to react with more than customary violence. Or, the plan might even have come from Pharisees disappointed with their leader. If so, it could have been known to Paul and been a factor in his conversion. Since we can only speculate as to who the conspirators were, it is enough to indicate what the plan was intended to accomplish.

The idea was to seize as many of Jesus' key disciples as could be squeezed into a small boat and to set them adrift without oars, sails or rudder. Simply to execute so many would have been risky even with the formalities of a trial. However, if the culprits were taken to sea and set adrift under the right circumstances their absence might go unnoticed. They could be towed out of the sight of land and abandoned without food or water right before one of the gales that regularly sweep along the Levantine coast.

A Design for Evil, a Potential for Good

This diabolical plan was carried out. On board were nine men and six women. While none of the Apostles was among them, most of the men are thought to have been among those seventy Elders whom Jesus sent on the preaching mission St. Luke describes (Ch.10:1-20) following the return of the Twelve. (Luke gives no indication of the Elders' names.) The passenger list recorded by the nineteenth century poet and historian Frederic Mistral[2] suggests there were four groups of disciples the conspirators were most eager to be rid of. One included the chief witnesses to Jesus' Resurrection. Another group consisted of those who, besides the Apostles, had been personally closest to Jesus.

The third group was those for whom he had performed the most renowned miracles. Finally were men of wealth and high station who had embarrassed the Establishment by giving up every benefit and following Jesus' life of poverty and self-denial.

As it turned out, the most important witnesses to the Resurrection *were* on that boat including Mary Magdalene; Mary Salome, the mother of James and John; Mary Cleopas, the Virgin's cousin, who was the mother of Jude and James the Less and perhaps Simon of Cana, a.k.a. Simon the Zealot. In addition were Martha and Lazarus, along with two women servants One servant was Marcella, who had served the Bethany family from childhood and who would make her home with Martha for the rest of Martha's life. The other was a young Egyptian named Sarah, who was Salome's servant. Sarah is still patroness to the gypsies who, each May, make a pilgramage to the fishing village where she served those two Marys with whom she is enshrined.

The Hitchhiker and Patroness of Gypsies

There is a touching story about St. Sarah. When her mistress was seized and taken to the seaside, she followed, unnoticed by the captors. When she realized what was happening, she leapt into the water pleading to join the others. Although the boat was already full to capacity, she was taken on board.

Lazarus, whom Jesus raised from the dead after three days in the tomb, was also captured because his was the miracle that, above all others Jesus performed, threatened the authorities most. Another man, though unnamed in the description of his miraculous cure in the ninth chapter of John's Gospel was also on board, Healed of congenital blindness in the Temple by Peter and John, we now know his name was Sidonius, and his nickname Restitutus, or "Restored." In addition were seven others: Cleon, Eutropius, Martial, Saturninus, Maximin, Trophimus and Joseph of Arimathea, only the last two of whom are named in the Gospels. However, we are already familiar with one of the other five, Maximin, the rich young ruler referred to in Matthew 19, Mark 10 and Luke 18, who "went away sorrowful: for he had great possessions." In the years of exile that followed, Maximin would be the one to whom the others chiefly looked for direction and support. This was especially true for Mary Magdalene and her community of women for whom he became protector and provider.

We know a good deal about the last two of the seven named above, both in the Bible and in ancient tradition. Trophime became the Bishop of Arles after traveling with St. Paul for several years. Joseph of Arimathea, in whose tomb Jesus was buried, was the Virgin Mary's uncle. He was the necessary male next-of-kin to whom the Crucified One's body could be released and who would provide burial.

A Journey Ended, A Ministry Begun

Nothing is known about the length of the journey or in what manner the fifteen castaways arrived at their journey's end. But arrive they did–all fifteen –near the mouth of the River Rhone. They spread out through Provence, for the most part taking Gentile names. The men lived singly, some distance from one another. The women divided into three households, one of which formed in after years, and all of which eventually included women converts. Despite the distances between them, all remained in touch. The women had the assurance of personal protection and care from the men living nearest at hand. Mary Cleopas, Mary Salome and Sarah settled near the place of landing. By remaining on a seaside strand near the mouth of Gaul's great river (to which Palestinians occasionally came) they could hope for messages and even visits from those they loved.

We have no knowledge that such hopes were realized. Mary Salome's son James may have passed the village later known as Saintes Maries de la Mer on his way to or from Spain, whose Apostle he became. But five years after their landing he was beheaded in Jerusalem, the first of the Twelve to die a martyr's death It is significant that, except for the Magdalen and for Maximin, the place where each went in the beginning became his or her lifelong home –each becoming the patron saint of that locality. This setting down of roots may be why our traditions of each have been accepted so broadly as historic fact.

The Bethany Family

Of the fifteen, only Lazarus is known to have been out of Palestine during the years between Jesus' Resurrection and Stephen's death. During that time he visited and preached in Cyprus, where he is remembered as its first Bishop. After arrival in Provence, he settled in Marseilles. Here again he served as Bishop, though only as a young man, for death came seven years later. His sister Martha, with the family's lifelong servant Marcella, settled in Tarascon, located on the Rhone nine miles north of Arles and forty-two miles northwest of Marseilles.

It appears that Mary Magdalene spent much of the next fourteen years in Gaul and Britain as a traveling evangelist, the principal witness to Jesus' Resurrection. She may well have spent long periods with each of her former boatmates, assisting them in preaching and teaching. About AD 52, the Magdalen formed a community of women living in a large cave just below a mountain top twenty-one miles east of Marseilles. This was forty-two miles from Tarascon, where Martha had a similar but more structured community. In the final decades of her life Mary and her companions gave themselves to prayer and meditation. Their abode has come to bear the name, *"La Sainte Baume, The Holy Cave."*

From this point Mary and Martha, though rarely together, were nonetheless in touch. They died one week apart, on the 22nd and 29th respectively of August in AD 84. Each was aware of the other's impending departure and had sent her farewell with the confidence of being joined with the saints above and with their Lord and Master.

Ministry of Trophime, Martial, Maximin, Restitut and Saturninus

Trophime had long since gone to Arles, the chief city of Gaul and the site of what in the Fourth Century would be the Western Church's first great Council. For several years before joining Paul, he lived in a cave in a rocky outcropping in marshy land three miles northeast of the city. Later the great Abbaye de Montmajeur would be built upon that site. Briefly stated, Martial–who had been St. Stephen's cousin –went to Limoges while Eutropius went to Orange. Maximin, the rich young ruler, first lived in Aix and later went to the place now called St. Maximin-de-la-Ste. Baume while Sidonius Restitutus, the one born blind, took Maximin's place in Aix and later retired to St. Restitut's. Saturninus went to Toulouse and died as a martyr, thrown down from the capitol while proclaiming Jesus as the Messiah. Cleon is the only one for whom there seems to be no record.

Ministry of Joseph of Arimathea, Jesus' Great Uncle

The last survivor –and most central to the record in Britain –was Joseph of Arimathea. The Greek New Testament describes him as being a disciple,* rich,* an honourable counsellor,* a good man and a just.* Fortunately, we know much more about him than what the Scripture tells us. An important tradition concerning him is confirmed in St. Jerome's Vulgate translation (published in AD 386) where he substitutes "noble decurion" for Mark's term "honourable counsellor." For military men, decurion was a rank next junior to centurion. In civil affairs, however, decurion was an honorific and could be applied throughout one's lifetime. Joseph of Arimathea was in direct line of descent from King David. He was also the younger brother of Joachim, the father of the Virgin Mary. Early in life he had entered the Empire's employ, serving as superintendent of tin mines in Spain. In time the stream tin played out and Joseph left Rome's employ, becoming a dealer in metals. For the last twenty years of Jesus' life on earth, Joseph traveled regularly to Britain, buying tin in Cornwall, lead in Somerset and copper in Wales and Scotland. Of the three metals, tin would be nearest at hand and chiefly sought. The closing of Spain's mines left Cornwall, in fact, as the world's chief source of tin until the first decade of the twentieth century.**

Though facilities for shipping via the Straits of Gibraltar were available on Phoenician and Carthaginian vessels, it is believed that Joseph transshipped his cargoes using strings of packhorses to cross Gaul. After debarking at Morlaix in Brittany, he would have followed

* Respectively John 19:38, Matthew 27:57, Mark 15:43, Luke 23:50
** It seems likely that James the Greater chose to evangelize Compostela at Joseph of Arimathea's suggestion because of friendships Joseph had with many still there.

a route through Limoges and Figeac, skirting the Massif Central on his way to Marseilles or Narbonne.

Beginnings of Ministry to the British

Because he was already well known in Britain, we can suppose that Joseph would have gone there from Provence at the first opportunity. And he did, for his arrival in Britain is described as taking place in the same year as the forced departure from Caesarea and the landing in Provence.[3] It is likely that Joseph's arrival in AD 37 was as an evangelist rather than as an Apostle, for his departure from the Holy Land, like that of his companions, was unplanned. We do have record of Philip's designating him Apostle to Britain, but that is believed to have occurred in Gaul in AD 63, following which Joseph returned to Glastonbury with eleven companions including his son, Josephes, for what would be his final years. While we have record of other Apostles in Britain following Joseph's arrival –including Aristobulus, Simon the Zealot, Barnabas, Paul and Peter perhaps in that order –it is Joseph who, from the first, has been honored as the Apostle to Britain and founder of the British Church.

It is also on record that Britain's King Arviragus, before becoming a Christian, gave twelve hides of land in acknowledgment of Joseph's ministry.[4] The famed Domesday Book records the grant itself, which took the property off the tax rolls until its confiscation by England's Henry VIII. Meanwhile that twelve-hide grant had provided for Joseph of Arimathea and the Twelve who joined him as anchorites. These were succeeded by others until Patrick of Ireland retired to Glaston and founded its Monastery, serving as Abbot until his death. Though the Twelve are said to have been sent from France by Philip the Apostle at the time of Joseph's consecration there in AD 63, it is hardly likely that Arviragus was not a Christian by that date. What seems more probable is that the grant was made in AD 43, when Rome's legions had invaded Britain, and the British and Celts were on the losing side of forty-three desperate years of war against the Romans.

A Link of the Bethany Family with the Gospel in Britain

There is one hint in ancient writings that, when Joseph of Arimathea went to Britain in AD 37, Lazarus may have gone with him. There is also the possibility that if this happened, Lazarus' sister Mary Magdalene went there as well. The evidence in his case hangs on one fine point; with her it is little more than speculation. In parts of Britain –notably East Anglia –a great many parish churches are named for Mary Magdalene. The reason could parallel that in South Wales and the border counties where more than a hundred churches are named for the British princess St. Eigen or Eurgain. Eigen was the elder daughter of the Pendragon Caradoc; she is said to have been a Christian before being taken to Rome as a captive in AD 51. After her return in AD 58, she founded many Welsh parishes as well as the earliest Christian monastic life. We know that Mary Magdalene preached widely in the years between AD 37 and AD 52, perhaps as readily in Britain as in Gaul. It is therefore very possible that many congregations in East Anglia and elsewhere took her name as their spiritual founder. Yet if true, it would put reason itself to the test since within a few centuries many of Anglia's Christians –and perhaps all of its churches –may have disappeared with the coming of Anglian and Saxon invaders.

In Lazarus' case the thread of tradition is his mention in Welsh Triads handed down from ancient times. Ten are ascribed to Paul, who on good authority spent as much as two years in Britain. One Triad only is ascribed to Lazarus, but it could be enough.[5] It is the only writing to have been left by that saint, who had so few years remaining for the exercise of his ministry. The title of the Triad here cited is:

The Three Counsels of Lazarus:
"Believe in God Who made thee;
Love God Who saved thee;
Fear God Who will judge thee."

Newcomers from the Palestinian Homeland

Inevitably, it was not long before the word of the castaways' safe arrival got back to Palestine. Not only had they survived the rigors of the sea, but they had landed in a favored colony of Rome and gone to various parts of Gaul with the expectation of remaining in touch with one another. The first to find them appear to have been Marcellus and Elizabeth, coming in response to word from their son Martial.[6] They joined him in Limoges and remained there for the rest of their lives. Also about that time came Parmenas,[7] a deacon whose ordaining is described in Acts 6. After some years as resident protector for Martha's community in Tarascon, he went to Avignon, eighteen miles to the north. Still later he preached in Asia Minor, and in AD 98 was martyred in Philippi.

The most unexpected change of scene came for the little publican of Jericho, Zacchaeus.[8] From his arrival in Gaul, Zaccheus became a hermit remembered as St. Amadour, *lover of souls*. His hermitage was a cluster of caves on the face of a cliff above the River Ouysse. a tributary of the Dordogne. Rocamadour, as it came to be called, was not far from the road used by Joseph to travel to and from Morlaix. It also would have been used by Martial to and from Limoges. Since, in local tradition, both men are associated with Amadour, and since Zaccheus was not a castaway on that boat, his arrival may have occurred some years after Joseph went to Britain. Elsewhere a tradition that Zaccheus briefly and reluctantly succeeded Peter as Bishop of Antioch, also supports a later date for Zaccheus' arrival.[9]

Increase in the Jerusalem Church Comes from the Homeland[10]

Whether they came to Gaul as castaways or to take part in the life and ministry of those exiles, all described thus far must be identified as part of a Church seemingly rooted in that land by chance. They were disciples of Jesus, yet they were in Gaul neither by act of the Apostles nor with the knowledge and ordering of any but those of the Jerusalem Church.

The following are also believed to have been Jewish converts who come directly from the Holy Land. Apart from Gratian, of whom we have explicit information, the others are thought to have been given Apostolic authority before leaving Palestine or, already in Gaul, received it spontaneously from Apostles or Apostolic men traveling in that region.

Frontinus (or Fronto) was the first Bishop of Perigeaux and **George**, a priest in his diocese. Both came from the Holy Land, one of the two living till about AD 100.

Julian, First Bishop of LeMans, died in AD97 after forty-five years' episcopate.

Sabinus and Potentianus. were Martyrs and patron saints of Sens, Sabinus being its first Bishop. Both came from the Holy Land, and are said to have been among Jesus' Seventy Elders.

Gratian, First Bishop of Tours, is described as coming from the Holy Land and having Apostolic authority, presumably of James.

Bishops Chosen from Among Gaulish Converts

Following are Gaulish (and presumably gentile) converts, a second generation of Christians but still of the first century. These are believed to have been consecrated and assigned by authority of Apostolic men or by Bishops of the first generation:

Feroncius, First Bishop of Besancon.

Eutropius, the Martyred First Bishop of Saintes.

Austrogesilus, the First Bishop of Bourges.

Austroclinian and **Alpinian**, who accompanied St. Martial into Gaul, spending their lives preaching in the area of Limoges.

Clair, the First Bishop of Nantes in Armorica or Brittany.

Crescens, Paul's companion, whose apostolate included the founding of the Church in Dauphine in Gaul and Mentz in Germany before his martyrdom about AD 100 in the East.

Denis, First Bishop and patron saint of Paris, martyred with two of his clergy, Rusticus and Elutherius.

Memmius (a.k.a. Menge), **Donation** and **Domitian**, the first three bishops of Chalons-sur-Marne.

Eugene, martyred successor to Denis as Bishop of Paris.

Regulus (a.k.a. Rieul) a Greek from the East, sent as missionary to Arles and later as First Bishop to Senlis in the north of Gaul.

Taurinus, First Bishop of Evreux and Bayeux in Normandy.

Xystus, Martyr and First Bishop of Rheims.

Bishops from Britain a Part of First Century Gallican Mission

The following list includes Bishops serving in Gaul and nearby transalpine lands who are known to have come from Britain. Considering their numbers, placement and evident coordination, we can presume the existence of an Apostolic Church already in Britain by the latter part of the First Century. These men were missionary bishops who in all respects seem to have fit that description:

Mansuy or **Mansuetus**, a Scot, the First Bishop of Toul, known as the Apostle of Lorraine; died in AD 89.

Suetonius Beatus, Apostle to the Helvetians, arrived near Interlaken c. AD 85, in what is now Switzerland. Of noble birth, Beatus was baptized in Britain by Barnabas and very likely ordained by Barnabas' brother, Aristobulus. His companion and servant was Justus, also a local patron saint. Beatus' death may have come as early as AD 96 and certainly no later than AD 113.

Maternus, Eucharius and **Valerius**, all at Treves from AD 50 till the closing years of the century. They were, in that order, the first three Bishops of Treves (Trier), Constantine's capitol and are all said to have come from Britain. Unlike the others, however, Maternus was not himself a Briton. He is said, in fact, to have been the widow's son at Nain —raised up by Jesus from the dead (Luke 7:11-16). Maternus, after relinquishing his post to Eucharius, became the First Bishop of Tongres in Belgium. All three died as martyrs before the century's end.

Places of Pilgrimage in Early Gallican (Jerusalem) Church

To speak of ordered, catholic churches as Gallican is not to beg the question of their eventual ordering in and by the Roman Church. It is to point out that they all appear to have had their founding and their initial ordering in the Jerusalem Church, and some seem to have been founded before there was a church at Rome. In each, the initial preaching of the Gospel and the attendant ordering as part of a Gaulish Church was wrought by Jewish Christians, who as disciples of Jesus, acted on their own because of the circumstances in which their mission began.

The Abbey Church of St. Victor, Marseilles, built in honor of a Roman soldier martyred in the third century, is near the entrance of the old harbor. It has the appearance of a massive crenellated fortress with tower. Beneath, in ancient crypts, the first generation of Christians worshipped with Lazarus as their bishop. Those crypts were also used as burial places for early saints including Lazarus. His remains were removed to the cathedral city of Autun in AD 1054.

The Royal Collegiate Church of St. Martha, Tarascon is on the waterfront just north of the old city and adjacent to the 15th Century Tarascon Castle. It still bears the name given it prior to the French Revolution, when it ranked with the great Cathedral Church of Notre Dame de Paris. Unlike those of other saints, whose tombs and reliquaries were despoiled during barbarian invasions, Martha's tomb appears to have been untouched. It is located in a chapel built in her lifetime which became a crypt chapel of successive churches dedicated to her memory. Assisted by the family servant Marcella and for some years by Parmenas the Deacon, her ministry was in large part the practical one of hospitality and concern she had shown in Palestine.

Saintes Maries de la Mer is the name given to the village on the Mediterranean shorefront where Mary Cleopas, Mary Salome and her servant Sarah lived out their lives. The church of Notre Dame de la Mer was built in the eleventh century by monks of Montmajeur Abbey, following the style of St. Victor's Abbey in Marseilles. In the upper chapel are tombs and reliquaries of the two Marys. In the crypt chapel are the tomb and relics of Saint Sarah. As mentioned earlier, because she is the patron saint of gypsies, hundreds of thousands of Romany people come each year on her festal eve and day, May 24-25, and fewer on her mistress Salome's feast day, October 22.

La Sainte Baume, the Holy Cave of Mary Magdalene, is linked with Rocamadour as the two most favored spots for pilgrimage in the south of France. Driving from Marseilles via the route through Gemenos is an unforgettable trip. Here a well-kept but narrow road threads through a series of steep ascents, dizzying drops and narrow bends up and over the sheer face of the Massif de la Ste. Baume. The drop along the north face is equally spectacular. Beyond the village of Plan-d'Aups-Ste.Baume are two footpaths leading to the Holy Cave (2,105 ft. elevation) and the chapel on the crest 156 feet above it, called Holy Pilon for the cairn of stones placed there in ancient times. The Magdalen, with her community of women penitents, lived in the Holy Cave from AD 52 until her death in AD 84.

Eutropius, who may be the same Eutropius who, as First Bishop of Saintes, died a martyr's death, went to Orange site of the Celtic Aurasio where, in 105 BC, the Roman legions were so decisively defeated. Though the subsequent victory had been won near Aix, 75 miles away, it was upon the site of this defeat that a Triumphal Arch was raised, land grants given to Army veterans and the finest Roman Theater still standing, built for their use. Orange became a permanent legionary camp of veterans, a ready and seasoned reserve living directly in the path of possible invaders who might come again around the Alps through Gaul.

Narbonne, Rome's provincial capital for Western Gaul, received the Gospel from Sergius Paulus, who as the deputy governor of Cyprus, had been converted by St. Paul during his First Missionary Journey in AD 45 (Acts 13:12). The founding of his church, The Basilica of St. Paul Serge, was unrelated to that of the castaways in the Rhone

Valley, and his ordering may have been at the hands of Paul the Apostle. Paul Serge's arrival at Narbonne undoubtedly took place long before Trophime left Arles to accompany the Apostle Paul on his Third Journey, which began seventeen years after this conversion.

The Basilica of St. Maximin is located twenty-three miles east of Aix in the town of St. Maximin-la-Ste. Baume, named for the Magdalen's protector and for the Holy Cave ten miles to the north where her community of penitents lived. The Gothic edifice was built upon the site where Maximin buried the Magdalen and where he in turn was buried. In its crypt are reliquaries of Mary Magdalene, of Maximin and of St. Marcella, Martha's servant.

Seventy-five miles northwest of Aix, not far from the River Rhone, is the village of St. Paul-Trois-Chateaux, where Restitutus, the "man born blind," seems to have settled at the initial dispersal of castaways. He was there for many years, but when Mary Magdalen took up residence at La Sainte Baume and Maximin moved to St. Maximin-la Ste. Baume as protector for her community, Restitutus may have retired to Aix as Maximin's Vicar. If so, we have no knowledge as to how long he may have served there. His burial took place in what is now the ninth century Church of St. Restitut, large indeed for the tiny village of St. Restitut clustered around it only three miles from St. Paul-Trois-Chateaux. During the religious wars, Restitut's tomb was rifled, his body burned and its ashes thrown to the winds.

The Primatial Church of St. Trophime is Arles' cathedral church, situated in the heart of the ancient city not far from the Amphitheater and the Emperor Constantine's later Palace. When Trophime returned from his travels with St. Paul, he did so as Arles' first Bishop. In his cathedral are his tomb and reliquary as well as a reliquary containing the skull of St. Stephen, brought by him from Palestine.

History's Focus on Arles

Arles, the point where the Rhone was bridged to provide a Rome-to-Spain highway, became the favored port for commerce on Gaul's largest river but began as an outpost of the Greek Colony of Marseilles, the favored seaport for traffic with Gaul. During the Second Punic War, Marseilles, as Carthage's commercial rival, sided with the Romans. Later, when the Celto-Ligurians of Gaul became a threat to Marseilles, the Romans were asked to come to the aid of their ally, which they did, but it meant that Marseilles was no longer a partner, but a subordinate power. When Rome's triumvirate broke apart, Marseilles sided with Pompey while Arles provided Caesar with twelve ships for his campaign. Marseilles thus fell from favor, while Arles became the pre-eminent city of Gaul with Nimes and Avignon sharing its wealth and prestige. Arles was still at its peak of eminence when Constantine built his palace, giving it a "presence" equalled only by that at Treves, whose great church and palace were built for him and his mother, the Empress St. Helena.

Given Arles' importance to the Church in Gaul, let us review its later years. Two sets of documents are helpful in this regard. One is provided by a noted historian, Rabanus Maurus, a pupil of St. Alcuin and Archbishop of Mainz (d. AD 856).[11] The other consists of two letters from Bishops of Rome to those in Gaul, one written in AD 417 and the other in AD 450. The second letter was by Bishop Leo I or Leo the Great at a time when Lyons was seeking preferment above Arles in that province.[12] He reminded the nineteen bishops under his jurisdiction that Arles must remain the metropolitan see for the Viennoise province. It was at Arles, Leo pointed out, that the Gaulish Church had been established by St. Trophimus. It was from that site that the Apostle Peter's authority would continue to be in force for Gaul.

The earlier letter had been concerned with the same matter. Zosimus, the Pope at that time, put it fluently to all the bishops, "One must not derogate from the old privileges of the Metropolitan of Arles,* to which Trophimus, a bishop of the first rank, was sent from this see and from whom the faith spread like a river through the whole of Gaul."[13]

This tribute, coming nearly 400 years after Trophime's arrival, underscores his contribution to the Gallic Church. Yet the date and circumstances of Trophimus' arrival at Arles raise the question as to

*Between AD 314 and AD1275 fourteen additional councils were held at Arles.

whether it could truthfully be said that Trophimus "was sent from this see," meaning Rome. It must already have been decided that the claims on behalf of Lyons' pre-eminence were unacceptable at Rome because Lyons' apostolic authority was derived from St. John rather than from St. Peter. Regardless of the merits of Lyons' claim as against Arles', it is evident that Rome's own claim of metropolitical authority had begun for all of Gaul if not the Western Church. The broader perspective may be served in several points made by Rabanus four centuries later in his Life of St. Mary Magdalene. He tells how the Provencal mission came to branch out, saying it was by the guidance of the Holy Spirit rather than by apostolic ordering. He also describes how, following Paul's acceptance by the Apostles in AD 47, the following assignments for apostolic mission were agreed upon:

"Thomas and Bartholomew were assigned to the care of the East,

Simon and Matthew to the South,

Philip and Thaddeus to the North,

Matthew and James to the middle of the world,

John and Andrew to the provinces of the Mediterranean, and

Peter and Paul to the kingdoms of the West."[14]

A Curiosity in Maximin's Appointment by the Apostles

Following his description of the Apostles' assignments, Rabanus goes on to say that in Paul's absence Peter chose twenty four of the eldest and best to carry out the Church's mission in Spain and Gaul —seven of these to Spain and seventeen to Gaul. Those in Gaul were assigned to ten provinces and seven provincial towns —which in ecclesial terms became ten dioceses and seven archdeaconries. All were placed in the care of Maximin, who, it was agreed, was "illustrious by his power of miracles and of teaching, and *chief of the Christians next to the Apostles*[15] (emphasis mine). A curiosity in Maximin's assignment is that while he was and remained an elder (which is to say, a presbyter) nearly all of the leaders of his dioceses and archdeaconries were bishops. Rabanus lists them by name —Serge, Paul, Austregisilus, Gratian,

Sabinus, Valerius, Eutropius, Frontinus, Trophime, Martial and Julian being among them. A problem for the historian is this: that Rabanus' own episcopate came at a time when the concept of Church order had been substantially developed and carefully defined. Considering this, one may ask how Rabanus could have uncritically reported on an assignment so pertinent to later polity in East as well as West.

A few possibilities come to mind:

1) Rabanus' scholarly background may have been influenced by the Druidic principle of adherence to the Truth, "let the chips fall where they may."

2) He may have felt free to describe the structure headed by Maximin because it was similar to that of the Irish and Scottish Churches, where presbyter-abbots were often senior to bishops.

3) The Church in Gaul, like that in Britain, had been so identified with the Celtic social character —and so linked historically with Eastern church tradition —that Rome's centralizing polity provoked an ambiguity in Gallic thought and custom.

4) Rabanus may have regarded himself more the historical scholar than the prelate, and in fact have had opinions on prelacy that ran counter to the norm.

5) Even in his time the Church in northern France was more essentially Gallican than Roman.

Any or all of these possibilities could have affected Rabanus' concept of society and Church, as well as his manner of presentation.

❧ Chapter 8 ❧

The Jerusalem Missionary Church

Rabanus Maurus (AD 776-856), a pupil of Alcuin, served as Abbot of Fulda and Archbishop of Mainz, and possessed the most encyclopedic mind of his age. He was learned in Latin, Greek, Hebrew, Syriac and Chaldee. His *Life of St. Mary Magdalene*, a beautifully illuminated manuscript, is one of the treasures of Magdalen College, Oxford, and includes a Life of St. Martha as well. In it Rabanus describes the use of earlier manuscripts and records (now long gone) and from various sources is able to give a significant recital of the words and deeds of Jesus' disciples complementing what is contained in the Acts of the Apostles. Rabanus mentions the name, for example, of the woman who touched the hem of Jesus' garment and was healed. It was Martha, a Phoenician woman from Caesarea Philippi. Except for Rabanus we would not know the Bethany family had other homes than the one near Jerusalem. One was *in* Jerusalem, another at Magdala on the Sea of Galilee, still another in Bethany (a.k.a. Bethabara) on the River Jordan. It was at the estate in Magdala that that the sisters invited Jesus and the Twelve to dinner and where, "cumbered about much serving," Martha asked Jesus to bid Mary come and help her.[1]

What Rabanus adds is that the Seventy were there as well, along with "a large following of illustrious women." These included Joanna and Susannah, who helped the stewardess Marcella serve guests.

It was here, on another occasion, that the Blessed Virgin and Jesus' brethren came seeking him while he was addressing a multitude. Concerning the "certain woman" described by Luke as saying to Jesus, "Blessed is the womb that bore thee" (Luke 11:27),[2] Rabanus tells us it was the same Marcella. He also says that Jesus and the Twelve were staying at the Bethabara house in the family's absence when he informed them of Lazarus' death. It was to the house at the Bethany-near-Jerusalem that they hastened and where, upon arriving at the tomb, Jesus raised Lazarus from the dead.

Many Bible students have believed Mary Magdalene to be a different person than Mary of Bethany, though the latter ascription is not used in the biblical text. If we consult the Church Fathers, we shall find Tertullian, Ambrose, Jerome, Augustine, Gregory, Bede, Odo, Bernard and Thomas Aquinas in agreement with Rabanus Maurus that Mary of Bethany and Mary of Magdala are one and the same. Rabanus' *Life of St. Mary Magdalene* starts by reviewing the family background.[3] The mother's name was Eucharia, a descendent of the royal house of Israel. The father, Theophilus, was a prince of Syria who had been governor of its maritime province. The family possessed much wealth, many servants and the estates already mentioned. By the time of Jesus' ministry both parents had died. Martha as the oldest had been vested with the care of these properties, which in the case of Bethany-near-Jerusalem included most of the village as well as the family home.

For centuries there have been those who contend that before her conversion the Magdalen had been a prostitute. Luke says only that she was a sinner (Luke 7:37; 8:2).[4] He adds that she was one of several women out of whom Jesus cast evil spirits —in her case, seven. According to Rabanus, Mary was a young woman of extraordinary beauty who had left her sister and younger brother to live in Magdala, where she had her home and a circle of friends. Whether she lived as wife or mistress to a wealthy man of that city is not known. But it is evident that her manner of life had been viewed by her family with sorrow and chagrin.

Rabanus tell us that the biblical "woman in the city" who washed and anointed Jesus' feet was the Mary both of Bethany and of Magdala. He speaks of Martha as being a relative of Simon the Pharisee, in whose home this took place. The possibility seems to exist then that Martha, being considerably older than the others, may in fact have been a half-sister. Regardless of Mary's life-style, she would have been known in Simon's household as an occasional if not entirely welcome guest. So there were two foot-washings, or rather a washing and an anointing, performed by Mary on Jesus. One followed her healing and forgiveness. The other became the opening scene of Holy Week, with Mary serving Jesus in one sense how he would serve his disciples, yet betokening his Passion and death so soon to follow.

Perhaps the most apt translation of Jesus' words to Simon are those of the Jerusalem Bible. They indicate a prophetic recognition of what God accomplished in Mary rather than an assertion of Jesus' authority, "This woman has poured out her tears over my feet and wiped them away with her hair... She has been covering my feet with kisses ever since I came in... She has anointed my feet with oil. For this reason I tell you that her sins, her many sins, must have been forgiven her, or she would not have shown such great love." Then he said to her, 'Your sins are forgiven. Your faith has saved you; go in peace.'"

Other Traditions of the Jerusalem Disciples

Rabanus also cites several legends of the Provencal castaways that merit our attention. In one he describes how, in her final hours, Mary Magdalene sent a messenger to tell Maximin that the members of her community were bringing her to his village to make her last communion at his hands. On hearing this, Maximin set off immediately carrying the Blessed Sacrament. The women of her community had come in haste, taking turns carrying the dying saint. He found them not far outside his village. It was there at the roadside that Mary made her last communion.[5] *Le Petit Pilon* –the Little Cairn, marking the spot–has, for nearly two thousand years, been the site of pilgrims' prayers and devotions.

Another legend has found its way into a current guidebook on Provence. It tells how, seven times a day, the angels are said to have carried Mary Magdalene from her Grotto up to Le Saint Pilon, "so she could listen to the music of Paradise." Having had a bit of fun at the expense of the faithful, it goes on to say how those who make the effort to climb to Mary's place of meditation will find an unsurpassed view. It names the nearby mountains one by one as though to ask, "Is this not as beautiful as what Mary was looking for?" What the guidebook could say but does not, is that on a clear day the Alps' highest mountain has always been visible from the Grotto as well as the Summit -180 miles away.

What truth might lie behind the legend? A fable for children could be an elaboration on what Mary may have done for herself. The pilgrims' path from the Grotto to the Holy Pilon winds along below the cliff for nearly half a mile before climbing to the crest. It then doubles back on itself to arrive at what is now a Chapel, 156 feet above the Cave. Yet there has always been an obscure path skirting the cliff the other way which is great deal steeper, but no more than 200 yards in length. Mary Magdalene, as well as certain of her fellows may have used this shortcut,. Those seven daily trips to the top may have been the model for the format for monastic worship the Church would one day follow. Its scriptural basis is found in Psalm 119:164, "Seven times a day do I praise thee; because of thy righteous judgments."

More from Rabanus on Mary and Martha

Quoting at length from a paraphrase of two chapters:[6] "St. Maximin, having gone to Aix, began to sow the good seed of the heavenly doctrine in the hearts of the Gentiles, giving himself, day and night, to preaching, prayer and fasting, so that he might bring the unbelievers of that country to the knowledge and service of God.

"Soon the preaching of the Gospel produced a new harvest of the faith, and the blessed Maximus at the head of his Church at Aix, shone forth by the many and Divine excellencies of his miracles.

"With him, and in the same Church, St. Mary Magdalene, the special friend of the Saviour, gave herself to contemplation; for since she had chosen, with so much wisdom, the better part, which she had found at the feet of her Lord, this, as He had promised, was never taken from her.

"But, full of anxiety for the salvation of the souls for whose sake she had come westward to the very ends of the earth, she often desisted from the joys of contemplation, in order to preach to unbelievers or to confirm the Christians in their faith, 'Out of the abundance of the heart the mouth speaketh', and this made her preaching a true Divine meditation. She herself was ever an example to sinners of genuine conversion –to penitents the certain hope of forgiveness –to the faithful of loving sympathy, and to all Christian people a proof of the Divine compassion.

"She would point to her eyes as those which had washed with her tears the feet of her Saviour, and had seen him first when he rose from the dead –to her hair which had wiped His sacred feet –to her lips which had kissed them, not only during his life here, but even after His death and resurrection –to her hands which had touched them and anointed them."

"St. Martha also, with her companions, preached the Gospel of the Saviour to the people in the cities of Avignon and Arles, and among the towns and villages which were on the borders of the Rhone in the province of Vienne. She chiefly bore testimony to all that she had seen touching the person of our Lord –to what she had heard from His lips when publicly teaching –to what He had disclosed concerning heavenly powers –joining those with wonders (or miracles) of her own. First had been given to her, when necessity demanded, by prayer or by the sign of the Holy Cross, to cleanse the lepers, to cure the paralytics, to quicken the dead, to heal the blind, the deaf, the dumb, the lame, and all who were in any way diseased.

"Similar powers were granted to St. Mary who performed

miracles with an inexpressible graciousness when these were needed either to establish the truth of her words or to incite the faith of her hearers.

"Both St. Mary and St. Martha possessed a noble beauty, an honourable bearing and a ready grace of language that was captivating. Rarely or never did anyone come away from their preaching incredulous or without tears. Their very look appeared able to inflame others with the love of Christ or to fill them with true contrition.

"They were abstemious in food and drink and discreet in their clothing; Mary, indeed, providing herself with too little food and clothing after losing the corporal presence of the Lord of salvation. The matrons, however, who lived with her and had a great affection for her, provided sufficiently for her necessities.

An Oddity Involving St. Maximin

It would appear from our later knowledge of Maximin and Mary that the above is a recital of their later years in Provence. So far as we know, Maximin was identified with Aix for eleven years before being placed in charge of the Church's mission in Gaul and Spain. Three years after this appointment he moved his ministry twenty-three miles to the village that now bears his name. His purpose there was to be no more than a day's walk from Mary Magdalene and her companions. Yet though Aix has from ancient times been a substantial and wealthy place —later renowned as the royal capital of Provence —there are no churches in that city that bear Maximin's name, no relics that the faithful could point to as proof of his life and ministry in Aix. Why not? Only two reasons come to mind. It could have been due to disappointment on the part of people there that Maximin had moved his household elsewhere and perhaps deputized another to take up his pastoral cares. Had he stayed at Aix, its church could have been the Primatial Church of Gaul instead of the church at Arles. The mountain air, the hot springs, the baths, the nearby site of Rome's greatest victory, the city's very centrality —all could have lingered in people's minds as suggesting why

Maximin should have remained there, allowing himself after death to be so honored.

The other reason is simpler. It may be that though loved and admired, Maximin did not spend enough time at Aix to be well known or for jealous thoughts to arise. His commissioning by the Apostles as Vicar General for Spain and Gaul, as made clear by Rabanus, can hardly be questioned,[7] "The chief, St. Maximinus, went to Aix... where, too, Mary Magdalene finished the course of her wanderings." This, however, could only have been the end of the beginning.

What may be implied is that for many of those first eleven years Maximin traveled with the Magdalen from place to place as her companion and protector. This possibility would not only be reinforced by his failure to be memorialized at Aix, but by the need for careful protection that such a woman must have —one whose witness was of great importance to the Church. The same want of a memorial applies as well to Lazarus at Marseilles. All the castaways but Maximin and Lazarus were provided, after death, with a vivid recollection of their ministry in the dedication of churches and memorials. For those two, however, there is no remembered record that we can see or read about. Where Lazarus served as first bishop is a church dedicated to a later saint. Where Maximin had first served is a Cathedral Church dedicated to the Holy Savior. In a way these two exceptions to what otherwise became the custom may be our best proof that the two spent much of their ministries away from where they are now remembered. At the same time, the naming of churches for the others and the continued presence of their relics would seem to reinforce the historical fact of their being where tradition says they were. The historic likelihood of their presence is furthered by the eagerness with which devotees in every age have risked their lives for the protection, preservation and later recovery of what, after its dishonoring, had remained.

Continued Increase in Provence of the Jerusalem Church

As Rabanus tells it, after the Magdalen had formed her Grotto community, Martha built an oratory in Tarascon where she lived for seven years, "her food being edible roots, green herbs and fruits." Yet to refresh herself more than once in the day she considered as wrong for herself, but not as wrong for her friends and neighbors. For considering that this daily fast would only be a suffering for herself and a burden to those who stayed with her, she was ever mindful of her old hospitality. "And because God loveth a cheerful giver, so He took care that like an inexhaustible fountain, the stores in her cellars, though daily emptied by her generosity, should never be exhausted; for the faithful, seeing her delight in giving, contributed so much the more, and without any care of her own, she was always able to give abundantly."

Rabanus adds, "Her clothing was rough. During seven years she simply wore two garments gathered together by a girdle of horsehair. Her feet were naked and she wore on her head a white cap of camel's hair. Branches of trees and vine leaves, over which was placed a coverlet served her as a bed, while her pillow was a stone."

During this time, Maximin "came from [Aix] to Tarascon, in order to see St. Martha... With similar intention and at the same hour came Trophimus, bishop of Arles, and Eutropius the priest of Orange, none expecting the arrival of the others, but all coming together by the inspiration of God, who disposes all things delightfully."

"The sainted heroine received them with honour, entertained them liberally and insisted on their stay and, on the sixteenth day of the kalends of January they dedicated to our Lord and Saviour as a church the house of the most blessed Martha —a house already rendered sacred by her deeds and virtues and conversation."

A year or so before Martha's death "a persecution arose in Aquitaine among the Gentiles," and a great number of Christians were thrust into exile. Among these Frontinus, Bishop of Perigeux and Georgius of Veliacum, fled together to the blessed Martha at Tarascon. She, with her usual charity, kindly received them, showed them every generosity, and honourably studied to retain them with her, until they were permitted to return to their own dioceses.

"When they were just ready to depart, Martha said, 'O bishop of Perigeux, you must know that next year I shall leave this mortal body. I beseech, if it please you, that you will come to bury me.' To which the bishop replied, 'I will come, O daughter, if God permits it and I am still alive.' " Following their departure, "She then lay down on her couch of branches, and was consumed by fever through the whole of that year, 'as gold is tried in the furnace.'"

We have already described how the Bethany sisters departed this life in AD 74, one week apart. Rabanus tells us that not only was Frontinus able to bury Martha as promised, but that among those present for her burial were several who had come a great distance and would be returning to the East.[8] Parmenas, her earlier protector, came from Philippi (where he would soon be martyred), bringing with him Epaphras and Sosthenes, who like Trophime had evangelized with St. Paul. He also brought two Christian women referred to by St. Paul in his letter to the Philippians, Syntyche and Euchodia. In it he described them (Chapter 4:2,3) as "my fellow-laborers, whose names are in the book of life." The others may have heard of Martha's illness and desired to come with Parmenas to pay their respects to the much-loved sisters.

A Modern Scholar's Witness, Supplementing Rabanus Maurus

For the Jerusalem Church in Gaul, one book by an English author is eminent above all others, both for comprehensive treatment and for careful, detailed and honest scholarship. *The Coming of the Saints*, by John W. Taylor, was first published in 1906 by Methuen & Co. A physician and surgeon, medical school professor, co-founder in 1883 of the Gynecology Society of Great Britain and accomplished as a poet and musician, Dr. Taylor had engaged in many years of study in libraries and in travel, seeking not only written but oral sources of tradition. Revised editions of his work were published in 1911 and 1923. Following his death, succeeding editions have been issued by the Covenant Publishing Co. Ltd., most recently in 1969. While there are several fine books dealing with the Early British Church, none deals so effectively and conclusively with its Gallican counterpart as does Dr. Taylor's.

I think it fair to say that Taylor's work may stand for years to come as the principal source for study and research on the Gallican Church as perhaps the first fruit of the Jerusalem body. Having visited nearly all the places in France, Switzerland, Germany and the Low Countries described by Taylor as having sprung from that mission, I have found it to be free from factual errors. This in itself is remarkable, since so much of his research involved a quest for ancient and localized tradition. His evaluations appear to be as reasonable and "up to date" as when he set them down a century ago. Because of widespread cultural confusion in our own day and the lack of scholarly interest either in memory-work or objective presentation, it seems reasonable to believe his findings are as sound and true as we can hope for in years to come.

The Importance of Reliquaries for the Historical Record

Regardless of religious belief, it will be evident to the reader that Christians will be of two minds regarding relics of the saints. On one hand will be those for whom relics –if truly that –are precious and of great importance. Such folk will go to considerable effort and expense to visit holy places for meditation and worship in company with the saints –looking to the spiritual and esthetic delights that go with pilgrimage. On the other hand will be those who recoil from any expression in the presence of the departed, other than solemnity and reverence. For them it will be almost axiomatic that any visible expression other than reverential good manners may lead to a veneration that borders on idolatry and that may encourage a superstitious adoration. Rather than comment on these views, I shall cite a few of Dr. Taylor's observations. Be reminded that his pilgrimages were lengthy and leisured. They involved travel by ship, railway, horse and carriage, lengthy stays at hotels and inns, visitation to holy places one day at a time. Be reminded also that these came in an era when Christendom was an accepted reality as well as a carefully defined and universally admitted state of mind. My visitations, by contrast, were done with a weather eye on wrist watch and wallet. I did not undertake it so much as a personal "trip to Mecca" as to check on the truth and the validity of what I had read of a Provencal Mission whose history and growth patterns differed so considerably from those in other places. My concern for relics differed so much from that expected of pilgrims that I must turn to Dr. Taylor, whose comments may enable readers to understand the relation of relics to personal religion and life in the Spirit:[9]

"The pilgrim... will not refuse to listen to the voices of almost countless generations of his predecessors... They did not undertake pain and difficulty and danger for the sake of foisting a lie upon posterity, and the luminous cloud of witness which their memory forms about each sacred shrine has not only light within itself, but undoubtedly throws some light on the object of their veneration and devotion."

Writing at a time when the effects of the French Revolution were far more in evidence than today, Taylor adds,[10]

"In France of today it is quite... impossible to determine the truth or falsity of *The Legends of the Saints*... Critics and apologists have done much to tarnish if not destroy the freshness and beauty of the ancient story. So, if we go on pilgrimage... I think it safer to follow in the wake of the older pilgrims –to stand with them in the holy places, and do nothing to forfeit that spirit and atmosphere of which the subject is really worthy."

Regrettably, I felt forced to confine myself to facts rather than devotional possibilities. As a pilgrim-in-haste on a tight budget, given scant time for prayer and meditation at the holy places, I have to thank the inner voice that said, "Find and photograph the churches. Find the reliquaries and where possible take pictures in which the saints' names can be clearly read. The history of those saints and their churches will be better proven by the photographs you have taken than by any written word."

Let me say why that intuition seems to have been sound advice. Wherever one goes, the same excuses will be given –whether from guidebooks, guides or local know-it-alls. They'll inform you that the kind of written proof historians insist on cannot be found earlier than the ninth century, for –as they will tell you –it was only then that local records began to be kept. Yet that fact can be misleading, for there was more literacy in the first three centuries *anno Domini* than in the last seven centuries of that first millenium. The entire history of northern and western Europe during that thousand year period was one of violence and terror. The persecutions throughout the Mediterranean world –i.e. the other parts of the Empire –brought centuries of absolute horror.

Therefore the only dependable history of any locality must be what those who grew up and remain there can tell you. For each of those whom my wife and I met –sought out specifically for purpose of the writing of these pages –it went like this, "Our Lord's disciples came in the first century and brought the Christian faith. They settled in Provence and won souls to Christ and died here and were buried. In all the places where they'd lived we built churches honoring their names. Their graves were given reverence and protection. But our history was a constant round of violence. First came the pagan Romans, then the Vandals, the Visigoths, the Teutons, the Huns, the Ostrogoths, the Sueves, the Arabs, the Northmen in that order. All came through France in their turn not only killing our people but destroying our churches, robbing our graves, dishonoring our dead. When the looting ended and the invaders had gone their way, those of us who were left gathered what we could find of the relics and hid them until we could rebuild our churches. The same continued during the religious wars –the Huguenots and the Reformers, the French Revolutionaries, the Marxists and the Nazis. And this does not include persecution by the State itself, when we were killed for being Christian. Our most vividly remembered history is what happened to the churches and the relics of the saints. We don't need books to prove it. All who have interest in their forebears know what happened and will tell you the same story. It's a diary that's open to all–in Provence, in France and everywhere– the story of what had happened in the places where each of us grew up."

A Visit to First Century Sites in the Trans-Alpine North

We have already described Rocamadour as of enormous interest for pilgrimage from the earliest days. When St. Amadour's tomb was opened in 1166 his body was found to be uncorrupt. The same has been discovered at the tombs of many other saints, but none so well known to us from the Scriptural record. The biblical promise applied uniquely to Jesus (Psalm16:11), "Thou shalt not leave my soul in hell; neither shalt thou suffer thy holy one to see corruption." Yet the promise has been fulfilled –at least in part –for other saints, and for reasons that must remain beyond our ken. Regrettably Zaccheus/ Amadour's tomb was rifled by Huguenots in 1562 and his body, still uncorrupt, was burned. Following custom grown from instincts of devotion, his charred bones were sought out and returned to the Saint Amadour Crypt. A few days' pilgrimage to Autun and Vezelay in France, to Interlaken in Switzerland and Trier in Germany brought delight, not only for their historic associations but for their scenic beauty. Taylor describes these spots at length –the first two because of their association with the disciples in Provence, and the latter two because of their founding by First Century missionaries from the British Church.

Concerning Saint Lazarus and Autun

Little could be done in the building and adorning of churches during the centuries while Rome's official policy for Christians was one of extermination. Nearly three centuries of persecution would end in AD 313 with Constantine's Edict of Milan. Yet even with Christianity as the established religion, little could be done in the trans-alpine regions so long as the land and people were subject to violence and disorder in every generation.

When at last the Church was free to grow and flourish, there came the building of churches meant to stand through the ages. Most referred to in these pages date from the twelfth or thirteenth centuries –with at least one in the ninth century and one in the third or fourth. St. Lazarus' remains were brought from Marseilles to Autun in 1054 and placed in the Cathedral Church of St. Nazaire. In 1146 they were transferred to the newly-completed Church of St. Lazarus, where they remain today. Fragments of his ancient tomb are on display in the nearby Rolin Museum. Grouped around the fragments is a magnificent set of statutes depicting the grief-stricken Martha, Mary Magdalene and Andrew returning from his tomb.

Concerning St. Mary Magdalene and Vezelay

Though built as one of the principal places in Europe for pilgrimage, Mary Magdalene's relics occupy a modest place near the high altar. What remains of her basilica, after destruction at the hands of French Revolutionaries, is a beautifully proportioned structure. Thirteenth century Vezelay was not only eminent for visitation, but one of four departure points for pilgrims bound for Compostela in Spain. Along with Mont St. Michel, Rocamadour and the Magdalen's own Sainte Baume, it continues to be for pilgrims one of the holiest and best-loved places in France.

Saint Beatus, Apostle to the Helvetians

Were it not for a missionary who came from Britain with a devoted servant around AD 85, the Apostle to the Swiss would be St. Gall, who, en route to Italy with St. Columbanus in the sixth century, was forced to remain at Lake Constance because of illness. But Suetonius Beatus did come to Lake Thun in the First Century, teaching, preaching and working miracles till the day of his death no later than AD 113. While his ministry is recalled chiefly at Interlaken, Beatenberg and Unterseen, the cell where he lived can still be seen near the lake's eastern shore.

Like Trophime, Zaccheus and Mary Magdalene, Beatus and his servant Justus lived in a cave —more truly a chain of caverns. The Beatus Cave may be explored today to a depth of half a mile. In it is not only his burial place, but that of Justus who continued in his ministry after Beatus' death. While neither is shown in Rome's *Book of Saints*, traditions found in Britain and Interlaken agree as to certain facts concerning Beatus. It is held that he came from Britain, was nobly born and had given away his wealth before coming to the Alpine region. The British record is that he was baptized there by Barnabas, whose brother Aristobulus was Peter's father-in-law and who went to Britain as Paul's Apostle. Beatus' name was taken by the nearby village of Beatenberg as well as by Beatushaus, the new hall of the Roman Catholic parish church at Interlaken.

Maternus, Eucharius, Valerius –Martyred Bishops of Treves

We have already noted that these three are said to have come from Britain about AD 50.[11] All lost their lives as martyrs before the century ended. Eucharius and Valerius died at the hands of a Celtic tribe, the Treveri, in Treves –the modern Trier, which is the oldest city in Germany. Maternus was martyred at the hands of the Tungri in what is still known as Tongres, 85 miles northwest of Trier in what is now Belgium. All three are buried in Trier. Eucharius' and Valerius' tombs are in the crypt of St. Matthias' Church. Maternus' tomb is in the crypt of the cathedral founded by Constantine in the twentieth year of his reign. The Dom in Trier is by far the oldest church we have referred to. Much of it dates back to the third and fourth centuries.

Some Considerations Concerning Constantine

We know that Emperor Constantine the Great had palaces in Trier and Arles and went to Rome no more than a few times in his life. But he seems to have ruled effectively from Trier and Arles. Why, halfway through his twenty-six year reign, did he move the seat of government from Rome to the former Greek colony of Byzantium?

It's likely that Constantine had no more interest in the city and its institutions than had any of his predecessors after the end of the second century. It had been more than three hundred years since a once virtuous and industrious people had handed over their governance to despots and nearly two centuries since an emperor had himself been a Roman. After the death of Commodus nearly all of the emperors were non-Roman, men who rose to posts of command in legions made up almost entirely of soldiers recruited from subject peoples.

Even without this shift, the transfer of power and authority from Rome to Byzantium made sense. Except for Rome, all of the Empire's great cities, the historic centers of culture and most of the Empire's population were in the East. The new capital, renamed Constantinople, was, of all the Empire's cities, the most central and soon became and remained for hundreds of years after Constantine's death, the Empire's greatest city. By AD 750 its population was second only to the capital of China, Ch'ang-an, now Sian (Siking) in the province of Shensi. Even in AD 900 –a hundred years after the coronation of Charlemagne –Constantinople was still "the world's first city, its commercial and cultural center."

As it turned out, Constantine and Charlemagne had much in common though their reigns were separated by five hundred years. The one was essentially a Celt, the other a Frank. Yet they derived nature and nurture from a Christian background and each was royal born. Their peoples, though of difference lineage, did not differ greatly; each had grown to live by grace, when to be Christian involved suffering and deprivation. Not only by faith but by geography they were native with their capital cities –Trier and Aachen –only 75 miles apart. Their subjects had such pride for, and devotion to, a monarch of such character and achievement as to confer the appelation "the Great." Each could regard themselves as a people upon whose history their nation's future would consist.

For Constantine, Britain may well have been "home" in the sense of being his native and ancestral land. His father was a general officer of Rome, Constantius Chlorus, already distinguished for his military ability and his able and gentle rule as administrator of his native Illyria. When Constantine was a year old his father was pressured into divorcing his mother Helena, a British princess, to marry the step-daughter of the Caesar of the West, whom Constantius would succeed when the new father-in-law became Augustus of the Western Empire. The promise was kept and Constantius became Caesar (Vice Regent) of the West in AD 293. Though this took place during the worst of all persecutions –when Diocletian was Augustus of the East and the senior of two rulers –Constantius was apparently able to stave off the persecutions, and especially in Britain. (It is now thought, however, by many that the persecution of St. Alban and as many as 10,000 others, attributed formerly to the Diocletian years, actually took place during the Decian persecutions in AD 249-50. If so, Constantius' reign was entirely praiseworthy if brief. It would allow St. Helena, though no longer his wife, to have played an ongoing role in nurturing the Emperor's compassionate nature, making her a significant factor in his life and that of her people.)

The Part That the Empress St. Helena May Have Played

We have already referred to Helena as a princess of Britain, descended both from Caradoc and Arviragus, who served in succession as Pendragon, charged with Britain's defense in the war following Rome's invasion in AD 43. Helena was the daughter of King Coel of Colchester ("Old King Cole"), in the sixth generation of descent from each Pendragon and in the third generation of descent from King Lucius, during whose reign Christianity became the established religion of the land. Helena's claim, however, has been disputed by Roman Catholic scholars and the currently irreligious, based on a rumor that her mother had been the daughter of an innkeeper in Illyria. This is mentioned here in passing, later to be dealt with more fully. Suffice it to say that Rome's finest historian, along with several others, has long since taken the Britons' part in a matter that has been ready grist for revisionists. Cardinal Cesar Baronius, (1538-1607), the Vatican Librarian who spent twenty years writing Rome's first critical history *Annales Ecclesiastici* in response to Protestant claims, was on familiar ground when he wrote,[12] "The man must be mad who, in the face of universal antiquity, refuses to believe that Constantine and his mother were Britons, born in Britain." When Constantine was five his father became Caesar of the West, and the son was sent as hostage for his father to the eastern court. At fourteen he was elevated by Diocletian to the first order of tribunes, being stationed with legions along the

Danube. When, after a change of emperors, the new Augustus dragged his feet in returning the hostage, Constantine took prompt action. Now seventeen years of age, he escaped, taking the swiftest post-horses with him so as to avoid recapture. He crossed the whole of Europe in record time, joining his father at Boulogne just as Constantius was crossing the Channel to engage an army of Scots and Picts on behalf of his British subjects. In York, with the battle yet to be won, Constantius Chlorus sickened and died. At the age of eighteen Constantine won that battle and was hailed as Caesar by his legions. In short order the legions' choice was conceded and made official. Seven years later, at twenty-five, Constantine became not only the Augustus of the West but the sole Emperor of a reunited Empire.

An important reason for Constantine's choice of Trier (or Treves) for his palace, may have been the holiness of the site, rendered so by the bloodshed of a great many Christian soldiers. Had he come to the throne earlier, the site for his rule could well have been Lyons where, in a single day in AD 208, Irenaeus and nineteen thousand Christians had been put to the sword. Here in Trier, in three October days of AD 286, thousands of Christians died.[13] The slaughter began when a division of the Theban Legion, refusing to sacrifice to the Emperor as a god, was put to death by order of the prefect. In the following day the burgomaster and eleven leading citizens were beaten with rods and beheaded. On the third day a vast crowd of men, women and children —most of the populace of Trier, all proclaiming Christ —were butchered by the soldiers who had so recently murdered their own. At Lyons the River Arar had been renamed the Saone for its crimson hue. From Trier, in that later persecution, the Moselle was blood-red as far as Neumagen, more than twenty miles downstream. It can hardly be doubted that the massacre made a deep impression on Constantine's father —even more so on Helena who was still his wife and in later years, as Empress, built her palace and its adjoining cathedral there in Trier. The bloodletting came in the first year of Constantius' predecessor Maximian's rule as Augustus. It was two years before Constantine would be born and seven years before the compassionate Constantius became Caesar of the West.

For the Gallican Episcopate: a Misdating of Beginnings

Though ahead of ourselves, our purpose in part has been to provide a brief view of what the Church in France and the Low Countries was already becoming. A more immediate reason for skipping from the end of the first century to the beginning of the fourth is that this is what many if not most historians have already done for the Church in France. Many of those seeking to recount the Church's history there have assigned to the third century what ancient oral tradition still declares to have been first century bishops. A difficulty with such historical revision is that without leaving those bishops where tradition places them, there's no explaining how the Church in Gaul grew at such an extraordinary rate. By way of contrast, there has been no historical revision of any kind in Spain, and the ancient tradition is accepted in its entirety. The seven apostolic men declared in Rome's *Book of Saints* to have been sent to Spain by Peter are identical with those whom Rabanus Maurus has informed us were sent by Peter in Paul's absence. They were Torquatus, Thesiphom, Secundus, Indalecius, Coecilius, Esicius, and Euphrasius. The reason for historians' failure to challenge the Spanish tradition is that almost nothing is known about these men, either as to where they went or what they did. All that is known in the Roman Church's histories is that these seven men —some Greek and some Italian —were sent to Spain as apostolic men. Their success was enormous. The Church they founded grew with great rapidity in that same century. Yet of these seven missionary bishops sent to Spain, the location and work of only one can even be described. This was Torquatus who went to Cadiz. For lack of knowledge about the others —even as to where they were —all are memorialized with a single feast day, May 15. All are shown as first century bishops and none as martyrs. The *Book of Saints* says of them, "No reliable details of their Apostolate have come down to our times, though each of the first founded Spanish Churches has traditions regarding it."[14]

Proofs of a First Century British Church

In our Preface we spoke of the unwillingness of professional historians to acknowledge the *fact* of an Early British Church as well as their inability to consider anything handed down by oral tradition. Such reluctance becomes an indictment when we consider what happened at the Medieval Councils of Pisa (AD 1409) and Constance (AD 1417), when the French and Spanish bishops challenged the English bishops' right to priority in order of seating. The latter Council, after long consideration, awarded precedence to the English on the ground that their forebears, the British, had received the Gospel "immediately after the Passion of Christ." The decision was reconfirmed for the Councils of Sienna (AD 1424) and Basel (AD 1434) and the matter never raised again.

The following chapter will give the trained historian more reason to consider the substance of the British tradition. The best evidence presented thus far is that we have historic record of British bishops serving on the Continent between AD 50 and AD 100. Concerning these referred to –Maternus, Eucharius, Valerius, Mansuetus and Beatus –there is no clear evidence as to where their Apostolic authority came from. What, for the first three, speaks against Peter's having authorized their consecration is the probability they were on the scene at Trier before his arrival in Rome. Mansuy may have been consecrated in Britain by Joseph of Arimathea following Joseph's consecration by Philip or by Aristobulus who, though thought to be Peter's father-in-law, was consecrated by St. Paul. If Beatus was indeed an Apostolic man, he could have been consecrated by Aristobulus, for his baptism in Britain was at the hands of Aristobulus' brother, St. Barnabas.

L.S. Lewis states that a Briton, Marcellus, who was martyred in 166, was the third Bishop of Tongres and first Archbishop of Treves or Trier. (This is the princely Archbishopric that for centuries dominated the Gallican Church and of whose succession we have full record.) Lewis tells us further that most of Trier's Archbishops in those early centuries were British born and bred.[15] For its effectiveness in proclaiming the

Gospel, we can believe the refugee church of Jesus' disciples and the Culdee ministry launched by them among Brittanic and Goidelic Celts was the instrument of God's purposes through all of transmontane Europe as well as the British Isles and Gaul.

Chapter 9

Saints in Caesar's Household
(The Jerusalem Church in Rome)

In 1723, some workmen in Chichester, while removing earlier foundations from a building site, found a stone bearing this inscription:

NEPTUNO ET MINERVAE TEMPLUM
PRO SALUTE DOMUS DIVINAE
EX AUCTORITATE
TIBERIUS CLAUDII COGIDUNI
REGIS LEGATI AUGUSTI IN BRITANNIA
COLLEGIUM FABRORUM ET QUI IN EO
A SACRIS SUNT DE SUO DEDICAVERUNT
DONANTE AREAM PUDENTE
PUDENTINI FILIUS

The English translation is, "The College of Engineers and its sacred ministers have, with the approval of Tiberius Claudius Cogidunus, Augustus' king-legate in Britain, at their own expense and in honor of the divine household (the imperial family), dedicated this Temple to Neptune and Minerva, the site given by Pudens, son of Pudentinus."

With its discovery, the "Chichester stone" became one more historic item by which traditions of the Early British Church can be matched and evaluated. Rufus Aulus Pudens Pudentinus was a senator and military tribune attached to the staff of his kinsman Aulus Plautius. His mansion in Rome would be the first–and remains the oldest–of Rome's churches as well as the site of its first catacomb. The cornerstone, which provides proof of Pudens' service in the invasion of Britain can be seen on the east side of North Street a few doors north of Chichester's Cathedral, at eye level in the Council Chambers' outside wall.

Another historic item is the following citation long acknowledged as one of two earliest references to Christians found in classical writings. It is from Tacitus' *Annales*, dealing with a lady of high station charged with a capital offense,

> "Pomponia Graecina, a woman of high rank (the wife of Aulus Plautius, who, as I have mentioned, was granted an ovation for his British campaign), was accused of foreign superstition and was handed over to her husband for trial. He followed ancient precedent in hearing a case which involved his wife's legal status and her honor in the presence of members of the family, and pronounced her innocent. Pomponia's long life was passed in unbroken sadness; for after the death of Julia, Drusus' daughter, she lived forty years in the dress of mourning with only sorrow in her heart. This escaped punishment in Claudius' reign and thereafter was turned to her glory."

The citation gives us occasion to observe how such material may be handled by Church historians in relation to the "politically correct" writing of another era. It is quoted from Bettensen's *Documents of the Christian Church*[1] along with commentary from Furneaux[2]:

> "The retirement and sobriety of a Christian might well appear a kind of perpetual mourning to the dissolute society of the Neronian period."

St. Peter's Church at Plymtree in Devon The church dates from the 12th century. One of its panels depicts Joseph of Arimathea. It is one of two paintings to have survived the Reformation era's destruction of religious art.

Ancient Yew Tree in churchyard of St. Peter's Next to the church's entryway is a large stone cross marking a mass grave where the bodies of the victims of the Black Death (1348-50) were buried. One third of Britain's people died in those three years. Yew trees were planted in churchyards to keep cattle at a distance.

వ **All photos were taken by the author** వ

CHURCH OF ST. JUST IN ROSELAND It is said locally that Joseph of Arimathea and Jesus came up St. Just's Creek in a boat anchoring in the "pool." Close by is the ancient church set against a hillside with tropical trees and fragrant vegetation.

VIEW FROM THE VILLAGE OF EAST LOOE IN CORNWALL In the distance is West Looe and St. George's Island (Lamanna). These two Looe villages hold a tradition of a visit by Jesus with his great uncle Joseph of Arimathea.

St. Mawes on the River Fal in Falmouth There is a tradition that Jesus and Joseph of Arimathea landed on the strand here at Falmouth town, crossed a stream and climbed Smithick Hill.

Padstow Bay On Cornwall's north coast the Camel River meets the Atlantic. The bay became a haven for those wishing to ride out a storm. In ancient times it would have been well known to merchant traders such as Joseph of Arimathea.

THE JESUS WELL Located near Padstow Bay. No present tradition exists of a visit by Joseph and Jesus, but the well's name suggests a lost tradition, for all through Britain, wells are named for the holy men and women who used them.

SLAUGHTER BRIDGE The bridge derives its name from the battle in which King Arthur's nephew Sir Modred inflicted on Arthur the head wound that would kill the king, while Modred himself died at Arthur's hand. The wounded king was then carried to the Isle of Avalon where he died.

King Arthur's Castle   Ancient tradition says these ruins atop Tintagle Head were the castle of King Arthur–Britain's great hero-king. Some believe the ruins to have been a monastic house of the British Church.

Cliffs near Tintagle   View from Tintagle castle of the caves and cliffs north of Tintagle on this north Cornish coast.

The Chalice Well   The author, photographed at the well, which is located on Chalice Hill in Glastonbury, Somerset. Around this well Joseph of Arimathea and eleven companions are said to have dwelt as anchorites. Chalice Well is so called because of the legend that the Holy Grail was later buried there. Closer to tradition is the possibibilty that after Joseph's death in AD 82, two cruets were buried there that contained "the sweat and blood of the great prophet Jesus."

(Opposite) Chalice Well-Pool and Garden
The outpouring of the well can be seen on the right side.

St. Michael's Mount (**two views**) The Mount is near Marazion, in the southwest corner of Cornwall. Like Mont St. Michel in France it is a tidal island. The early Romans knew the Mount as Ictis. The island's use in the tin trade goes back by a demonstrable five thousand years. British miners brought wagonloads of tin to the island at low tide for a later exchange with Jewish traders. The island housed a Benedictine abbey from 1135 until the Reformation.

CLOISTER OF ST. TROPHIME AT ARLES IN PROVENCE

This Romanesque church and former cathedral was built between the 12th and 15th centuries. St. Trophime lived northeast of Arles as a hermit, later traveled with St. Paul for several years, and returned to Arles as its bishop. Arles was the chief city of Gaul and in the 4th century the site of the Western Church's first great council.

ST. VICTOR'S, MARSEILLES Marseilles was the site of Lazarus' ministry until his death after seven years as Marseilles' first bishop. This church is named after the local soldier saint and martyr, Saint Victor. He was one of four Third Century soldiers who met here to worship in caves earlier used by Lazarus. Lazarus and his sister Mary Magdalene are honored here in the Confessional of St. Lazarus, in the lowest level of the church's catacombs.

TRIER CATHEDRAL

Trier is Germany's oldest city, and its cathedral is the country's oldest church. Trier was already 1,300 years old when the Emperor Augustus (63 BC–AD 14) fortified it as Rome's farthest northern outpost. The Emperor Constantine built this cathedral next to the chapel of his royal mother St. Helena. Above the altar stand sculpted figures of Maternus, Eucharius and Valerius – the cathedral's first three bishops.

EARLY TOMBS, CHURCH OF ST. FRANCISKIERCHE   Below are the tombs of Eucharius and Valerius in the crypt of the Church of St. Franciskierche in Trier. Maternus is buried in nearby Trier Cathedral. These first three bishops of Trier were missionaries from Britain, as were nearly all of Trier's bishops and archbishops during the first three centuries.

GLASTONBURY TOR is a hill at Glastonbury, Somerset, England, which features the roofless St. Michael's Tower. Tor is a local word of Celtic origin meaning "conical hill." Glastonbury Tor was one of three centers of Druid worship in pre-Christian times. The others were Caerleon (Wales) and Aumbresbury. In later years these three became the centers of the British Church and its worship. The terraces are thought to have served for an encircling procession, ascending and descending the hill.

LAKE THUN This alpine lake near Interlaken, Switzerland is where Suetonius Beatus came as a missionary around AD 85. Known as St. Beatus, he is said to have been a Briton of royal blood. He was converted in Britain, ordained by Aristobulus and sent as an apostle to Switzerland.

St. Laurence Church, Priddy Twelve miles north of Glastonbury Tor is the tiny village of Priddy where tradition holds of a visit by Jesus. The story is that Jesus as a young man traveled on a Phoenician vessel from Tyre and spent a winter here due to inclement weather. This tradition at Priddy takes the form of an oath on a valid claim, "That's as certain as that Our Lord walked across Priddy's Green."

Mr. Bertie Weeks In Priddy, the author met with this gentleman during his exploration of the simple local tradition of a visit by Jesus. Mr. Weeks told how his grandfather had told him of this tradition using the local sayings of certitude, "As sure as Our Lord was in Priddy" and "As sure as Jesus walked upon Priddy's earth."

ROCAMADOUR Rocamadour has its beautiful setting in a gorge above a tributary of the River Dordogne. Ancient tradition holds that its beloved hermit St Amadour (*lover of souls*) was actually Zacchaeus, a tax-collector Jesus had met in Jericho. It is said that he lived his life as a hermit in one of the caves lining this cliffside.

BASILICA OF ST. MAXIMIN

Located near Aix-en-Provence, this Basilica was begun in 1295 on the site of an earlier abbey church of St. Maximin. Four sarcophagi in the crypt are believed to contain some of the remains of Mary Magdalene and others, including St. Maximin. Maximin was a protector of Mary Magdalene begining with her return to Provence in 52 AD. Following her death, Maximin became archdeacon of most of Gaul.

St. Restitut

This Romanesque church located in a small village by the same name on the east bank of the Rhone north of Avignon has a funerary tower built over the tomb of St. Restitut. Sidonius Restitutus (St. Restitut) worked with Maximin in Aix-en-Provence.

Collegiate Church of St. Martha

Located in Tarascon ten miles north of Arles on the Rhone, this church was consecrated in the 10th century, when the body of the saint, the sister of Mary Magdalene, was said to have been found here.

Saintes-Maries-de-la-Mer

Located less than a hundred yards from the Mediterranean is this legendary church of the St. Marys of the Sea. The church commemorates the landing place of the small boat set adrift from Palestine without oars, sails, or rudder that contained Mary Magdalene and Martha; their brother Lazarus; Maximin; Mary Salome, the mother of James and John; Mary Cleopas, the Virgin's cousin and others. Also on board was a young Egyptian named Sarah, who was Mary Salome's servant. Sarah is still patroness to the gypsies who, each May, make a pilgrimage to the fishing village where she served the two Marys with whom she is enshrined.

La Sainte Baume (The Holy Cave) Ste-Baume is the name of a cave in Provence where, according to local tradition, Mary Magdalene along with her companions spent the last years of her life. In her final days, anticipating her death, she "came down unto the plain" to receive her last communion from St. Maximin.

Cave interior Inside the cave is a shrine with relics of Mary Magdalene, brought from St. Maximin-la-Ste-Baume abbey. The cave itself is roughly a hundred feet deep, wide and high. A summit rising 156 feet above the cave provides a magnificent panorama of the region.

CHICHESTER CATHEDRAL

Located in Chichester, in Sussex, England, the cathedral was founded in 1075. It was at this city and at Colchester that in AD 43 the Roman landings took place. The discovery in 1723 of the Pudens Stone, nearby the cathedral, gave evidence that Pudens, a military tribune and senator and St. Paul's half-brother, was involved in the Roman invasion of Britain. Pudens' home in Rome was subsequently the site of Rome's first and oldest church.

ST. ANNE'S LIGHT stands at the entrance to Falmouth harbor, a port on the River Fal on the south coast of Cornwall. It was to this point that traders in ancient times came directly from Brittany. The discovery of sunken vessels with datable artifacts confirms the Brittany- Cornwall sea traffic that existed well before the Christian era.

BANGOR-AP-DEE, a village in the ancient district of Maelor in Wales, situated on the banks of the River Dee. A monastery was established here in about AD 560. At the time of its destruction by a Saxon army in AD 616, the monastery was the largest in Britain. According to the scholar Bede, 1,200 monks and hundreds of scholars were murdered, and every building and manuscript was destroyed.

THE MENAI STRAIT, a 14-mile-long stretch of tidal water, separates the mainland of Wales from the island of Anglesey. At the time of Rome's attack on Britain in AD 43, this island was the center of Druidic studies. In AD 61, a Roman legion crossed this strait and killed 5,000 unarmed men and women. When the news reached the British, there followed a bloodbath that took the lives of 100,000 Romans and their British collaborators.

What neither historian may have been aware of is that ancient tradition holds Pomponia Graecina to have been the sister of the British Pendragon Caradoc. While arranging the marriage of a family member to an enemy's top general seems odd, ancient Kings were their own foreign secretaries, and royal intermarriage was more beneficial to the cause of peace than self-serving diplomacy or a holding of hostages.

Bible and Tradition Point to Pudens as St. Paul's Half-Brother

Of recent scholars dedicated to the study of the Early British Church, the most dependable and helpful may have been the Rev. R.W. Morgan whose *St. Paul in Britain*,[3] was originally published in 1860 and the Rev. L.S. Lewis, longtime Vicar of Glastonbury, for his *St. Joseph of Arimathea at Glastonbury*[4] published in 1922. Both books were written when oral tradition was still respected as a reliable source of history, and each received new editions and many later printings. Morgan's earlier work, *The History of Britain from the Flood to AD 700*, is of singular value as a compendium of what lore was still obtainable when it was first published in 1857. His quest for Pauline tradition in Britain took many years to recover from written and oral sources.

A further discovery came long after Morgan's time. It confirms and in some detail adds to his conclusions. This is *The Face of Christ*[5] by the Rev. C.C. Dobson, onetime Vicar of Hastings. His purpose was chiefly to draw attention to the work of Thomas Heaphy, an artist who had labored in the recovery of ancient artistry in the more than 700 miles of Roman catacombs. Dobson also called attention to a tract overlooked by scholars, *St. Paul and Britain*, written by Edwin Wilmshurst and published by T. G. Willis & Co. of Chichester. Its author told of having discovered an ancient tradition in Rome and Tarsus of St. Paul's family background. What follows is largely drawn from Wilmshurst's leaflet.

The first of Paul's people to have settled in Tarsus was his grandfather, a wealthy merchant of the stock of Benjamin who, soon after his arrival, purchased Roman citizenship for himself and for his descendants. Paul's father, David, died while still a young man. In time Paul's mother Praxedes (or Prassedes) married a rich and honored Roman who had come to Tarsus on private business. Her new husband, Senator Pudentinus, had vast estates in the Umbrian countryside, with four hundred servants to help with the care of his property. They made their home in Rome and in time had a son, Pudens. Many years later—after Pudens' marriage to Caradoc's daughter Claudia —the family mansion in Rome would, for seven years, be home to the captive British royal family and the place of worship for the city's Gentile Christians. The tradition is that Pudens' and Claudia's four children received their faith at the knees of the Apostles.[6] This is unlikely to have taken place during the years of the Caradoc family's presence in Rome (AD 51-58), for neither Peter nor Paul had arrived there yet. More likely, it happened during the intervals when Peter and Paul were in the city. Paul could have been the children's teacher during his own two years of house arrest in Rome, ministering to the Gentile Christians there as well. Alternatively, Peter could have taught them while a guest in their home. His own congregation of Jewish Christians met at the home outside the city of Praxedes' sister, Priscilla, a wealthy Jewish matron. (Wilmshurst confirms this fact, adding that this aunt was not the Priscilla described in several of Paul's letters as the wife of his tentmaker friend Aquila.)

While the relationships referred to in this chapter may appear to be "bits and pieces of Scripture," taken together they should dispel what doubts we might have as to Pudens' and Paul's blood relationship. In his Epistle to the Romans, Paul sends greetings to twenty-six people by name. Three are described as kinsmen, Andronicus, Junia and Herodion. Four others, worthy of note, will be cited shortly. Paul makes no mention of an Aunt Priscilla, neither does he mention his mother by name, nor actually call Rufus (Pudens, that is) his brother. We must remember however, that Paul is unlikely even to have met his half-brother—or his stepfather, who by this time may have died. It is likely that as a "pharisee of pharisees," and disapproving of his mother's marriage, Paul may have gone through many years of anger and disappointment. Now, however, not even having met the brother from whom he has so distanced himself, he can send this greeting

(Romans 16:13), "Salute Rufus, chosen in the Lord, and his mother and mine." It is one of only two instances in the New Testament, where one who has converted to Christ is described as "chosen in the Lord." The other instance, in Acts 9:15, is Paul himself.

There is another significant greeting (verse 10), "Salute them which are of Aristobulus' household." Aristobulus was Barnabas' brother, said also to have been Peter's father-in-law.[7] By the receipt of this letter, Paul knows Aristobulus will be absent from Rome because, he had already sent him as Apostle to Britain.[8] Finally, there is the omission of a greeting to Peter, who, if he had been in Rome, would surely have received one. This epistle was sent in AD 60, the same year that Peter's First Epistle was written from Babylon. In that letter Peter describes the places where, until then, he presumably had been—namely Pontus, Galatia, Cappadocia, Asia and Bythinia.

This sums up Paul's greetings to those in Rome two years before his arrival. However, we cannot fail to speak of the last such greeting Paul would send shortly before his death in his Second Epistle to Timothy—the one in which he says, "I have fought a good fight. I have finished my course. I have kept the faith." His closing words come after this verse (4:21), telling of those who are with him at the end and who themselves send greeting. One is Eubulus, who is said to have been Caradoc's cousin. In addition Paul adds greetings from "Pudens and Linus and Claudia and all the brethren." These greetings from those relatives newly knit to him by marriage and still present in Rome as members of Britain's royal family though no longer captive. (In AD 59 some had chosen to remain there when the rest of the family returned to Britain.) These are almost certainly the remnant of those he referred to earlier when, in closing his Epistle to the Philippians (4:22) he wrote, "All the saints salute you, chiefly they that are of Caesar's household." Since Caradoc's capture had not taken place on the battlefield, but while sleeping and through betrayal by his own, his presence among the Romans added nothing to their glory. For this reason as well as to honor Rome's most respected enemy, the Emperor, who had exceptional ties with the family, was their sponsor and protector even conferring his name upon Caradoc's beautiful and accomplished younger daughter, who like her aunt Pomponia, had grown up with the name of Gladys.

A Question Mark Hovering over the Church at Rome

We could wonder what St. Luke had in mind when he sat down to write The Acts of the Apostles. Considering that there are eleven Apostles at the start while only one remains present and in chains in the final chapter, the Acts' sub-title could have been, "How the Gospel Was Carried from Jerusalem to Rome."

However, if that were the book's general theme, a problem presents itself. The first baptized Christians in Rome appear to have come from Britain–in which case a more realistic theme might be, "How the Gospel Was Carried from Jerusalem to Rome by way of Glastonbury or Llantwit Major," the way-station, depending on whether it was Joseph of Arimathea or Aristobulus who baptized Caradoc's children and perhaps his father and sister.

Although Peter and Paul are universally held to be the founders of the Roman Church, its founders can more explicitly be said to have been captive evangelists from Britain. We have no strictly historical proof that Peter was ever in Rome, and only that final chapter of Acts to substantiate that Paul was there. Given that these were indeed the Apostolic founders, the evidence of their presence is then entirely based upon oral tradition. That the British captives were the first Christians in Rome is implied by two of that Church's most respected historians. Cardinal Baronius wrote the following concerning Pudens' home, the Titulus* or parish church,[9] "It is delivered to us by the firm tradition of our forefathers that the house of Pudens was the first that entertained St. Peter at Rome, and that there the Christians assembling formed the Church, and that of all our churches the oldest is that which is called after the name of Pudens." The Jesuit historian, Robert Parsons, says, "Claudia was the first hostess or harbourer both of St. Peter and St. Paul at the time of their coming to Rome."[10]

The earliest date given for Peter's coming to Rome, AD 42, is offered by St. Jerome, who contended that Peter went to Rome to rid the city of the Simon Magus whose fraudulence he had exposed eight

---

*Later to be called Pastor Hermas', Hospitium Apostolorum, yet always St. Pudentiana's Church, adjacent to the St. Prassedes' Chapel named for her younger sister.

years earlier in Samaria, as recounted in Acts 8. But Jerome is given no support for what by his time had become an apocryphal legend. Another statement of Jerome's–that Paul arrived in Rome in AD 56–is supported by many scholars both ancient and modern. If true–and it does fit conveniently between Paul's Second and Third Missionary Journeys–it allows Paul eight years for contact with them, including two with Pudens' family and two nearby while under house arrest. While we have less evidence for Peter's early arrival, there are later and historically acceptable records concerning the Apostolic order of the Roman church; moreover, they involve these Apostles and no other. One is from Irenaeus, the Bishop of Lyons martyred in AD 180, who regarded himself as bound to Rome though his orders came from the Eastern succession of St. John:[11]

"The blessed Apostles, (Peter and Paul), having founded and built up the church (at Rome) committed into the hands of Linus the office of the episcopate.)"

Of this Linus, Paul makes mention in (2 Timothy 4:21) to which, lest there be question as to Linus' identity, we add this verification from Clement of Rome, the city's fourth bishop:

"Sanctrissima Linus, frater Claudiae (Saint Linus, brother of Claudia)".[12]

In addition we have corroboration from *The Apostolic Constitutions* of consecrations of bishops by Peter, Paul and bishops of the Jerusalem Church in areas of our immediate concern:[13]

"Concerning those bishops who have been ordained in our lifetime, we make known to you that they are these: James the Bishop of Jerusalem, the kinsman of our Lord, upon whose death the second was Simon the son of Cleopas, after whom the third was Jude the son of James. Of Caesarea of Palestine, the first was Zacchaeus who once was a publican. Of Antioch,

Euodias, ordained by me, Peter; and Ignatius by Paul. Of the Church of Rome, Linus, (the brother) of Claudia, was the first, ordained by Paul, and Clemens, after Linus' death, ordained by me, Peter. Of Corinth, Lucius by Paul."

There is a discrepancy between the statements of Irenaeus and Peter in that Peter says Linus was consecrated by Paul alone, rather than by them both. It could be the case that Irenaeus, aware of the joint responsibility shared by Peter and Paul assumed that such consecrations would be carried out jointly. But given the extent of the two Apostles' necessary travel, their inability to be in constant communication and their need to trust one another in all humility, it seems likely that they had a mutual agreement from the beginning–that each would accept the other's judgment and decisions. It would mean the endorsing of every action made by either in the absence of the other. The result would be that an action of either Apostle would, in effect, be the act of both.

To return to Peter's and Paul's presence in Rome then little more can be known other than that they died there, and even that is hearsay. What this implies is that, for the determination of the historicity of tradition in the Roman Church, "ground zero" must be what we know of Pudens' and Claudia's family in Rome, of the house in which they lived from the year AD 52 on, and of the ministry that existed there on the part of Pastor Hermas, said to have been a disciple of St. Paul. All else seems to be derived from oral tradition; these, slender as they are, appear to be facts. Caradoc, his father Bran, and his children Cyllinus, Cynon and Eurgain along with the latter's husband and attendants, returned to Britain in AD 59, taking with them two Jewish Christians as evangelists. The rest of the household continued *in situ* as the principal family of the Roman Church, living in its central quarters. If Paul arrived in AD 56, as is claimed, we may accept it, but as hearsay by comparison with the central fact. Of the Pudens household, all but Claudia died as martyrs. After Paul's beheading, his remains were placed in the Pudens' family plot on the Via Ostiensis alongside those of Bran's father Llyr (Caradoc's grandfather, fictionalized by Shakespeare as King Lear), who had died while in Rome as a hostage.[14] Their bodies would be joined by the others', one by one until, in Constantine's time and by his action as a member of the same family, the ground and Church of St. Paul's Without the Walls would be consecrated.

The Giving of Princesses in Marriage

We must anticipate, for a bit, the progress of Rome's war against Britain. When it began in AD 43, Britain's armed forces were divided between Caradoc, king of the Silurian nation in Wales, and Guiderius, the new high king of Britain. When Guiderius was killed at the Medway in the second day's fighting, he was succeeded by a younger brother, Arviragus, who was inexperienced in battle. By unanimous choice Caradoc was made Pendragon by the war council, with Arviragus casting the first vote and serving the under-king who would be his superior "for the duration." So difficult for the Romans were the battles of the coming days and so costly the crossing of the Thames that messages of dire emergency were sent to the Emperor. In a few weeks Claudius arrived, bringing two additional legions with their auxiliaries as well as a cohort of elephants. The fighting had continued intermittently and the armies were near Colchester when Emperor and reinforcements arrived there. Two days of continuous fighting ensued. The first day at Coxcall Knolls, was admirably handled. Caradoc held ground against Aulus Plautius, Vespasian and Gnaeus Geta, three of Rome's most competent and seasoned generals. That Britain's foot-soldiers were firm before Rome's usually invincible infantry was due to the superb skill and ferocity of British charioteers. On the second day, however, at Brandon on Teme, the elephants came on the scene. Their odor panicked the Britons' horses and pandemonium ensued. It was a propitious time to offer a truce, and having Claudius there, the Romans did so.[15] In the two weeks' discussions that followed, the Emperor offered his natural daughter, Venus Julia, in marriage to Arviragus while Aulus Plautius asked for the hand of Caradoc's sister, Gladys. Both requests were accepted, though for the time being as betrothals rather than espousals. Yet though unions such as these involved factors that do not apply today, we have no reason to regard these and others that would take place as not being love matches. These two seem to have been solemnized during a later truce of six months' duration when the principals went to Rome. Once married to Plautius, Caradoc's sister become known as Pomponia, to which Graecina was added because of her love of Greek literature and fluency in that tongue. That truce in Rome is also thought to have brought about the marriage of Arviragus with Venus Julia who as Venissa would became a much-loved British queen. After their father's capture and while in Rome, both of Caradoc's daughters would marry Roman nobles. Pudens and the younger daughter married two years after the captives' arrival, by which time she was sixteen and had taken the name of Claudia. Six years later all four of their children had been born, and Claudia was toasted by the poet and epigrammist Martial as the most beautiful woman in Rome and its most gracious hostess. Several volumes of Claudia's odes and hymns became prized possessions of a library in Britain till their disappearance in the Middle Ages. Caradoc's older daughter appears to have been the last to marry, being accompanied on their return to Britain by her Roman husband, later Lord Salog of Sarum. Considering that on Caradoc's capture his younger cousin Arviragus assumed the pendragonate, it was many years before Arviragus could make good on a promise made at the time of his betrothal. When hostilities ended in AD 86 and Arviragus was able to shed the mantle of pendragon, resuming that of high king, he built Gloucester as the royal city of his realm.

An End to Claudius' Truce, Resuming of the Fray

The other commitments made during the Colchester truce were negative. Two tribes chose to stand apart from combat, paying tribute to the Romans. They were the Iceni and the Coritani, a sub-tribe of the Belgae near the Channel and the most recent migrants from the continent. For the next five years the whole might of Rome's imperial forces was arrayed against the rest of Britain as the only nation in the Western world not yet within the Roman fold. According to the

Roman historian Suetonius, thirty pitched battles (according to the Greek Eutropius, thirty-two) were fought, with the British forces holding firm in every case.[16] In one other, Arviragus sustained a total loss to Vespasian, the general who became Emperor on Nero's death. Eight days later though Caradoc and Arviragus turned the Roman's victory into a disastrous rout.[17] Vespasian was captured in his tent at the knife-point but his son Titus, following a hunch, rushed in with a cohort, dispersing the captors and saving his father's life. (This was the same Titus, who in AD 70, during his father's reign and prior to his own succession as Emperor, sacked and leveled Jerusalem stone by stone.)

By AD 48 the war was still going badly for Rome and Aulus Plautius, Vespasian, Geta and Titus were successively recalled. Writing of this period forty years after the events being cited and while his father-in-law Agricola was military governor and still trying to conclude the war, Tacitus stated, "The Silures reposed unbounded confidence in Caractacus, counting the many drawn battles he had fought with the Romans, the many victories he had obtained over them."[18]

With the commanding general's recall, the six months' truce described above was proposed and agreed to. Again it was at the request of the Romans. Caradoc and Arviragus journeyed to Rome, along with Aulus Plautius, his new bride and other family members. Aside from the two marriages, there was little that could be achieved. A recollection of that visit is found in an address to the Roman Senate where Caradoc stated that he had "ordered every tree in Siluria to be felled, that the Romans might no longer allege it was the British forests rather than British valor that hindered their victory." There is an anecdote as well from the historian Dion Cassius, "When Caractacus was shown the public buildings of Rome, he observed, 'It is hard to believe that a people possessed of such magnificence at home should envy me my soldier's tent in Britain.'"

Upon the close of this truce Ostorius Scapula, the new Roman commander, already having a line of fortresses behind him, moved the battle westward into the mountains of Wales. Every step of the way was contested by the fierce Silurians and Ordovicians, whom the Romans never subdued. A succession of frequent encounters took place lasting through the winter, and at its end, near Caerleon, a Roman division was cut to pieces.

In AD 52 the battle that terminated Caradoc's career took place at a strategic spot where he was prepared to risk fighting in the open. There was little room for chariot or cavalry maneuvering, and the superior weapons, armor and tactics of the Romans led to their victory. Though Caradoc and many of his men escaped, his wife and daughter Gladys were captured and in short order the entire family. Caradoc crossed the width of Britain, taking refuge with a cousin, Queen Cartimandua of the Brigantes at York, who, unbeknownst to him, had entered a client relationship with the Romans. Awakened in his sleeping chamber, he found himself in chains. On hearing of the victory and Caradoc's capture, Claudius ordered the entire family to be brought to Rome. The city provided the greatest parade ever seen there, three million people lining the streets to see the captive British warrier. Caradoc's approach was described in the words of one historian, "Roma catgenatum, tremuit spectare Brittanum, "Rome trembled when she saw the Briton, though fast in chains." Quoting Tacitus, Morgan describes the spectacle:[1]

"The trial and speech of Caradoc are familiar to every schoolboy. With an unaltered countenance, the hero of forty pitched fields, great in arms, greater in chains, took his position before the [convened Senate and] tribunal of the emperor and thus delivered himself,

"Had my government in Britain been directed solely with a view to the preservation of my hereditary domains, or the aggrandizement of my own family, I might long since have entered this city as an ally, not a prisoner; nor would you have disdained for a friend a king descended from illustrious ancestors, and the dictator of many nations. My present condition, stript of its former majesty, is as adverse to myself as it is a cause of triumph to you. What then? I was lord of men, horses, arms, wealth; what wonder if at your dictation I refused to resign them? Does it follow that because the Romans aspire to universal dominion, every nation is to accept the vassalage they would impose? I am now in your power—betrayed, not conquered. Had I, like others, yielded without resistance, where would have been the name of Caradoc? Where your glory? Oblivion would have buried both in the same tomb. Bid me live, I shall survive for ever in history one example at least of Roman clemency."

Such an address as this, worthy a king, a soldier, and a freeman, had never before been delivered in the Senate. Tacitus thought it worthy to be reported and immortalized by his pen. Its spirit reminded him of the old republican times, a spirit long since extinct. The custom at these "triumphs" was that at a certain spot on the Sacra Via the captive kings and generals should be removed from the procession, cast into the Tarpeian dungeons, there to be starved to death, strangled or decapitated, and their dead bodies dragged by hooks to the Tiber." Clemency for Caradoc turned out to be the sole exception to what, from first to last, was Rome's normal practice.

While we cannot fail to appreciate the remarkable courtesy shown by Emperor and Senate to the British, in the back of their minds could have been the fear that putting Caradoc to death, with or without his family, would make the course of the war all the more difficult. Upon Caradoc's word not to take up arms once more upon his return to Britain, he and his household were allowed to live in the Palatium Britannicum for seven years, free to enjoy the city and the revenues from their Silurian estates. As to the continuance of the war, we have this from Morgan's volume *St. Paul in Britain*,

"The defeat at Caer Caradoc and the betrayal of their sovereign, had served not to intimidate, but to infuriate and rouse to greater efforts, his subjects in Britain. The Silures elected his cousin Arviragus his successor in the pendragonate. The Romans were beaten back across the Severn. Disaster followed disaster. Tacitus, loath to dilate on the misfortunes of the imperial arms, sums up the reverses of the war in a few expressive lines: 'In Britain, after the captivity of Caractacus, the Romans were repeatedly conquered and put to the rout by the single state of the Silures alone.'"

Caradoc's Sons: Head of State in Wales, Head of Church in Rome

In AD 59 Caradoc's captivity came to an end, and with his father Bran, sons Cyllinus and Cynon and daughter Eurgain he returned to Britain. Cyllinus would succeed him as king of the Silurians and though Caradoc was pledged not to bear arms, they were subject to the Pendragon Arviragus in other respects. Llyn or Linus would succeed Peter and Paul as the first Bishop of Rome.

While Caradoc's descent in Rome would cease with the martyrdom of its entire second generation, his descendants in Britain would continue to be members of the island's royalty to the present day. His great grandson Lleiver Mawr (Lucius the Great), whose queen was Arviragus' great grandchild, was the high king of Britain during whose reign the land became officially Christian. (According to Bede this came to pass in AD 156) Lucius reigned seventy-seven years, from AD 124 until his death in AD 201. His baptism had come in the year AD 139 at the hands of his first-cousin-once-removed Timothy, who had been Pudens' son and Paul's nephew —named in honor of the uncle's well-beloved disciple. Timotheus was survived only by his younger sister Praxedes, who died last of all, in the same year as her brothers. In the family burial ground, along with Llyr and Paul at what later became St. Paul's Without the Walls, had been laid Linus in AD 79, Pudens in AD 96, Claudia in AD 97, Pudentiana in AD 107, with Euodias perhaps along the way. Novation in turn received the martyr's crown in June of AD 139 while Timothy was baptizing Lucius in Britain. Timothy died in August after his return to Rome, and Praxedes thirty days later, in September. They were the last to call the Titulus their lifelong home, the last of Pudens' and Claudia's line.

That venerable house on Mons Sacer, known since the first century as St. Pudentiana's Church, has at its entry, carved in characters corroded by age, an inscription in Latin of which the following is a translation:

"In this sacred and most ancient of churches, known as that of Pastor, dedicated by Sanctus Pius Papa, formerly the house of Sanctus Pudens, the senator, and the home of the holy apostles, repose the remains of three thousand blessed martyrs, which Pudentia and Praxedes, virgins of Christ, with their own hands interred."

British and Gallican Churches,
The Early Years

Let us sum up what has been said of the British Church from the start. Joseph of Arimathea is believed to have arrived in Glastonbury in AD 37, ministering there till his death in AD 82. There is good reason to believe Lazarus, Martha and Mary Magdalene were with him at the beginning –Mary perhaps for several years. Whatever the case, they returned to their fellow-evangelists in Gaul and by their holy witness and holy lives become foundation-stones of that sister church.

Neither the Gallican Church nor its British counterpart got its start under apostolic ordering. Their origin came jointly, and it seems appropriate to accept that the Britannic and Gallican churches –which is to say the Celtic churches –found their carnal origin in the conspiracy to destroy many of those closest to Jesus. It was an action that God, in his mercy, decisively and providentially overruled. Both churches' sense of being may, as a consequence, have been that of the biblical remnant. The Gaelic name for such a Church, whether in Britain, Gaul or Ireland, was Culdich or Culdee, signifying a castaway or excluded body having no certainty of position or place. Its self-image could be like our imaginings of Jesus' kingdom as "not of this world."

At their joint beginning, both churches evangelized Gentiles rather than Jews. In Gaul it may have been for fear that if they directed their attention to Jews the knowledge of their survival might get back to Palestine. (We have already noted that several of the castaways adopted Gentile names.) In Britain it could have been that there were few if any synagogues to whose members the Gospel could be preached and through whom the Gospel could be more widely heard. Whatever the reasons, these Culdee churches evangelized Gentiles from the start.

Back in the Holy Land, the Twelve continued to have their reservations about evangelizing Gentiles. They wanted to be obedient to Jesus' instructions, and there was, as yet, no "go-ahead" sign from the Lord. This uncertainty ended with special revelations to Peter and Paul and the fact that Gentiles were already being baptized in the Spirit. In AD 46, at the Council of Jerusalem, their time of waiting for Israel's response was brought to an end. The Savior's Great Commission came in force.

Philip's Consecration of Joseph of Arimathea as Apostle to Britain

Our dating for Joseph of Arimathea's apostolate comes mainly from Freculphus, who was Bishop of Lisieux in Normandy in AD 850. He tells us that when the Apostle Philip visited Gaul in AD 63, Joseph crossed the Channel to see him. P hilip consecrated Joseph as Apostle to Britain and sent him back to Glastonbury with twelve companions, one of whom was Joseph's own son Josephes. We know from other sources that Joseph's daughter Anna joined them at Glastonbury about that time. Both children married into the British royal line, bringing to it a direct descent from King David, whose offspring in time included the Christian courts of Europe. This was in accord with the promise given through Jeremiah (33:17), "Thus saith the Lord, David shall never want a man to sit upon the throne of the house of Israel."

Though occupied with the Roman invasion and not yet a Christian, Arviragus had given a large tract of land around Glastonbury in support of Joseph's ministry. It continued as a Royal Grant for what in later centuries became Glastonbury's great Benedictine Abbey of St. Peter and St. Paul. The Domesday Book confirms this grant of "XII hides of land which have never paid tax." Following Joseph's consecration and for another 400 years, this center of British and Celtic Christianity embraced twelve circular huts, wattled, thatched and grouped around a chapel built earlier by Joseph of Arimathea. Joseph's chapel had incorporated, as its sanctuary, a still earlier hut. It was similar to the others but larger, and said to have been built by Jesus during one storm-bound winter when, as a young man, he was serving on a vessel of Tyre.

When Joseph returned from Gaul with his son and eleven new companions, he and those eleven became anchorites. They and their successors lived in these huts as a community of individuals having one life, one goal, one liturgy, one routine. The twelve could not have spent all their time in prayer and meditation, however. They had to be active in teaching and preaching Christ, for, by the time the first of their four centuries as a community ended, Britain's high king and his entire dominion were officially Christian. London was Lucius' chief city, Winchester the civil capital of his realm with archbishops at London, Caerleon and York.

Three hundred years later the Abbey was founded, and work on its monastic house begun. The founder was St. Patrick, who returned to the land of his birth about AD 460, having already devoted twenty-eight years to the conversion of the Irish. Patrick was the monastery's first abbot. With him came his favorite disciple, St. Benignus or Benen, the onetime psalm-singer at Armagh who was Patrick's successor in that see and who resigned as Armagh's archbishop in order to accompany his friend and master to Glastonbury. At Patrick's death in AD 464, Benen succeeded him as the monastery's second abbot until his own death five years later. William of Malmesbury, who was Bede's successor as superlative historian to the Saxon Church, tells us that St. Bridget, the "Mary of Ireland," came to Glastonbury as a young girl to be with the two saints during Patrick's final years, returning to Ireland after their deaths.

Aristobulus (Arwystli Senex), Paul's Designee as Apostle to Britain

Joseph of Arimathea is regarded everywhere as the founder of the British Church. However, Aristobulus must have been Britain's first Bishop, arriving early enough to convert Caradoc's children and his father Bran in the years prior to their captivity in Rome. It is likely that he came to Britain with them at the end of the six months' truce in Rome in AD 48, during which time Caradoc, his sister Pomponia, her husband Aulus Plautius and perhaps others of Caradoc's family could have been at Pudens' house in Rome. At that time Paul may have been there as well, providing Aristobulus' consecration. The timing fits in with what we know of Paul's schedule, for his First Missionary Journey had ended in AD 46 and his Second did not begin till AD 52. There is the possibility that St. Paul used this occasion to make the trip to Britain that we are aware of, for Pudens appears not to have been in Rome at that time and not yet "chosen in the Lord." Though it is more widely thought that Paul visited Britain between his first and second imprisonments, my own opinion is that he went to Britain (even if not to Spain) in AD 48 at the conclusion of the truce. That would have given him a year or two to meet and convert his brother, to help with the beginning of Aristobulus' work in the evangelizing of Caradoc's war-torn kingdom and to visit the several places where tradition and supporting evidence of ancient writings say Paul visited and preached. These included London, Paul's Wood near Portsmouth and Bangor-ap-Dee in Wales, an abbey he is said to have founded. Bangor would later be known to St. Benedict and St. Hilary of Poitiers as "the mother of all monasteries." Historically it may indeed have been the first. It was by far the largest in Britain at the time of its destruction in AD 616 by a newly-Christian Saxon army. At that time more than twelve hundred monks were murdered as well as hundreds of scholars, all of them unarmed. Every building was burned and every manuscript destroyed.

Assuming Aristobulus arrived at Britain in AD 48 in company with Caradoc, his ministry would be enormously important to the British Church. His presence would have helped to fill the gap brought about by the royal family's captivity abroad. Given his death among the Ordovici as occurring in AD 58, he had ten years to accomplish in Glamorgan, Monmouth and Brecknock what took Patrick twenty-eight for the whole of Ireland.

Arwystli Sows Seed, Eigen Waters, Welsh Reap the Harvest

Later records of the Church in Wales give some idea of the nature of Arwystli's achievements in character as well as numbers. The Benedictines' register of saints in Wales shows an astonishing number of saints among the Silures of Gwent and an even larger number in Brecknock. His opportunities could hardly have been improved on. The Welsh were in the midst of a desperate war. Their leadership was flawless. Caradoc, like his descendant Arthur, was the ideal soldier-king. His family was loved and admired. His father Bran had been no man of war and in earlier years had turned over his kingly office to Caradoc, becoming arch-druid of the kingdom. By the time of their capture, Bran had become a Christian. Unlike other lands, where Christianity is supposed to have grown "from the bottom up," for Britain and Ireland it would be the reverse. The Druids became Christian following their kings' and arch-druids' conversion. Those at the top set an example from the start –of obedience, fidelity and simplicity of life. Aristobulus served as Caradoc's spiritual alter ego throughout his ministry, and the fire of faith was burning brightly by the king's return from Rome.

The rightness of Aristobulus' decision to leave that fruitful field and go into the mountains prior to the Caradoc family's return is confirmed by what happened in later years. Despite the war's increase in intensity and violence, the dimensions of ecclesial growth were amazing. It was the difference between starting a national church "from scratch" and having an already-eminent religious structure succeeded by a truer and more glorious one –with the earlier one remembered as a stepping-stone. With St. Eurgain (Eigen) as benefactress, the Welsh Church grew rapidly both in parish and monastic aspects of community. Because her brother Cyllinus was newly chosen king of the Silures and her brother Linus was Bishop of Rome, Eigan had an unparalleled opportunity to set an example for her people. It is well known that in the second and third centuries there were great monastic choirs or cors at each of the three ancient arch-druidical centers –Caerleon, Glastonbury and Ambresbury near Stonehenge. The practice of having the Psalter chanted continually as an echo of the heavenly choir seems to have started in Wales under Eigen's sponsorship. The best proof we can find for that supposition is that its first century usage was not at Caerleon (where one might expect), but at Cor Eurgain. (later Llan Illtyd). The Welsh Church's first woman saint was already in residence there, seeking the perfect form of musical expression for human voices in the worship of Almighty God.

As for Aristobulus, it does not matter that Welsh tradition fails to treat its beloved Arwystli Senex (Arwystli the Aged) as a martyr. His death among the Ordovici came too quickly for him to have been heard and for any resistance to the Gospel to be articulated. The Ordovici were fierce men who hated Rome, and that was doubtless held against Arwystli, who had come from there. He was almost certainly bullied to death on his arrival so he could not technically be called a martyr, though the Roman Church called him that. Before long, so did the Ordovici.

Arwystli the Sole Martyr in Conversion of Bryt and Irish Celts

What is uniquely significant is that Aristobulus' death appears to have involved the only bloodshed during the conversion of the British and Irish peoples. (This refers to surrendering their Druidic faith for that of Jesus Christ.) Patrick, in his writings, refers to death threats made by Druids angry with his teaching. A similar opposition was found in Britain, but in all those years involving evangelism and conversion there were no martyrdoms in either land at the hands of Druids. In later centuries a great many Irish and British (as also English) would pay the price of holding to their faith. Here, however, those who sought the lives of fellow Christians –whether (as Catholics) for heresy or (as Protestants) for treason –were following a doctrine of human freedom more restrictive than that which permitted Druids freely and without restraint to adopt the religion of Jesus Christ.

What of the other Apostles? Peter and Barnabas are thought to have visited in Britain, with the evidence for Peter including written as well as oral tradition. Yet in neither case is their presence considered to have been more than brief. Peter is said to have preached at the site of London's earliest church, St. Peter-upon-Cornhill, founded by King Lucius in AD 179 as well as at the site of Westminster Abbey and following that occasion to have had the vision referred to in 2 Peter 1:14, "Shortly I must put off this my tabernacle, even as our Lord Jesus Christ hath shewed me." Barnabas is remembered as having baptized Beatus after that nobly-born Briton had spent his patrimony in redeeming Helvetians from slavery, so that they, as freemen, could return to the homeland he would be evangelizing. One other Apostle who is said to have died as a martyr in Britain was Simon the Zealot. But there is also a tradition holding that Simon was martyred on the Adriatic coast. Our local tradition holds that Simon was put to death at a legion camp in Caistor in Lincolnshire during the Boadician War.[However his death came by crucifixion, which means that he was killed by Roman soldiers rather than by the Britons. The same is true of the persecutions that took place near the end of the third century beginning with St. Alban. These likewise were persecutions of already-Christian Britons at the bloody hands of a pagan Empire. Arwystli's was the sole martyrdom of a Christian by Druidic Celts. Ireland's slate was completely clean.

Correspondence Between King Lucius and Bishop Eleutherius

A matter of questionable facts and interpretation is the note-worthy event in AD 183, during the reign of King Lucius, wherein he inquired of the Bishop* of Rome concerning the governance of the Church in his kingdom. There is no record of his message, and it may have been verbal rather than written. The bishop to whom it was delivered was Eleutherius, twelfth in the line of succession from St. Peter. The clerics who visited Eleutherius as envoys were Medwy

*The term *bishop* is used here rather than *pope* because the term *pope*, signifying *supreme bishop*, was bestowed and put in force by Emperor Phocas in AD 610. Gregory I declined it, but it has since been used for all of Rome's succession.

and Elfan, the former being Lucius' theologian who, two years later, succeeded Theanus, the then-Bishop of London. After meeting with Eleutherius, they returned with a written reply, a copy of which comes from Roman sources. The returning envoys were accompanied by Dyfan and Fagan, both British clerics trained at Avalon (Glastonbury), and seemingly sent as a gesture of Eleutherius' good will. Unfortunately the slant given this event since the Reformation by Roman apologists has been that Lucius wanted to know how to go about being instructed and baptized with the intention of bringing his people into the Roman Church, a claim not surprisingly denounced by Cardinal Baronius, for it cannot have been what Lucius was asking. If Bede is correct as to the date of establishment, by the time Lucius sent his inquiry, the Christian religion had been the national faith of the British for twenty-eight years, with Lucius a baptized Christian for forty-four. Moreover, proof of the falsity of this claim is found in the text of Eleutherius' own message. The bishop was not giving permission to start a church, but advice on how to run one. I quote significant portions of J.W. Taylor's translation of Eleutherius' letter to Lucius,[1]

> "We are always at liberty to reject the Roman laws and those of Caesar, not so the law of God. By the divine mercy you have recently received this law and the faith of Christ in the kingdom of Britain. You have both parts in your power in the kingdom. From these, by the grace of God, through the Council of your kingdom select the law, and by this, in the patience of God, rule the kingdom of Britain. You are the deputy or vicar of God in your kingdom...
> "Assuredly the Christian peoples and nation of the kingdom are sons of the king. They are under your protection, and live at peace...These are the people of the kingdom of Britain whom...though separated, you ought to hold together, bound in concord and peace to the faith and law of Christ and holy Church, to unite, to recall, to cherish, to hold in your hand, to protect, to shelter, and always to defend from wrongs and evils and enemies...

"God Almighty grant you so to reign in your kingdom of Britain, that you may reign with Him in eternity, whose vicar you are in the kingdom that He hath given you."

Traditions of Jesus' Presence in Britain

Two things should be pointed out in regard to what may be said here about Our Lord and his Virgin mother as well as about her mother, St. Anne. It is our purpose to inform the reader –to tell what is locally believed in addition to that more widely known and to refer to extra-biblical narrative provided it does not conflict with the Bible.

It needs also to be stressed that whatever may be found in ancient tradition that casts new light on important matters cannot be so important as to distract attention from the saving knowledge on which alone the faith is based. What is written here may add to our knowledge of the past and also hopefully add to our understanding of the relationship between God and man, especially in regard to a Communion of Saints in obedience to a Lord "whose service is perfect freedom." If one finds joy in what is brought to light here, let it be that and nothing more. If one has doubts, let it not be a cause for anxiety or disappointment.

I have described my surprise and delight when, after five years in the sacred ministry followed by a year's graduate study in Canterbury, I found hints of an unheard-of and undreamed-of history. Those hints were like stories from childhood filled with splendor, wonder and romance. First was the tale of Jesus' boyhood visit to Britain with his great-uncle Joseph of Arimathea and possibly with the Blessed Virgin. What concerns Mary may be treated as legend until our data can more clearly be seen as fitting into the picture. Some local traditions recall the Virgin as accompanying Joseph and Jesus, but more speak of Joseph and Jesus as though they were alone.

Yet even without specific record of the Virgin's presence in Cornwall, it must continue to be a historical possibility. Joseph of Nazareth, the Virgin's spouse, was many years her senior, and may have died soon after the Holy Family's visit to Jerusalem when Jesus was twelve. If Mary, as a widow, had not come with her uncle and her son on the voyage to Britain, it could have been a matter of hardship, for her parents were no longer with her, and she had no other children.* One reason for her to remain a background figure during the visit could be the inappropriateness of a recent widow being present while the men of her family were following the merchant's trade in different settings. Yet considering the ease and excitement of travel in the Augustan Age, it is hard to imagine Mary's not being with Jesus and Joseph, but we can see why she might be inconspicuous to those without eyes to note the holiness of her presence.

As to the visit itself, it seems at this point to be unquestionably historic. While it is not validated by matching traditions in Galilee, as is Jesus' voyage to Somerset as an adult, the nineteen local Cornish traditions known to the writer appear to validate one another. They treat Joseph and Jesus in the same way –the one being a well known merchant and the other a grand-nephew who came only once, but made an indelible impression. In addition is the fact there are no local traditions in any places other than where, in the first century, tin was either mined or traded. It can be said as well that the local traditions tend to validate themselves. While I have earlier described some of the local variants, the following is a list of where they are found. The Cornish mining areas where these traditions exist are Ding Dong, Nancledra, St. Day, Redruth and Carnon Downs. The points from which tin was shipped are East and West Looe, Lamanna, Talland, Polperro, Polruan, Fowey, Place Manor, St. Just, Falmouth, St. Michael's Mount, Marazion, Penzance and Mousehole (pronounced Mowz'l).

Further, to repeat an earlier anecdote, whatever uncertainties I may have had as to the historicity of Jesus' visits to Britain disappeared some years ago when a travel agent in Texas called me to ask if I'd be interested in a trip for clergy to the Holy Land. When I spoke of my consuming interest in the present work, she exclaimed, "Oh I know all about that," and told me that during training, the first thing told her was that Jesus, both as boy and man, had gone to Britain –and that this was common knowledge in Lebanon as well as Britain. To emphasize

---

* It is generally accepted that the *brethren* of Jesus mentioned in Matthew 12, Mark 3 and Luke 8 are not siblings, but cousins –children of Cleopas and Mary Cleopas.

the widespread knowledge –in the Holy Land –of what it had taken me decades to discover, she added, "Everybody in Jerusalem knows about that –everyone, at least, who is in the travel business!"

Saint Anne in Brittany

It was not until many years after hearing of these so-called legends in Cornwall and Somerset that I learned the Virgin's mother, St. Anne, the patron saint of France, had been born and bred in Brittany. Her home village of Palud was on the Atlantic coast some twenty miles south of Brest an area where, as shown in Sir Martin Gilbert's *Atlas of Jewish History*, there were already substantial Jewish communities. Little more is known of St. Anne other than that she and the Virgin's father, St. Joachim, were living in Palestine when Mary, at the age of fifteen, was married to Joseph of Nazareth. Soon thereafter, following the death of Joachim, St. Anne returned to her Breton village to remain for the rest of her life. She is said to have been visited by Jesus while he was serving on that Phoenician ship. During the visit to Cornwall in Jesus' boyhood, those on Joseph's ship could in decent weather have seen St. Anne's home while sailing past Palud's bay. It is inconceivable to think of their not stopping by for a lengthy visit, especially if the ship were Joseph's own.

Happily the fact of St. Anne's being in Brittany could account for the Virgin's absence while Joseph of Arimathea and Jesus were in Cornwall buying tin and overseeing the ingots' storage in the vessel's hold. During these weeks of activity, Mary's time could well have been spent with her mother in the village now called Ste. Anne de-la-Palud. We can point to no proof of this other than its logic and what is known about St. Anne. Her tradition in Brittany is similar to that of Christ's in Cornwall –a precious narrative to be hidden from strangers but otherwise spoken of freely so that the young might glory in the knowledge. Those who refer to St. Anne with delight and pride-of-place are chiefly the nuns of orders having schools in Brittany and Normandy. Another such school operated by French nuns is described by L.S. Lewis as being at Alexandria in Egypt.[2] The knowledge was the more surprising to him because it dealt with Mary in Britain rather than Anne in France. This came from an elderly Mrs. Cottrell of Penwerris in Cornwall, who as a girl had studied at their convent school. She described the nuns as being members of the old French *noblesse*. Lewis adds, "She said she had been told by the sisters that Saint Joseph of Arimathea brought the Blessed Virgin to Britain, and that she had died there. . . It could only mean that among the French there lingered a tradition that the Blessed Virgin had come to Britain, and that her *Koimesis*, or falling asleep, took place there."

We are also told that the lighthouse at Place Manor in Cornwall was built in 1835 upon the foundation of an ancient chapel dedicated to St. Anne. That would be in keeping with the close relationship between the Bretons and the Cornish. Their fishermen used to work together, having common forebears and no more than minor differences in speech. They shared facilities and markets until the Cornish tongue finally disappeared a century and more ago. The lighthouse, however, still marks the nearest anchorage in Britain for anyone sailing from Palud. It is 150 miles across the Channel on a northerly course with no need to tack given a steady west wind.

A stern reference to St. Anne comes from Gladys Taylor, who has written extensively on the ancient traditions in Greater and Lesser Britain,[3] "The very strong Breton traditions concerning St. Anne, the mother of the Virgin Mary, having resided in Brittany, are too important to be dismissed.' Intriguingly, she quotes the prophet Amos (9:9) in the very next paragraph, "I will sift the house of Israel among all nations, like corn is sifted in a sieve." The verse may tell why, in Chapter Five, we found so little to demonstrate a connection between the Israelites and Celts. The sifting, like George Herbert's and Long-fellow's divine grist, would come about "slowly and exceeding small."

Refuge in Avalon for St. Mary the Virgin

Marguerite Steedman, who died in 2001, was a journalist and historian who devoted more than sixty years of study to the Cornish and Somerset traditions. Her prize-winning 1962 novel, *Refuge in Avalon,* dealt honestly and truthfully with the material, given the limitations placed on a work of fiction by a conscientious historian. The plot took Joseph of Arimathea to Gaul in that boat of castaways –having the same companions we have named. Apart from fictional characters introduced to teach and dramatize, the story ends with Joseph's arrival at Avalon. He was now alone, the ultimate refugee as it were. Avalon was the one place where a prominent person hated by the Jews and wanted by the Roman authorities could not only be safe, but free. Yet there are unanswered questions not concerning the fictitious, but the real. Why did Joseph not remain in Provence? He had been the castaways' chief stay; what would be the point of his leaving them? Why would a man of his age place importance on reaching a place so protected by nature that no Roman, Saxon, Danish, Viking or Norman sword would ever be wielded there? Why this place of ultimate security when every one of his companions would have thought it more important to remain in Gaul?

As one having had for years a consuming thirst for this history and finding it in puzzling fragments, I find myself, here and now, to have been one with eyes to see and ears to hear who failed to understand. The secret has been with us all along and I have discovered it only at the moment of writing. Joseph of Arimathea was gripped by necessity to head for Britain from the moment of his arrival in Provence. Why? Because unknown to us and possibly to our scholarly sources, the Virgin Mary had been in that boat! It is possible, though not likely, that her captors had placed her in it without knowing who she was. Following the landing in Provence, her uncle could have had only one thing in mind –to take her to a place where she could be safe from the harsh hands of Roman justice and agents of the Temple. The place must be Britain –still outside the Empire –and the village must be Avalon. Joseph would undertake the journey with no other intent than to devote the rest of his life to Mary's care and protection. As it turned out, according to uncertain legend backed up by one clear tradition, she would die fifteen years after their arrival, but Joseph would remain as guardian of a place for so long sanctified by her presence –and this regardless of the doctrines and devotions that would in time be extended in her honor.

Having arrived at this judgment, I have two options. One is to "go back to square one," revising the passenger list of the castaways' boat and adjusting the text accordingly. The other is to allow the mysteries of the faith to remain until in God's time the concealed may be revealed. I choose the latter, since there is no way of proving what is apparent here. At the least it gives an agenda for the remainder of this chapter. We can make a fresh start with this speculation –that Joseph, in taking leave with the Virgin from the other castaways, asked the Bethany family to accompany them and after their arrival at Avalon to return by themselves to Provence. And seemingly they did this; there is slender evidence of such an escort's being provided. The Magdalen, however, may have remained with Jesus' mother until after the Virgin's death. Based on evidence to be cited below, Saint Mary the Virgin appears to have died in AD 52. By the following year Mary Magdalene was back in Provence. With Maximin's help and under his protective care, she established her community at la Sainte Baume. That community could be very like one started by Joseph of Arimathea eleven years later in Avalon.

Before considering evidence of the Virgin's life and death at Glastonbury, let us consider such evidence and opinions as might call this theory into question. First is the fact that while on the Cross, Jesus gave his mother into John's care. One reason for such bestowal could be Jesus' foreknowledge that John, alone among the Twelve, would survive for such an undertaking. There is evidence, however, that John at one point transferred Mary's care to Joseph of Arimathea, who as male next of kin was, in any event, legally her guardian. We also have the Scriptural text as a reminder that after the Crucifixion John took the Virgin not to *Joseph of Arimathea's home*, but to *his own*. Neither of these possibilities could have meant much for long. When that boatload of Jesus' disciples was set adrift, John was already underground with the other Apostles. His mother was in that boat. His brother James had already left for Spain and would be martyred on his return. As for Zebedee, their father, there are no further references to him in Scripture or tradition. So being with "John's own" *could* mean being with John's mother, Mary Salome, as well as the others in that boat.

Three other facts require us to be open to the possibility that the Virgin spent her last years at Avalon. One is that the tradition of Mary in Ephesus, while based on that passage in John, is vague –not fleshed in with details. What links Mary with the Eastern Churches is their doctrine of her Dormition or Falling Asleep of the Virgin. That teaching, like the Roman Church's teaching of her Assumption into heaven, is based on theology rather than on history. That is to say, there is no evidence of time, place or circumstances of death, or whether she was assumed in her earthly body or in a resurrected body following death to this world. Whatever happened, therefore, to the Virgin could have occurred as readily at Glastonbury as in Ephesus or Jerusalem. What the Glastonbury tradition does provide –which the other two do not –is a time and a place as well as fact of death and burial in a known location.

Let us now consider the evidence that the Virgin lived, died and was buried at Avalon. We may be blessed by the fact that only one person seems to have given a positive statement on the matter –and by the fact that even this statement, coming several centuries after the events described, must be treated as hearsay. It leaves us without the need to resolve a matter that is best unresolved as one of the mysteries of the faith. What is of benefit to us is the witness of one man given readily on many occasions –and backed up by the supportive, but indirect, witness of many others. As a result we can hardly fail to consider Glastonbury as one of the holiest places on earth. Aside from the bloodied and beleaguered Holy Land it could be the holiest there is.

We begin with the letter Augustine of Canterbury is said to have written to Gregory the Great in Rome. It describes a church Augustine had not seen but had heard about. He described it as "constructed by no human art, but by the hands of Christ himself... The Almighty continues to watch over it as sacred to himself and to Mary, the mother of God." What an astonishing thing to relate! What could it have meant? Very possibly it was beyond the power of either man to deal with –in which case it could have been set aside and forgotten. (But it was not forgotten; we have the above quote from Augustine as a reminder and a challenge.)

We continue with David, the patriarch of the Welsh Church. After his consecration as Archbishop of Menevia, he determined to build and dedicate a stone chapel enclosing the ancient wattle Church. On the night before the cornerstone laying, David had a vision in which Jesus told him not to do this thing, saying that He had long since built the church and dedicated it to His Virgin Mother. He closed by saying that what David had planned would therefore be a profaning rather than a blessing. St. David canceled the plan, later building a galilee (a connecting passage) joining the Old Church to the Abbey.

We now come to the principal witness not only to supposedly historic facts about Mary, but to the meaning of Joseph's presence. His name was Melchinus or Maelgwyn of Avalon —famous as a historian and bard, living in the middle of the fifth century. Maelgwyn is known to have been St. David's uncle and a cousin of King Arthur. It was said of him that "he was before Arthur"; some people have believed that he was the Merlin of Arthurian legend. Whatever else he was, he was a scholar of note whose writings have carried a considerable authority. In one fragment of his work Maelgwyn describes the multitude of saints who, buried in Avalon's sacred soil, have "awaited the day of resurrection under the protection of the Mother of God."

The facts of Mary's presence appear to have been secret —or very private —knowledge until Melchinus wrote them down. Yet it can hardly be doubted he wrote of things known to some, and there can be no question as to what he meant. Maelgwyn's first statement concerning her was starkly simple, "The Ealde Chyrche was built over the grave of the Blessed Mary." In giving tribute to the Virgin's uncle, he wrote, "Joseph of Arimathea, the noble decurion, received his everlasting rest with his eleven associates in the isle of Avalon... He has with him two white vessels of silver which were filled with the blood and the sweat of the great Prophet Jesus." The vessels are thought to be the historic elements that in legend have become the Cup of the Last Supper, the Holy Grail.

Elsewhere Maelgwyn wrote of Joseph of Arimathea's chapel and of its adjacent cemetery and of their precious burials. The meaning of some passages is obscure and in need of helpful interpretation. But there can be little question that he is speaking with knowledge and understanding, and that it is our task to find his meaning, "The isle of Avalon greedy of burials... received thousands of sleepers, among whom Joseph de Marmore from Arimathea by name, entered his perpetual sleep. And he lies in a bifurcated line next the southern angle of the Oratory made of circular wattles by 13 inhabitants of the place over the powerful adorable Virgin." In describing St. Mary's Chapel, Maelgwyn set down these words, "In this church they worshipped and taught the people the Christian faith. After about fifteen years Mary died and was buried at Glastonbury. The disciples died in succession and were buried in the cemetery."

Other and Later Evidence Based on Maelgwyn's Words

A curiosity relating to Joseph of Arimathea is that while no one at any time seems to have doubted the fact of his ministry in Avalon, as early as William of Malmesbury's time (the 12th century), doubts were cast as to Joseph's significance to the picture. William, as a careful historian, was content to document what he could be sure about. In Joseph's case he had to acknowledge existence of doubts and his own decision to limit himself to what he could state with authority. Where we quote William below, we can acknowledge Joseph as object of some uncertainty, but at the same time, his recognition as an important figure. It is significant that when printing was invented, two of the first three books to be printed in English were lives of Joseph of Arimathea. The following is a brief reference to the Virgin, taken from Richard Pynson's metrical *Life of Joseph of Arimathea*. It gives a basis for the dating of her death. Adding its 15 years to Gildas' dating of Joseph's arrival in AD 37, we are given an approximate date of AD 52:[4]

> "Now hear how that Joseph came into England;
> But at that time it was called Brytayne,
> Than XV yere with Our Lady, as I understande,
> Joseph wayted styll to serve her he was fayne,
> So after hyr Assumpcyon, the boke telleth playne;

With Saynt Phylyp he went into France,
Phylyp bad them to go to Great Brytayn fortunate."

We cannot ignore the fact that not only many kings and queens, but many of the leading figures of the Church are buried at Glastonbury. Their very presence bears witness to the importance and holiness of the place. These include Patrick, Benen, David, Gildas and Aidan, all of whom were buried at Glastonbury in the small Chapel of St. Patrick, built especially for Irish pilgrims.

Further testimony may be seen in the way Avalon and St. Mary's Chapel, as holy places, have been respected differently. In post-Reformation years, it was common for those wanting finished building stone to help themselves to what was in the Abbey. Yet the Lady Chapel, roofless, without flooring and fallen into decrepitude, seems never to have lost a stone except for a portion of one wall, which may have fallen rather than been carried away.

We have also mentioned how from the time the Christian faith came to Glastonbury, its village and Abbey have never been the scene of warfare, looting or pillage, with one exception –its wanton seizure and the wanton killing of its abbot at the order of Henry VIII, himself the descendent of Joseph of Arimathea. We know of the murder by brigands of a party of Irish pilgrims –but it took place at Shapwick, five miles short of their hearts' and souls' desire. Likewise during Somerset's Pitchfork Rebellion came the Battle of Sedgemoor, before which the Duke of Monmouth's rebels camped in the Abbey ruins. But the shedding of blood at Sedgemoor took place six miles away.

What seems worthy of note in this connection is that at the nadir of Alfred's reign, when his rule was reduced to no more than a few hundred acres of Somerset swampland, his hill fort of last resort appears to have been the tiny Mump Burrow–some ten miles from Glastonbury and no more than 80 feet high. How much more defensible would the Tor have been, and how easy for Alfred and his remnant to have gone there. Yet so holy was this Avalon to Alfred as to monarchs before and after that it would be unthinkable that sword be drawn or blood shed in any part of Britain's holiest place. As a Merlin could have told him

–or for that matter many others –Mump Burrow had similarly been blessed by St. Michael, the proof of such blessing being that Alfred held out in that place through the most difficult of times to set an example of Christian kingliness to Saxon and Dane alike. The one wicked use to which Glaston's abbey and its community were put was at the Dissolution of Monasteries, when this greatest of abbeys was closed down, its treasures seized and its abbot hanged, drawn and quartered on the Tor.

For a final piece of evidence pointing to the physical presence of the Virgin we can regard the obverse side of the Great Seal of the Abbey, in use from AD 1400 until the Dissolution in AD 1539. On the seal's face are three of its abbots, Patrick, Dunstan and Benignus with a Latin inscription translated as, "The holy bishops three, assurance give to thee." On the reverse are three female saints, Katherine on the left, Margaret on the right, the Virgin in the center, holding the child Jesus in one arm and with the other holding what appears to be a flowering Glastonbury thorn, with this inscription,

"Testis adest isti, scripto pia genetrix Xti –Glastonie,[5]
"The holy mother of Christ the Word is here in Glastonbury
   as witness."

Proposed Solution to Mystery in Maelgwyn's Script

A mystery remains from Maelgwyn's time at to the meaning of "linneae bifurcatae" in two of his quotations. A literal translation has it that Joseph's body lies in the southern angle of the *bifurcated line* of the Oratorium of the adorable Virgin. Bifurcated line, as in "straight line" or "plumbline," seems to carry no meaning whatsoever. Neither does the Latin *linea* meaning "linen garment." Miss Steedman has a proposal which I cite with her permission. She believes the word *lineae* has come from a misspelling of what could have been the original term, *lignea*, meaning wood or wooden. Accepting this, the translation may come clear. Joseph of Arimathea may have been buried beneath the floor in a corner of his chapel, in a "ligneae bifurcatae" or *split-wood* coffin placed *over that of the powerful adorable Virgin* (emphasis mine)." In death as in life he sought to place himself between her and whoever or whatever could bring her harm.

Guardedness of References in Avalon to the Blessed Virgin

We may note the oblique and guarded way in which all these references have been offered –except for Maelgwyn's. There seems to have been a universal disposition to protect the Virgin. One way to effect this would be in symbol and euphemism rather than in language such as Maelgwyn's. Glastonbury Abbey has been called *Domus Dei –the House of God*, implying a unique presence of the Almighty. It is curious that the *Domesday Book*, using that same term, adds a kind of alias, *Secretum Domini, the Lord's Secret*. It is equally curious that during the Middle Ages Britain itself was referred to as "Our Lady's Dowry." These are oblique and guarded, conveying a significance beyond the ordinary meaning of the words. In another context this could express a gnostic supposition. The use here is unlike that, however. It suggests no more than a desire to keep all of us at a discreet distance from this most precious and vulnerable of saints.

We have referred to William of Malmesbury's readiness to confine his scholarship to what was altogether available and open to study. Yet with regard to the holiness of Joseph's Chapel and the spot where the Virgin is thought to have been buried, he is the soul of discretion and indirection. He speaks of the pavement tiles in the holy place, adding gently and with diffidence "under which if I believe some sacred secret to be contained, I shall not be doing an injury to religion."

It is very possible that Joseph of Arimathea saw his task as a *kenosis*, a self-emptying that might leave his own presence at Avalon very nearly as unnoticed as the Virgin's. That could provide a kind of protective coloration of benefit to both. His ministry to Saint Mary and –after her departure, to her memory sacred to that place –might require the work of Joseph the Apostle to give way to that of Joseph the Guardian and Protector of Saint Mary the Virgin Mother of Our Lord.

British and Gallican Churches,
The Early Years (continued)

Before we return to the British scene following Caradoc's release from captivity, let us reflect on Rome's dealings with Britain during the ninety-eight years between Julius Caesar's withdrawal in 54 BC and the beginning of the war now in its eighteenth year. Because its chief historians say nothing about Rome's dealings with Britain in those years, it has been widely assumed they were years of accommodation. A study made in 1871 by William Henry Black, F.S.A. found many indications that during Augustus Caesar's reign there was calculated aggression. Rome's means-to-an-end included conspiracy, bribery and intrigue, the scenario being that of "divide and conquer."[1]

Britain's record at all times is evident in what its Triads tell us. Whether during war or peace, they tell of virtue and vice on the part of leading figures. In being personal and specific rather than abstract and open to later revision, the Triads are like Holy Scripture; they view events as with the eyes of God, showing a sense of divinely-given standards. Like the Scriptures, they provide maxims of behavior fitting for every generation. If Tacitus and Suetonius overlooked the period, it is because it was an era of bark-and-growl-without-the-bite. Besides, they were too young to give attention. Neither would be studying or writing history until the time of Trajan.

Our material for the period at hand comes from two literary figures, Virgil and Horace, who were the Emperor Augustus' contemporaries and well known to him. Moreover, they had nothing to lose by disclosing what he planned and carried out, which is to our advantage. Virgil and Horace made clear what Augustus' mind and policies were. We are not told whether he set foot on British soil, but there is evidence of commando-like incursions on a number of occasions. British captives were brought as slaves to Rome and given a visible part in public entertainment. Tribute money was paid by British kings. Hostages were brought into Caesar's household from several British kingdoms. Two such lads, according to tradition, were Coriolanus,* (Cynvelin) the father of Arviragus, and Bran, the father of Caradoc. It is thought that these two sons may also have spent a few youthful years as hostages in Rome.

When Tiberius became Emperor, Rome's aggressive policy is unlikely to have changed. Under Caligula it escalated to the flash-point when Rome's armies were brought to the Channel, expecting to embark. Sensing mutiny, Caligula called the campaign off by playing the buffoon. He doubled the soldiers' pay and announced a triumphal procession in Rome at which, in place of a laurel wreath, he wore a garland of seaweed while dragging a captive King Neptune in chains behind his chariot. A timely assassination allowed the madman to be replaced with a strange and awkward Claudius, who nonetheless chose competent and responsible subordinates. When the British high king Guiderius sent a delegation asking extradition from Rome of two fugitive princes found guilty of treasonous dealings with Caligula, it provoked a war far more savage than what Julius Caesar had attempted on his own.

---

*In his *History of Britain*, R.W. Morgan states that when Horace had halfway persuaded Augustus of the folly of a planned invasion, the Emperor gave audience to King Coriolanus, who as a youthful hostage had been reared in his household. Morgan states (v. pp. 97-99) that as a consequence, Augustus called off the invasion and reduced to a light tariff the heavy duties on British exports to the Continent.

Rebellion of a Client People, the Iceni

We have already described how the Iceni, a people in what is now East Anglia, decided during the Claudian truce in AD 43 to become a client kingdom and thus entitled to Rome's protection. Soon the worthlessness of that protection would be evident to every Briton. Things came apart when Seneca, a friend of Nero and a man of great wealth, called in an enormous loan made years earlier at usurious rates to Prasutagus, the Iceni king. When the king's council asked for time, Nero ordered the Roman prefect, Caius Decius, to seize all property belonging to the state and its ruler. Prasutagus had just died, and though his will left half of his estate to Nero, the prefect seized it all. When the widowed Queen Boadicia protested, she was stripped and flogged and her two daughters raped by a mob of soldiers. Subsequent to the brutality and in violation of the Claudian treaty, Decius ordered the seizure of all property belonging to Icenian nobles. Word flew abroad, and, despite the Icenis' earlier betrayal, Britons flocked from every quarter to take up the queen's cause against the hated Romans.

Nero Enforces Julius Caesar's Wish to Eliminate the Druids

At the same time as Nero's order to Decius, a harsher and even more serious command was sent to Suetonius Paulinus, governor of Britain and chief of Rome's forces in the West. He was directed to march with all speed to the Menai Straits in northwest Wales and to cross to the Isle of Mona (Anglesey) which for centuries had been the heart of Druidic studies and religion. Upon arrival, he was to extirpate the Druid's priests and priestesses, bards and ovates as well as other men, women and children. And this he did. All were killed —more than five thousand souls. Every altar was leveled to the ground and the Druids' sacred groves felled and burned. No weapon had ever been allowed on the holy island, so there could be no armed resistance. The attack began at night while the Druids stood their ground holding torches aloft, uttering imprecations against the Romans and calling on God to avenge the outrage to the island's sanctity.

By the time news of the Druids' massacre got around, Queen Boadicia had been joined by some 120,000 men bent upon avenging her country's honor —either killing the Romans or driving them into the sea. They met the Queen at Leicester and moved on to Colchester, where an enormous temple had been built on the site of their meeting with Claudius at the time of truce. A force of retired veterans (for whose settlement Rome had seized the people's land) held out for two days, but the city was burned, with death coming to every Roman and Briton found there. Having destroyed Colchester, they now turned to Verulamium (St. Alban's). Along the way they were intercepted by two thousand men of Rome's ninth legion, hastening from Lincoln to stem the tide. The mob swarmed around the legionaries and killed every one who was afoot. Only the cavalry escaped in company with the legion's commander, Petilius Cerealis, who in later years succeeded Suetonius as military governor.

By now Boadicia's forces included some 230,000 people consumed by man's two ancient curses, guilt-by-association and the blood lust of the vengeful. They descended upon a London packed with frightened Romans and fearful Britons. By the time they arrived, its Roman defenders as well as all who were able to flee had abandoned the city which was destroyed by fire. Every remaining person was put to the sword. By the time Boadicia's forces had finished with the city, more than 70,000 Romans had fallen either in garrison or on the field. The British dead numbered tens of thousands more, including a great many innocent victims. The artist who did the monumental painting of Victoria (Boadicia), must have had Dio Cassius' words in memory. Describing her meeting with followers at Leicester, he writes,[2]

"Her stature exceeded the ordinary height of women —her appearance brought terror —her aspect was calm and collected but her voice had become deep and pitiless. Her hair fell as low as the hips, in long golden tresses, collected round the forehead by a golden coronet. She wore a Tartan dress, fitting closely to the bosom, but below the waist opening in loose folds as a gown. Over it was a chlamys, or military cloak. This was her usual attire. On this occasion she carried also a spear."

We quote Victoria's prayer in part as Dio gives it,[3]

"I rule over Britons little trained in craft, but born and trained to the game of war —men who in the cause of liberty stake down their own lives, the lives of their wives and children, their lands and property. Queen of such a race, I implore thine aid for freedom —for victory over enemies infamous for the wantonness of the wrongs they inflict, for their perversion of justice, for contempt of religion, for their insatiable greed. Never let a foreigner bear rule over me or these my countrymen! Never let slavery rule in this isle."

What followed was a painful blow to the cause of freedom when its defenders followed their instincts rather than the precepts by which liberty is won and maintained. Tacitus says there were two more[4] engagements after London, while Dion speaks of many. Whichever it was, the final battle was a resounding echo of what happened to the Teutons at Aix-en-Provence 163 years earlier. Though Rome's two remaining legions included only ten thousand men, with Boadicia's many times that number, the combined legions held their formation across a wooded defile that could only be approached from the front —doing what their centurions and the rule book required of each and all. At the close of a long day of furious combat the British had lost as many as eighty-thousand dead to the legions' four hundred. There was no way the Romans could take advantage of their victory, however, and many Britons got away. It was enough that the Romans kept their hold on the island and that their subsequent treatment of Britons would be more respectful. Boadicia died in the last day of what must have been a protracted series of engagements, for the best evidence is that the final battle took place in Flintshire, two hundred miles from London.

A War Returned to Veterans of a Deadly Game

The outcome of the Iceni's rebellion had little impact on the course of the war. The leadership of the Britons now included Venusius, the displaced husband of Queen Cartimandua who had betrayed

Caradoc. A succession of Roman governors (still general officers on active military service) came and died or were recalled.[5] As a result of Rome's experience, Roman historians came to refer to Britain as "Ferox Provincia," *the Untamable Province*. Tacitus added (presumably with the Silurians in mind) that such people "could neither be coerced by any measures however sanguinary, nor bribed by any promises however brilliant, to acknowledge the dominion of Rome."[6]

Aside from Aulus Plautius, the one great general was Julius Agricola, whose first taste of the British War had been as a 21-year-old officer on the staff of Suetonius Paulinus. The year had been AD 61, when the Druids were massacred and the Iceni rose in wrath. Of that year Tacitus would later write,[7] "Neither before nor since has Britain been in a more uneasy or dangerous state. Veterans were butchered, colonies burned to the ground, and armies isolated. We had to fight for life before we could think of victory."

Agricola's entire military career was spent in Britain. In AD 69 he became commander of the 20th Legion, stationed at Chester.[8] In AD 78 the aging Vespasian appointed him Governor of Britain, which meant he directed the remainder of the active fighting. In the first three years he completed the reduction of north Wales and of the Brigantes' strongholds between Chester and York on the south and the Scottish border on the north. The year AD 81 brought the conquest of Scotland up to and including Glasgow and Edinburgh. The years AD 83 and AD 84 were occupied in probing and working toward the conquest of northern Scotland and involved fierce fighting with the Caledonian Celts led by a redoubtable and eloquent Calgacus to whom Arviragus —now too old for active service —had given command of the north. Late one night in the summer of AD 83, the Caledonians, after silencing its sentries, swarmed into the camp of the smallest of three legions. Only the quick arrival of Agricola's scouts and cavalry, followed by legionaries racing from a distance —all shouting war cries in Celtic style —averted a massacre. The climactic battle for the remainder of Scotland took place in AD 84. at a place known only as Mons Graupius. It left the Scots with so many dead that it would be forty years before they could once more be a threat. Ten thousand Caledonians died that day as against 367 Roman legionaries.

Agricola's Recall and Departure —and with it Rome's Dominion

What happened following Agricola's departure is more than a surprise. It is astonishing —a mystery whose magnitude in numbers could approach that of Israel's Ten Lost Tribes. The Encyclopedia Britannica's eleventh edition, the most thorough and dependable on matters of history and religion, has this to say,[9] "What frontier was adopted after Agricola's departure, whether Tweed or Teviot or other, is unknown. *For thirty years (AD 85-115) the military history of Britain is a blank.*" (Emphasis mine) Since we have no resources other than those of local tradition, we must note what Morgan has to tell us. Let us first, however, hear Tacitus' own "one liner" on what transpired after his father-in-law left for Rome and retirement,[10] "*Britain,*" he says, "*which was considered at last effectually conquered, was lost in an instant!*" (Emphasis also mine)

And the Land Had Rest from All Its Enemies Round About

R.W. Morgan states that immediately after Agricola's departure, a reorganized confederacy under Arviragus took the field anew. It included the Kymri, the Kymric Picts, the Caledonii of Western Albyn and the Brigantiaid. The new Roman Governor, Lucullus, was worsted at one place after another in the west and north and could offer no strong opposition anywhere to the forces of the aging Pendragon. The fortresses in the south built earlier by Aulus Plautius were assaulted and taken, the Thames crossed and London reoccupied. In AD 86, after forty-three years of war and more than sixty pitched battles, the Romans were expelled from their last holds in Kent. Rome's new frontier, therefore, was not Tweed or Teviot but once more the English Channel![11]

Arviragus was frail by AD 86, but his death would not come till three years later. Meanwhile, at his order, every Roman monument and every inscription that could be found from those war years was destroyed or wiped clean, and every Roman coin removed from circulation and destroyed. The thoroughness with which the task was accomplished has everywhere been evident, and that it was done on

Arviragus' authority and during Rome's supposed "occupation" can hardly be denied. When death came to the great soldier-king it could be said of him, as was later said of Washington, that he was "first in war, first in peace, and first in the hearts of his countrymen." Yet many who have written the history of the period seem not even to know who Arviragus was. His British name was Gweyrydd, while that of his brother Guiderius was Gwyddyr, and these names are even less familiar to historical scholars than are the Latin.

The record, as now offered at historical sites, seems to confirm in part what Morgan told us. Agricola's legion at York was transferred out of Britain almost immediately after the general's departure. The fortress in Scotland was permanently evacuated. There is vague reference to uprisings in the north. Of any remaining forces there is no record. We can only speculate that what Arviragus planned and achieved was an uprising of such universal immediacy that there was no possibility for relief because every unit was at all times occupied in combat. The Roman naval forces left behind by Agricola may or may not have been sufficient to remove those Romans who reached the beaches. The only feature that can be described as an accomplishment during thirty years of a cease-fire marked by mutual exhaustion is that the three legionary fortresses and a number of auxiliary fortresses were rebuilt in stone. But it is questionable whether any Romans were on the island during these years, and the rebuilding could well have come later.

Peace Treaty Follows Forty-Three Years of War and a Thirty Year Mutual Stand-off

Arviragus' son Marius (or Maric) had succeeded his father as Britain's high king with the father's death in AD 89. Though the war's military occupation came to an end in AD 86, a peace treaty would not be signed until AD 114 with the Emperor Trajan. With this signing Britain consented to become a provincial partner of the Romans on the following conditions:[12]

◻ That the Britons continue under their own laws and their native Kings.

¤ That Roman law be confined to such cities as chose to become municipia or colonies.

¤ That no Briton be disturbed in his hereditary estates.

¤ That three Roman legions be stationed at Caerleon, Chester and York, recruited wholly from British volunteers and for defense only and never to be ordered to serve on foreign soil.

¤ That in return, Britain agreed to tax itself three thousand pounds' weight of silver annually as its contribution to the general defense of the Empire and to place its forces under officers appointed by the Emperor.

Why Risk Turning Victory into Defeat?

Why, after nearly three generations of brave resistance to unlawful domination, would a nation of freedom-fighters give in by joining those they had opposed? It seems likely that, having won the enemy's admiration and esteem, the British might engage –willingly and with sound logic –in a relationship they could not be forced into. Having a bred-in-the-bone sense of self-worth, with rulers and magistrates held to be servants of the people, and applying checks and balances in restraint of power, the Britons had as much to give as to obtain. It was understood that the most important benefit would be the training of British youth in Rome's techniques of warfare and weaponry that had taken such toll on its countrymen. There was also a common concern among Britons and Romans about the increasing aggressiveness of barbarians beyond their borders. A system of joint defense became the only option when civilization itself appeared to be at stake. Lastly there was a personal element in the treaty. While the high king's father was the great Arviragus, his mother, the much-loved Genuissa, was the daughter of Claudius the Emperor of Rome. In terms of blood and culture, King Maric was a Romano-Briton.

The peace treaty had one profound weakness–a failure to guarantee the Britons freedom of religion. The Empire's policy continued to be an implacable hostility to Druidism and Christianity. It gave no protection for British legionaries against requiring the oath of allegiance to the Emperor and the burning of incense before his statue in acknowledgment of his "divinity." The most frightening scenario came when the legions vied and fought with one another – not in common defense against barbarians, but in determining whose candidate would rule as Emperor. In AD 114, when Maric signed the treaty, such a possibility seemed unthinkable. By AD 411, when all three of Britain's legions had gone to Gaul on such a quest and all three were destroyed in internecine quarrels, the situation was desperate, the more so because Rome itself had fallen. It was out of such desperation that Gildas Badonicus wrote his lament. Through those years when Britain was attacked by Saxons from the east and Picts from the north, "there were no males to meet the enemy but old men, cripples and boys under eleven years of age."[13]

The Persecution of British Christians in a Roman World

The standard histories fall far short of explaining what happened when Rome's persecution of Christians came to an island that for more than two hundred fifty years had had no martyrs. The dating of that persecution is uncertain. Charles Thomas suggests that the martyrdoms that began with St. Alban may well have taken place during the reign of Decius (AD 249-51) rather than of Diocletian (AD 284-305). If so, we can breathe a sigh of relief for Constantius, the husband of St. Helena and father of Constantine the Great, since he was a co-emperor with Diocletian and would have been partaker of his guilt. If we could rewrite the history we would do so, for the later date would contrast with this man's humane rule not only against the martyrdoms described in the standard histories, but a far larger number known in ancient times and described by Bede[14] as well as Gildas. The names of Alban and five clergy of the British Church have long been honored (following Bede) as "the earliest British martyrs," and are the only ones described in the Roman Benedictines' *Book of Saints*. But Gildas adds the names of Stephen and Argulius, successively bishops of London; Socrates, Bishop of York; Amphibalus, Bishop of Llandaff; Nicholas, Bishop of Penrhyn (Glasgow); Melior, Bishop of Carlisle; along with some ten thousand communicants whose names are known only to God —a thousand or so described as priests.[15]

First Christian Royal Family in First Established Christian Church

Below is a brief record of the British royal family[16] —altered to conform with textual discrepancies observed in Morgan's chart:

Royal Christian Dynasty of Ancient Britain, Beli to Constantine*

Beli the Great	100–70 BC
Caswallon	70–47 BC
Tenuantius	47–5 BC
Llyr	5 BC–AD 10
Cynvelin	5 BC–AD 30
Bran	AD 10–36
Caradoc	AD 36–60
Guiderius	AD 30–40
Arviragus	AD 40–90
Cyllin	AD 69–95
Linus	AD 67–79**
Cynon,Eurgain Claudia	
Maric	AD 90–120
Coel	AD 120–124
Lucius	AD 124–201
Cadvan, Prince of Cambria	
Strada the Fair	
Coel King of Colchester	AD 232
Helena	AD 248–328
Constantius, Emperor	AD 242–306
Constantine the Great	AD 265–326

*Dates of rule, high kings underlined
**Dates in office as Bishop of Rome

The Apostolate in Early Britain

From what has been shown thus far, we have a sure record of Apostolic ordering of the British Church in Aristobulus and Joseph of Arimathea. While Simon of Cana, Paul, Peter and Barnabas are believed to have been in Britain, and while we have record of several first century missionary bishops going to the Continent from Britain, we have no record of who may have consecrated whom except in the cases of Barnabas and Beatus, and these are no more than supposition. Yet we find all of these accepted in the *Book of Saints* as apostolic men, which is to say there is no reason to question the validity of Apostolic Order in the British Church. As for Gaul and Spain, we have record of the Apostles' ordering of Gaul and Spain, with Maximin as a Vicar General charged with oversight for the seventeen dioceses and seven archdeaconries provided at the start.

When it comes to Apostolic Succession, however, we accept the necessity of regularity both in the sequence of bishops for any given place and the catholicity of doctrine being held and proclaimed there. We find it most definitively in the Patriarchates of the Catholic and Apostolic Church. In the East it involved those of Jerusalem, Alexandria and Antioch, to which later would be added Constantinople, Athens and Moscow. In the West we are given the Church of Rome to which should be added the British Church whose founding preceded Rome's and whose archbishops were originally in London, Llandaff and Caerleon, with the Primate initially in London. Those properly ordered could be identified by their acceptance and participation in the Councils of the Early Church or by suitable records in their churches' registries or in historic material giving evidence of such records.

The British Church Represented at Early Councils

Apart from the Council of Jerusalem in AD 46, recorded in Acts 15, the first important Council was that called by Constantine in AD 314 at Arles. Three British archbishops were there —Restitutus of London, Adelphius of Caerleon and Eborius of York. These represented twenty-eight dioceses in the three provinces that by that time had been established.[17] We also have record of British bishops being present at the First General Council at Nicaea in AD 325 as well as the Council of Sardica in AD 347 and the Council at Ariminium in AD 359, respectively in Illyria and Italy. Such attendance compares favorably with that of other churches of the West, especially since all seven of the Ecumenical Councils were held in the East, centering in Constantinople. Admittedly, all we know is that there was a British presence at some of the above-named councils. Since many of the Councils left no record of bishops' names or dioceses, we must let it go at that. All we can claim is that the fact of certain bishops' presence can be regarded as evidence of catholicity on their churches' part and validity of their episcopal and apostolic order. But it is only half the story if we have no more than a general idea of who they were.

Lines of Apostolic Order in Britain

It is well known that the First Archbishop of Canterbury, Augustine, received Episcopal Orders from the Bishops of Lyon and Arles, whose own orders were derived from that of John the Apostle in the East. When in AD 666 the Augustine line of succession died out, the Seventh Archbishop, Theodore, received his orders from the Petrine line in Rome.

The Church of England would subsequently obtain, through its 60th Archbishop Henry Chicheley in 1408, the lineage of the Patriarchs of Jerusalem. Prior to his translation to Canterbury, Chicheley had been the Bishop of St. David's in Wales. David himself, prior to his earlier ordering, had been lay Abbot of a Welsh monastery. He and two of his priests, Teilo and Padarn, joined in pilgrimage to Jerusalem. On the night before their arrival in the Holy City, its Patriarch, John III, received a message from an angel directing him to consecrate the three pilgrims as Bishops for the Church in Wales. The Patriarch welcomed them and did as he was directed.

The historic fact of these consecrations was ascertained by the Saxon historian William of Malmesbury, from records in Glastonbury's library prior to the disastrous fire of 1184. As further proof, William could point to four gifts sent to David by the Patriarch after being assured of his return to Britain. They included a famous sapphire altar stone, a bell, a bishop's staff and a tunic of woven gold. All were given by St. David to Glastonbury's monastery before his death and burial in St. Patrick's Chapel near the Abbey church.

But there was an earlier Apostolic lineage for the British than the one referred to here, and it would be conjoined in any case with that of Patriarch John III. We can identify it as Apostolic but only *presumably* so because of the gap in time between that of Joseph of Arimathea and those in his succession whose names we first have on record. To make such an admission is not to cast doubt upon Philip's consecration of Joseph or of Joseph's being *the* Apostle to the British. It is that we have yet to learn the names, places and succession of apostolic men or bishops who exercised that ministry between the time of Joseph, who died in AD 82, and that of King Lucius' Establishment of the British Church a century or so later. It helps to state that we *do* have the names of many British bishops whose ordering has always been accepted as valid and whose lineage was that of Joseph of Arimathea. But from Joseph's death until the time of Good King Lucius the episcopal succession may have been limited to the company of anchorites whom Philip and Joseph together had established at Glastonbury. That community continued there for some 400 years, when its members were incorporated by St. Patrick of Ireland into the Benedictine Abbey in Glastonbury, of which he was the founder and first Abbot. The chart below shows the succession of eleven bishops in the Diocese of Llandaff from the British Church's Establishment to David's consecration as the 12th Bishop of that See. We have likewise, for the Archdiocese of London, nine such bishops, the last of whom was the Bishop Restitutus who, along with Archbishops of Caerleon and York, represented the British Church at the Council of Arles in AD 314.

It is possible that similar records may yet be found in such ancient centers as York, Caerleon, Winchester and Gloucester. But those named here, who served as archbishops or bishops from the time of King Lucius until that of St. David the Patriarch of Wales, are sufficient to certify from earliest days the Catholic and Apostolic nature of the British Church.

British Bishops' Orders Deriving from Joseph of Arimathea's:

Diocese of Llandaff	Archdiocese of London
1. Dyfan	1 Theanus
2. Ffagan	2. Elfan
3. Medwy	3. Cadar
4. Edelffed	4 Obinus
5. Cadwr	5. Conan
6. Cynan	6. Palladius
7. Ilan	7. Stephanus d. AD 300
8. Llewyr	8. Augulus d. AD 305
9. Cyhelyn	9. Restitutus d. AD 314
10. Gwythelyn	
11. Dyfrig (Dubritius)	
12. David	

We have already referred to several of these bishops. Medwy and Elfan were King Lucius' ambassadors to Bishop Eleutherius in Rome. Theanus was the Bishop of London whom Elfan replaced after his return to Britain. Dyfan and Ffagan were the priests (already schooled at Avalon) whom Eleutherius sent back to the British Church. The seventh and eighth bishops of London, Stephanus and Augulus, were among those martyred in the Imperial persecution, according to Gildas Badonicus[18] Regrettably, the dates assigned to their deaths, make it appear that their persecutions took place in the time of Diocletian (and on Constantius Chlorus' conscience therefore) rather than during Decius' reign. Finally, the name of Restitutus, the ninth Archbishop of London since Lucius' Establishment, appears —along with the Archbishops of Caerleon and York —as a participant in the Council of Arles in AD 314.

Lineage of Bishops in Gallican Church in Gaul

A matching list of bishops found in the Gallican Church includes several mentioned earlier as well as others serving during the first three centuries of the Church. These others do not by any means complete the list, for the names making up the second and third centuries are limited to those found in the *Book of Saints* of the Roman Church. Many —perhaps the majority —of these dioceses would appear to have received the Gospel originally at the hands of Jesus' disciples rather than from those with Apostolic ordering. For many dioceses, their first ordering to the episcopate was at the Culdees' (i.e. the Jerusalem Church's) hands.

What we perceive as characterizing the British and Gallican churches from the beginning is growth and commonality, even though they became different branches of the Church and were made up of different people. While it can be risky to make comparisons and out of them to draw generalizations, some truths can be perceived. The common threads between the Gallican and British peoples and churches seem to be these elements:

a) the Druidic background of their religion, morality and ideals;

b) their Brythonic Celtic heritage;

c) a Gospel brought to them by Jesus' *disciples* rather than by Apostles, along with such differences as that fact may provide in authority of Scripture, informality of ordering in a direct one-to-One relationship with God and;

d) a lengthy experience of Apostolic authority with Eastern patriarchates prior to coming under that of Rome.

Based on admittedly scanty evidence, we find signs of steady growth and of responsible adherence to the faith of Christ in spite of theological controversy and widespread persecution. What we can see of the British Church is that, while remote from others and hampered by hideous warfare, it appears to be not only Catholic and Apostolic, but One and Holy. Among the Gallican churches across the Channel the same seems to be true.

Gallican Church of Gaul, Helvetia, Low Countries and Germany

Below is a table of Apostolic men from 1st Century British Church and from the Holy Land, as well as Bishops ordained in in the 2nd or 3rd centuries.

City or Diocese	First Century	Second Century	Third Century
Aix-enProvence	Maximin	Autun	Amator
Arles	Trophime		
Auxerre		Peregrinus	Augustalis
Bourge	Austrogesilus	Ursinus	
Amiens		Firminus	
Besancon		Feroncius	Ferroleus
Bordeaux		Fort	
Chalons-sur-Marne		Menge	Donatian & Domitian
Evreux		Taurinus	
Le Mans	Julian		
Limoges	Martial	Austroclinian	Alpinian
Interlaken	Beatus		
Languedoc		Aphrodisius	
Lyons		Pothinus	Irenaeus
Marseilles	Lazarus		
Mende		Privatus	
Mentz	Crescens		
Metz		Felix, Patien	
Nantes		Clair	
Meaux		Sanctinu	
Narbonne	Paul Serge		
Orange	Eutropius		

Underlined: Apostolic men from 1st Century British Church.
Not underlined: Apostolic men from Holy Land

City or Diocese	First Century	Second Century	Third Century
Paris		Denis, Eugene,	
Perigeaux	Frontinus		
Poitiers		Victorinus	
Rheims		Xystus, Nicasius	
Rocamadour	Zaccheus		
St.Restitute	Restitut		
Saintes	Eutropius		
Sens		Senlis	Rieul
	Sabinus, Potentianus		
Tarascon	Parmenas		
Toul	Mansuy		
Tour	Gratian	Martin	
Toulouse	Saturninus	Sernin	
Tongres	Maternus	Martin	
Treves	Maternus, Eucharius,	Auspicius	Severinus
Veliacum	George		
Vienne		Denis, Verus	Florentius

If our comparisons, here and still to come, show more growth of the churches in Britain, France and Spain than in other countries, that is the way it was throughout the centuries (one exception being a Celtic Ireland). These three were the largest and most influential of the Transalpine churches –and in point of time the first.

If our comparisons center on British and Gallican churches rather than on, say, the Irish and Spanish, this could well be because the former involves the Brythonic and the latter the Goidelic Celts. Our most important reason for persisting in this line is that the case for an Early British Church hangs largely on what can be proved of the Early *Gallican* Church. The two are intimately related. Without the Gallican to add to the case for the early *British* Church, where fewer written records are available and where the Druidic reliance on oral history continues to be discounted by conventional historians, the search for the truly historic continues to be what for so long has been a daunting task. The fact that we can see and appreciate the commonality of character and interests these two Celtic Churches have had from the beginning makes "telling it like it is" considerably easier and the picture we arrive at as more accurate and true.

ᛒ   Chapter 12   ᛒ

A Cloud of Witnesses

The evidence seems to be overwhelming that there was in Britain, during the First Century, a fruitful branch of the Christian Church. It is likewise evident that however the verities of that Church's existence may differ from what has been proposed, *its reality* and *our picture of that reality* are far more compatible, one with the other, than with the doubtful sketch suggested by those whose output is limited by an imperfect and bureaucratic canon. At this point it would be sheer obstinacy to insist that the Gospel must have come to Britain later than it did and in the hands of Gentile converts going about their daily work. If we review the literature of those who in ancient times passed along hearsay knowledge of a Christian presence in Britain, we may consider one proposition the professionals have overlooked. The substance of that hearsay, regardless of where or when it was written down, is a single believable and integrated narrative, returned from East as well as West and over a broad span of time. It would seem to be of genuinely catholic tradition as measured by the Vincentian canon* even though its earliest transmissions came through memory and voice

---

* "That which has been believed everywhere, always and by all."

rather than through the occasional copying of worn and faded scripts. This is to suggest it is substantially true, especially where there is no evidence to the contrary and no reason to suspect a fiction. If those who have transmitted what is already common knowledge are known to have been scholars, saints or prelates of the Church, what they believe and report has a high probability of being genuinely historic. If there is reason to doubt, we may give them the benefit of that doubt because of who and what they were. Rather than confine their witness to an appendix at the back of the book where it could go unnoted and unread, let us allow these honored Churchmen to give their testimony here and now.

Witnesses to British Church's Founding by Jesus' Disciples

Tertullian of Carthage, after the Apostolic era the first great author of Christian literature, c. AD 196 tells us, "The extremities of Spain, the various parts of Gaul, the regions of Britain which have never been penetrated by the Roman arms have received the religion of Christ."[1]

Sabellius, Roman priest and theologian, c. AD 235, "Christianity was privately professed elsewhere, but the first nation that proclaimed it as their religion, and called itself Christian after Christ, was Britain."[2]

Origen of Antioch, c. AD 240, biblical scholar and perhaps the ablest theologian of the early Church, wrote, "The divine goodness of Our Lord and Saviour is equally diffused among the Britons, the Africans and other nations of the world."[3]

Eusebius, Bishop of Caesarea, known as the Father of Ecclesiastical History and an important participant in the Council of Nicaea, wrote c. AD 330, "The apostles passed beyond the ocean to the Isles called the Britannic Isles."[4]

Emperor Constantine the Great, in an epistle to the church is quoted as saying that "the Bishops from the City of the Romans, and Africa, all Italy, Egypt, Spain, Gaul and Britain... agreed at the Council of Nicaea to the keeping of Easter on one day."[5]

St. Athanasius, Bishop of Alexandria and indefatigable proponent of Nicene doctrine, in AD 353 describes the Churches of Britain as adhering to the faith of the Council of Nicaea;[6] c. AD 350 claims that British bishops joined with more than three hundred bishops at the Council of Sardica in AD 347 in supporting him against the Arian heresy;[7] in a synodical epistle in AD 363 states that at the First Council of Nicaea the Bishops of Spain, Britain, Gaul and from the East agreed to condemn Arianism;[8] c. AD 359, in referring to the Council of Ariminium in AD 350, mentions that the three British bishops in attendance, because of poverty, were helped from a common fund to pay their way home.[9]

St. Hilary, Bishop of Poitiers, ardent opponent of the Arians and supporter of Athanasius, in AD 358 wrote, "The apostles (went)... wherever it was possible to go, even in the isles of the Ocean built several tabernacles for God."[10] In later years he congratulated the Britons on having had no part either in the Arian or the Pelagian heresies.[11]

St. Jerome, biblical scholar, translator of Scriptures into Latin: c. AD 378, "From India to Britain all nations resound with the death and resurrection of Christ";[12] c. AD 385, "The Britons, who live apart from our world, if they go on a Pilgrimage, will leave the western parts and seek Jerusalem, known to them by fame only and by the Scriptures"; [13] c. AD 398, "Nor is it to be thought one Church of the City of Rome, another of the whole world. Both the Gauls and Britons, and Africa, and Persia, and the East, and India, and all barbarous nations adore one Christ, obey one rule of faith."[14]

St. Chrysostom, Patriarch of Constantinople and the Eastern Church's most noted preacher, writes c. AD 400, "The British Isles, which are beyond the sea, and which lie in the ocean, have received the virtue of the Word. Churches are there founded and altars erected. Though thou shouldst go to the ocean, to the British Isles, there thou shouldst hear all men everywhere discoursing matters out of the Scriptures, with another voice indeed, but not another faith; with a different tongue, but the same judgment."[15]

St. Augustine of Hippo, Bishop of Hippo and most noted theologian during the millenium after St. Paul, c. AD 408: "How many churches are there not erected in the British Isles which lie in the ocean!"[16]

Sozomen, Greek historian, c AD 414 in his *Church History* speaks of British Christians in the court of Constantius, the father of Constantine the Great.[17]

Theodoret the Blessed, Bishop of Cyrus in Syria, regarded as the ablest patristic expositor of St. Paul, c. AD 423, tells "of dwellers in the furthest west, both Spaniards and Britons and Gauls, coming to visit St. Simon Stylites at Telanisous near Antioch."[18]

Palladius, Bishop of Helenopolis c. AD 415, in his *Historia Lauriaca*, tells of the coming of British pilgrims to Syria and Jerusalem before AD 410.[19] His city, across the Bosporus from Constantinople and renamed in honor of Constantine's mother (herself a pilgrim for many years) would be a sacred spot for visitation while on the Pilgrims' Way.

Constantius of Lyons, c. AD 450,in his *Life of St. Germanus*, describes the saint as bringing relics of all the apostles and many martyrs to place in the tomb of St. Alban in Britain following the Diocletian persecution.[20]

Patrick of Ireland, in his *Confessions* c. AD 460 says he was born in Britain, the son of Calpurnius, a deacon, and grandson of Potitus, a priest.[21] These could only have been of the British Church.

Gildas the Wise, monk of Llan Illtyd and author of the first *History of Britain*, described by Archbishop Usshur as "auctor veracissimus,"[22] writes, "We know that Christ, the true Sun, afforded his light to our island in the last year of Tiberius Caesar (AD 37)."[23]

According to Michael Alford, S.J., in his *Fides Regia Britannica*, Nicephorus, Byzantine historian and Patriarch of Constantinople c. AD 800, in describing the Apostolic journeys, stated. "One reached Egypt and Libya, another reached the extreme regions of the Ocean, and the British Isles."[24]

Crakenthorpe, in translation from his Latin work. *Defens. Eccl. Angl.*, "Of our British Church it is certain that it was established several years before the Roman....Christ (says Gildas) granted his rays, that is, His precepts to this island, then numb with glacial cold, as we know in the last year of Tiberius Caesar. The birth of the Roman Church being (according to Baronius) on February 15, AD 45. Now learn to know from this, learn (I say) that the Roman Church is not the mother of our British Church, but the sister and a sister the younger by five (seven) whole years."[25] (The bracketed corrections are inserted because of revised estimates of Tiberius' dating.)

Witnesses to the Coming of Joseph of Arimathea

Cardinal Baronius, Rome's greatest historian, Vatican librarian and author of *Ecclesiastical Annales* (a thirty year work), shows under the year AD 35 the landing at Marseilles of those disciples named in Chapter Seven.[26] They further record Joseph of Arimathea's proceeding to Britain with several companions, and of his preaching there.[27] They quote an ancient English manuscript in the Vatican library on Joseph's mission to Britain and his death there.[28] They further quote William of Malmesbury on St. Philip's sending twelve missionaries to Britain to serve under Joseph of Arimathea,[29] and the king's gift to them of Ynys-witrin or Avalon (Glastonbury) and twelve hides of land.

Three other ancient manuscripts unite in saying that Joseph of Arimathea was the first to preach the Gospel in Britain. One is the *History of the Franks*, written c. AD 590 by St. Gregory, Bishop of Tours.[30] Another is the work *Fragmenta* of Haleca, the Archbishop of Saragossa.[31] The third is a letter written by Isidore, Archbishop of Seville (AD 600-636).[32]

Witnesses to the Coming of Aristobulus

Hippolytus, greatest of early Roman scholars, author of *The Apostolic Constitutions,* the *Didache*, etc., a schismatic bishop (probably of Greeks in Rome) honored nevertheless by the Roman Church both as saint and martyr; c. AD 210, in a published list of Bishops of the Church shows Aristobulus as "Bishop of the Britons."[33]

The Greek Menology for March 15: "Aristobulus was one of the 70 disciples chosen by St. Paul to be missionary bishop to the land of Britain. He was there martyred after he had built churches and ordained deacons and priests for the island."[34]

Haleca, Bishop of Augusta, "The memory of many martyrs is celebrated by the Britons, especially that of St. Aristobulus, one of the 70 disciples."[35]

St. Ado, Archbishop of Vienne in France c. AD 870, writes of March 17 as "Natal Day of Aristobulus, Bishop of Britain, brother of St. Barnabas the Apostle....He was sent to Britain, where after preaching the truth of Christ, and forming a Church, he received martyrdom."[36]

Achau Saint Prydain (*Genealogies of the Saints of Britain*): "There came with Bran the Blessed from Rome to Britain Arwystli the Aged, Ilid, Cyndaf, men of Israel, Maw or Mawan, son of Cyndaf."[37] Ilid is said to have been the founder of Cor Eurgain, later Llan Iltyd, the scholarly center of learning in south Wales.

Witnesses to the Coming of St. Philip to Gaul

St. Isidore, Archbishop of Seville,most learned man in Spain, c. AD 620, writes, "Philip, of the city of Bethsaida...preached Christ to the Gauls and brought barbarous and neighboring nations, seated in darkness and close to the swelling ocean to the light and knowledge and port of faith."[38] Martyrology of Jerome (either Jerome the translator of the Bible c. AD 378 or Jerome of Rome martyred AD 193);[39] This work is cited both by Isidore and by Julian, Archbishop of Toledo AD 680-690, as stating that Philip preached Christ to the Gauls. Julian repeats the citation in an exegesis of the Prophet Nahum.

The Venerable Bede, c. AD 700, in his *Book of the Saints*, assigns Gaul to Philip.[40]

Freculphus, Bishop of Lisieux in Normandy AD 825-851, wrote, "Philip of the city of Bethsaida (whence also came Peter) of whom in the Gospels and Acts of the Apostles praiseworthy mention is often made, whose daughters were also outstanding prophetesses, and of wonderful sanctity and perpetual virginity, as ecclesiastical history narrates, preached Christ to the Gauls."[41]

Witnesses to the Coming of St. Paul

Clement of Rome, the third Bishop of Rome (AD 90-99), consecrated by Peter, described by Paul (Phil. 4:3) as his "fellow-laborer"–well known to him and the Pudens family–writes, "Paul... was the herald of the Gospel in the West as well as in the East....And after he had been to the extremity of the West he suffered martyrdom before the sovereigns of mankind."[42]

Theodore the Blessed, Bishop of Cyrus in Syria c. AD 435, "Paul, liberated from his first captivity at Rome, preached the Gospel to the Britons and others in the West. (He) not only persuaded the Romans and their tributaries to acknowledge the Crucified and His laws, but the Britons also and the Cymry."[43]

Venantius Fortunatus, Bishop of Poitiers c. AD 600, author of such hymns as "Hail thee, festival day" and "Welcome, happy morning," speaks of Paul as "crossing the sea" and visiting "Britain and the extreme West."[44]

Witnesses to the Coming of Simon the Zealot

Dorotheus, Bishop of Tyre c. AD 303, wrote, "Simon Zelotes preached Christ through all Mauretania, and Afric the Less. At length he was crucified in Britain, slain and buried."[45]

Nicephorus, Patriarch of Constantinople, wrote c. AD 820, "Simon born in Cana of Galilee (and) surnamed Zelotes...traveled through Egypt and Africa, then through Mauritania and all Libya, preaching the Gospel. And the same doctrine he taught to the Occidental Sea, and the Isles called Britanniae."[46]

Greek Menology: The Menology of the Greek Church celebrates St. Simon's Day on May 10 and supports the statement of his having preached and been martyred in Britain.[47]

Witnesses Already Singled Out and Waiting to be Heard From

Since the chief purpose of this work is not to furnish an exhaustive study of the Early British Church, but to offer proof of its existence,

I shall, for the next two chapters, make use of an unusual reference work. Its subject matter extends back to pre-Christian times, yet it is readily updated. It is not a "history book" in the sense of being an organic record of the Church's life and activity. Rather, it is a record of individuals who have lived notable lives within that Church. Its full title is *The Book of Saints: A Dictionary of Servants of God Canonized by the Catholic Church: Extracted from the Roman and Other Martyroligies*, published by The Macmillan Company (New York) and A. & C. Black Ltd. (London) in 1922. Compiling was done by the Benedictine Monks of St. Augustine's Abbey at Ramsgate in Kent, a Roman Catholic order.

We are fortunate that this work was undertaken by the English Benedictines, a preeminent order in the country's history. Its ties with the restored Anglican Order of that name have been close for many years. Their conscientious work, jointly undertaken, has sought the restoration of unity and wholeness lost from the Western Church with the Reformation.

What is greatly helpful to us is that the monks have not only listed persons officially declared to be saints; they have included a far larger number of possible candidates for formal declaration of sainthood —almost every individual who has been the focus of local followings since early times. While the statistics, even for a goodly number, are only a small proportion of the total Christian population, they provide a sampling that can tell us much about the churches of which they were members. These compilations include not only people living during and after the Benedictines' arrival at Canterbury in AD 597, they offer data on hundreds if not thousands who lived and died in the three hundred years before the Canterbury mission began. This could not have been done to accommodate Patrick's ministry in Ireland, though it predated theirs by more than one hundred fifty years It is simply that evidence of those Christians and their holy lives was available to the Benedictines and could not be overlooked. Considering the paucity of names both in Britain and in Gaul during the three centuries earlier still, we must conclude it was not till the third and fourth centuries A.D. that there were sufficient records or even folk-memory of heroic souls to allow for compilation. What will be most strikingly evident as we discover their numbers "up front" in one locality after another is that in most cases the patron saint of a place or institution is likely to have been the founder.

The Benedictines' compilation allows us a general idea of growth and loss during years marked by aggressive warfare and displacement as well as religious persecution. The individual entries also tell us what the saints were like and who and what they were, e.g. Virgins, Widows, Nuns, Abbesses, Recluses, Martyrs, Hermits, Priests, Monks, Bishops, Abbots, Kings, Queens, Princesses, Princes, Penitents, Confessors. The entries name their teachers and their students. We learn who went to neighboring lands for sacred study or to serve as missionaries. While we are given few dates of birth, we have many dates of death as well as the centuries in which they lived and died. For most of these who are shown in *The Book of Saints*, it is comparatively easy to distinguish one from another; if we cannot date or otherwise identify them, we omit them from our computation. It is comparatively easy to distinguish male from female, Irish from British, Gallican from either of the other and one century from another. The Bretons, the Welsh and the Cornish are British, and their numbers may well reflect growth at the expense of those "other British" who, under attack by German invaders from AD 411 on, declined in numbers. The Scots, though originating in Ireland, are not designated as Scots till their arrival in Britain. The Bretons must be distinguished from Gallic, for their culture was British and even though they were "continentals" their peninsula was spared much of the violence suffered by Franks and Gauls as successive waves of invaders poured south through the rest of France after rounding the Alps. The Gallican Church is hardest to define, for here the Celt is fused with Frank. Yet the affinity between Celto-British and Gallican cannot be denied despite the fact that the latter has been identified with the Roman Church twice as long as the Celto-British church. The saints identified as Gallican may include those from Northern France, Switzerland, Germany and the Low Countries. Obviously–and regardless of who makes them–judgments as between Gallican and Roman will be less dependable and less definitive than for others.

Quite apart from our purposes, *The Book of Saints* is an important historical document. To browse through its pages is to stroll through an ancient but well-kept burial ground. Its citations may be compared with lines on old tombstones, narrating what has been distinctive about those thus remembered.

Our reason for showing statistics for British, Irish and Gallican Churches, and within the British for Breton, Cornish, Welsh and Scottish subdivisions (beginning with the fourth and ending with the thirteenth centuries) is in part to suggest their comparative size in numbers. Another reason is to make it evident when each church had its period of rapid growth and when growth leveled off. Both for Gallican and British the growth began with the first century, though we have no significant records other than a few names. (We know there were martyrs in the scores of thousands, though with few specific details.) For the British Church the growth periods shown in Table 1 will be the 5th through 7th centuries—as with the Gallican. The Irish growth will be most notable in the 5h through 8th and the Scottish and English from the 7th through the 12th and 13th respectively.

Table 1: Total number of Celtic Saints, identifiable by centuries, in *The Book of Saints* AD 400-1300.
At bottom is similar list of saints associated with the Roman Church's English mission.

Church	5th	6th	7th	8th	9th	10th	11th	12th	13th	Total
					Century					
Welsh	33	74	19	2				1		129
Scottish	5	8	20	7	7	5	5	4		61
Cornish	9	15	2							26
Breton	2	11	11	2	1		1		1	29
Other British	21	21	13	8	2		1			66
Iona, English		12								12
British subtotal	70	141	65	19	10	5	7	5	1	323
Irish saints	57	107	101	36	7	6	4	9	1	328

Church	5th	6th	7th	8th	9th	10th	11th	12th	13th	Total
					Century					
All Celtic Saints	127	248	166	55	17	11	11	14	3	651
Roman Church's English mission			78	76	26	24	17	21	10	252

One observation from the above statistics could be that each church grew rapidly, then declined in spirituality and numbers. Such is not the case. Christianity was the popular religion throughout this era, and the 13th century has widely been regarded as the summit of the Age of Faith. The "up front" numbers in Table 1 show the founders of parish churches and monasteries, a once-only happening in settled areas. The statistics also reflect a record of events. Those for "Other British," for example, point to an influx of Jutes in Kent, Saxons in central Britain and Angles in the north after the Legions' withdrawal in AD 411. The result: a flight of Christians, especially to Wales and Brittany. Subsequent invasion by Danes in the 8th century AD and Vikings in the 9th and 10th centuries AD brought death and desolation, and the same unwillingness to evangelize the enemy as had been true between Britons and Saxons. The northern record reflects the Scottish people's move from Ireland to Scotland. The facilitating ministry there was chiefly that of the Iona Community.

Table 2: Total number of missionary-saints from British Isles shown in *The Book of Saints* as serving between AD 500-1300.

	5th	6th	7th	8th	9th	10th	11th	12th	13th	Total
					Century					
BRITISH CHURCH TO										
France	4	1	3	6		1				15
Germany		3	1	1	1		1			7
Total	4	4	4	7	1	1	1			22

	5th	6th	7th	8th	9th	10th	11th	12th	13th	Total
					Century					
IRISH CHURCH TO										
France	1	3	8			1		5		18
Germany			6	11			1			18
Switzerland		1	2		1					4
Belgium			3	2		1				6
Holland	1		3							4
Total	2	4	22	13	1	2	1	5		50
ENGISH CHURCH TO										
France		7	4	1				2		14
Germany		3	14							17
Belgium			4							4
Holland		1	7							8
Norway							1			1
Denmark						1				1
Sweden					1	1	1	2		5
Total		11	29	1	1	2	2	2		48

Table 3: Functions filled by some saints shown in *The Book of Saints* and serving during years AD 500-1300.

Church	Bishops	Abbots	Abbesses	Kings	Queens	Hermits	Martyrs
British	74	54	2	7	3	30	21
Irish	111*	101*	8		23	7	
English	66	31	26	12	7	23	32
Gallican	198	96	25	8	5	23	51

*At least 27 served both offices at the same time.

Table 4: Native-born saints in Gallican churches with the number sent as missionaries from churches in the British Isles.

Missionaries to Gallican Churches			Total	Native-born	Total
	from		Missionaries	Saints	for Country
to	British	Irish	English			
French	15	18	14	47	363	410
German	7	18	17	42	48	90
Swiss		4		4	7	11
Belgian		6	4	10	23	33
Dutch		4	8	12	2	14
Danish			1	1	7	8
Norse			1	1	4	5
Swedish			7	7	6	13
Total	22	50	52	124	460	584

The early response to the Gospel in France, Germany and Switzerland is understandable; all were evangelized from the first century on. The Low Countries were next in order, followed by Eastern Germany, the Baltic area and Scandinavia. France received the Gospel, as we have seen, directly from Jerusalem. However, the evangelizing of the Gallic areas was joined by British missionaries during the early centuries with Irish participation from the 5th century AD on. As Table 4 indicates, the British and Irish, measured by the number of missionary saints, may have contributed more to the evangelizing of Germany, Switzerland and Holland than did the French —or for that matter, than the Germans, Swiss and the Lowlanders provided for themselves.

However, the Scandinavian kingdoms' knowledge of the Gospel came in remarkable fashion from Anglo-Saxons. It is true that Ansgar, "the Apostle to the North," was born in Amiens and made many converts in Denmark and Sweden. Yet after his death, his converts lapsed, and it was a century later that Scandinavia began its ultimate conversion to Christ. This ministry came almost entirely from the English, nine of whom are named in *The Book of Saints*: Bartholomew for Norway, William for Denmark and Sigfrid, David, Ulfrid, Aeschilus, Winaman, Unaman and Sunaman for Sweden. The chief native saints of Scandinavia during these years were Olav of Norway, Canute of Denmark and Olav of Sweden. All were kingly martyrs.

Table 5: Showing those listed in Tables 1, 2 & 4 who were women. These included martyrs and those engaged in continental mission.

Church	5th	6th	7th	8th	9th	10th	11th	12th	13th	Total
					Century					
Welsh	10	7								17
Cornish	1	1								2
Scottish	2		1		2	1				6
Breton		1								1
Other British	7	4	1							12
Brit. subtotal	20	13	2		2	1				38
Irish	14	13	7	4	1	1				40
Total Celtic	34	26	9	4	3	2				78
Anglo Saxon			23	13	3	10	2	1		52

Of these 130 women, 86 are shown as virgins and 42 as nuns. Two are shown as matrons and 16 as widows. Thirty-six are listed as from royal families as queens or princesses. Many came from families of recorded saints, 8 as daughters, 9 as sisters and 9 as mothers. Ten women—most of them Irish—lived as recluses in places as near as Cornwall and Scotland, and as far as France and Holland. 17 died as martyrs, though in several cases their names were the only way of identifying other and unnamed martyrs—all of them young women.

St. Ursula is remembered as a virgin martyr associated with the invasion of the Saxons. Many boatloads of young British women, attempting to escape to Brittany under the leadership of this royal princess, landed by mistake at the mouth of the Rhine and were put to death by warlike Huns. Scholars accept Ursula as their leader, but their numbers are thought to be considerably fewer than the eleven thousand described in medieval legend. That they were many, however, is borne out by the vast collection of bones ascribed to them and assembled floor-to-ceiling in a church-crypt in Cologne.

Table 6: Women included in Table 4 above –as saints of the Gallican Church in France and daughter churches

Church	5th	6th	7th	8th	9th	10th	11th	12th	13th	Total
					Century					
French	10	5	19	6	3	1	2	2		48
German	3	3	8	4	3		9	1	3	34
Total	13	8	27	10	6	1	11	3	3	82*

*There are no women shown in *The Book of Saints* as native to other countries and churches in Gallic Christendom.

However, the following recap from Table 3 above suggests the part played by women in the evangelizing of continental Europe.

Table 7: Part played by women of British Isles in evangelizing of Gallican Europe–items excerpted from Table 3.

	5th	6th	7th	8th	9th	10th	11th	12th	13th	Total
					Century					
British Church to										
France	4	1								5
Germany		1								1
Total	4	2								6
Irish Church to										
France	1	2	3							6
Germany			1							1

	5th	6th	7th	8th	9th	10th	11th	12th	13th	Total
				Century						
Belgium		1								1
Holland	1									1
Norway						1				1
Total	2	3	4			1				10
English Church to										
France		2	5	1						8
Germany		1								1
Total		2	6	1						9

In this record, as in those above indicating the ministry of men and women, the larger numbers in earlier centuries seems to point to a fuller commitment. This can be attributed to several factors. One would be the enthusiasm of new converts. In this case it would not only be sharing and proclaiming by individual women. Many might consider themselves as proclaiming Christ on behalf of a newly-converted nation. Another factor could be the individuality and venturesomeness so characteristic of the Celt; in the case of Christian enthusiasts this could be considered self-oblation. To these reasons might be added the readiness for martyrdom found in the earlier centuries in all places of which we have record. One occasion involves the several thousand Christian soldiers already referred to at Treves. Having pronounced their unwillingness to sacrifice to idols, they laid down their weapons and stood waiting —each in his turn to be slaughtered. Such a following of Christ–in imitation of his Passion–may be seen in the case of St. Sunnifa, the only martyr shown by name for the tenth century. She is described by *The Book of Saints* as a "Virgin Martyr; an Irish maiden whom tradition asserts to have been cast away by shipwreck on the coast of Norway together with other maidens her companions. There they appear to have led a life of seclusion and prayer." Their arrival followed by a number of decades that of St. Ansgar who, while sent to rekindle the waning faith of Norse Christians, did not himself die as a martyr. In God's providence it may have been the witting and willing sacrifice of these maidens that completed Ansgar's work. This seems to be why they are so honored.

A final item may personalize what otherwise is abstraction. All the British women shown here as having gone to France and Germany in the 5th and 6th centuries AD died as martyrs. Some had been sent as nuns by church authority to which they were obedient. Those who went as recluses did so as prisoners of Christ but of their own free will.

No one can be surprised by the thought that the pre-597 British Church gives the Church of England its only native taproot. Despite that body's Roman founding, its historic *figure* will have the appearance—and in some senses the reality —of a graft rather than a taproot.

Chapter 13

A Convoy of Saints

If Arviragus' son Maric, as high king, had signed a peace treaty requiring Britain to come to the Empire's defense in time of peril, the history of Britain might have been a different story. Rome had little bargaining power when its treaty with Britain was hammered out in AD 120. The Empire had poured its utmost resources into a forty-three year war that was already lost when they celebrated what they thought was its victorious conclusion. Perhaps out of mutual exhaustion they gave no thought to the war's official termination, for it continued (though without armed conflict) for another thirty-four years. Had Hadrian and Maric signed a mutual non-aggression pact instead of the one they agreed on, both peoples could have benefited. The Britons already knew enough about Rome's arms, armor, tactics and strategy to undertake their own defense. They knew enough of Rome's pagan religion and totalitarian politics to value God's justice and man's freedom above all else. The Romans by contrast had nothing to fear—and much to gain—from a people as principled and competent as the Britons had proved to be.

Yet the treaty was agreed upon and signed. The legions were restored, this time being furnished with Britain's own men. However, when, three centuries later, in AD 411 the legions were withdrawn, the British were tragically and desperately the losers. A want of attention to the nation's own defenses—and the growing readiness of legions (including the British) to use force of arms in choosing Emperors—led to the Empire's undoing and with it the Western Isles. A period like this could have been what Tacitus had in mind in one summarizing passage he wrote, "The Britons were gradually led on to the amenities that make vice agreeable—arcades, baths and sumptuous banquets. They spoke of such novelties as 'civilization,' when really they were only a feature of enslavement."

Meanwhile civilization's eastern boundaries were penetrated by successive barbarian hordes. Britain's soldiers died in *tours de force* undertaken in disregard of treaty restrictions. Early in the third century fifty thousand lives were lost when British legions, venturing on the Continent in support of their candidate for Emperor against a rival, were recalled from a costly defeat to win a still more costly victory against the Caledonians and Picts. In later years a British army was dispatched to Gaul to deliver Rome's allies from invading Sueves and Goths. Fresh from that triumph, they found victory come to naught still later when forces under the Duke of Cornwall turned against their countrymen. Now Britain was altogether undefended, for it had already asked for and obtained the removal of foreign legionaries remaining on its soil. With their army engaged in civil war—at distant Arles—the British were horrified to learn that the flower of British manhood had perished in one battle. Of those who survived, some made their way back to Britain. Most settled in Brittany rather than return to Greater Britain—perhaps as pensioned veterans on the Empire's payroll.

Considering the lack of political sagacity, it is remarkable that the first emperor to be called "the Great" was a direct descendant of Arviragus and Caradoc, that is, Constantine. His mother Helena, who during her son's reign would be Empress and co-ruler, was the castoff wife and widow of his father Constantius the Fair (Chlorus)—in his final years the Emperor of the West. It is likewise a curiosity that a later Emperor of the Romans, descended from Constantine and also a Briton, contributed much to the Medieval world's Arthurian Myth. This man, whom we may call Arthur the First, will be given a later appraisal. Constantine needs brief attention because, though British born and bred, he transferred the Empire's governing center from Rome to Byzantium. In so doing, he left a vacuum of power that would leave an unalterable mark on the course of Christian history as well as upon the faith itself. This said, we can focus on those men and women of whom we have unquestioned record, known to be saints of the British Church in its years of flowering and growth.

Influence of the Family on the Faith

One of the richest aspects of faith must be the influence of the parent on the child. Even in its secular expression it cannot be forgotten that the hand that rocks the cradle shapes the world. If we recall Marius' victory over the Teutons, we can understand why barbarian mothers would take their children's lives, followed by their own, rather than allow them to be slaves. Where our concern is with faith as well as freedom, we have a prime example in the Jews' Maccabean years (2 Macc.7), when seven young men in succession (and finally their mother) were subjected to horrible deaths before the others' eyes for their refusal to eat pork at the king's command. It was too late in the prophetic years for their doctrine and example to be incorporated in the Sacred Canon. Yet what that mother said to her sons by way of encouragement has great significance for those who treasure Law and Justice. She urged them to die bravely in defense of God's Law in expectation of the bodily resurrection that he must grant to those who have remained faithful and obedient to his Word. Whether in teaching or example, theirs is the only such case to be found in the Old Testament except for that recorded of Job in Scripture (19:25,26) and in the Burial Office, "I know that my Redeemer liveth, and that he shall stand at the latter day upon the earth and...though worms destroy this body, in my flesh I shall see God." We take note of these examples because of the millions of martyrs who died in the early centuries of the Church whose sacrifices can hardly have gone unrewarded. For similar reasons we have in mind those British saints who were daughters, sisters or mothers in families of saints. St. David's mother and aunt will be noted here, as St. Helena has been already. Patrick's mother, Consuessa, is believed to have been a sister of St. Martin of Tours—and *their* sister the mother of St. Ninian. We have no name for that aunt, but Patrick's sister, St. Darerca, had many sons of whom several became bishops in Ireland. Mention is made of saintly women in British families in order to suggest how and why monastic life in Britain—unlike that of the East—was already in effect at the Gospel's coming. The inclusion of family, clan and tribe in a monastic format had been the pattern of the Druids and is believed to have been put to Christian use by Caradoc's older daughter St. Eigen.

Some Families of Welsh Saints

The tradition of Martin's sisters and nephews is quite ancient, and because we know that greatness often runs in families, we have no particular reason to doubt it. Nor is it a surprise to find large families in *The Book of Saints*. Small ones seem to slip in unnoticed, but we draw attention to three. All were Welsh families, supplying saints over as much as three or four generations. One is that of Brechan of Brecknock, a chieftain of the Silurians. Brechan or Brychan was a fifth century king, twenty-seven of whose descendants are found in our reference work. Ten daughters and granddaughters are referred to as maidens—two of these as martyrs. The one listed as *matron* was the mother of the bishop-martyr, St. Cadoc. One son was martyred in Wales at the hands of raiders or invaders. Five of Brechan's descendants ministered in Cornwall and four in Brittany, all remembered in parish churches bearing their names. One in Brittany was an abbess. Another, a grandson, is remembered by two names—one in Cornwall and another in Brittany, where he later served as an abbot. Of them all, the best known was Dubritius or Dyfrig, St. David's predecessor as Bishop of Llandaff and the consecrator of King Arthur.

A second family of note was the Cunedda clan. Its founder had

returned from the British kingdom of Strathclyde Wales in the area
of what is now Glasgow in Scotland to the northwest part of present-
day Wales, where he became ancestor to the kingly line of Gwynedd.
This was the family from which came Wales' patron saint, David
(Dewi Sant), and the great King Arthur. Though *The Book of Saints*
speaks of fifty saints as descended from Cunedda, no more than a
dozen are actually listed as such, including several linked by marriage.
They include David's mother, Non or Nonnita, her sister Gwen and
Gwen's sons, Cadfan and Cuby. They include Arthur's uncle Gistillian
and Teilo, who was second in succession to David as Archbishop of
Menevia. However, apart from Ceitho, Eingan, Tyssel and Afan–also
in the family of Cunedda–we have no more knowledge of the remaining
Cunedda saints than of the seventy elders whom Luke tells us were sent
out by twos–but does not name.

The third great family was that of Patrick–contemporary with the
first generation of Brychans and Cuneddas. Patrick's people, though
Welsh, will be listed with the Irish for the same reason that many Scots
and other Irish are shown below with the British. There can only be
one reason for what otherwise would seem to be my inattention. Our
concern is not so much where the saints came from as to know who was
benefited by their ministry and, if they were martyrs, for whose benefit
they laid down their lives. One family of martyrs, either Scottish or
Irish, was put to death while in pilgrimage at the time of the Diocletian
persecution. Two sisters (their names unknown to us) were the first to
be martyred–in the Rhineland. Their brothers' deaths followed soon
afterward in Italy, Gunifort's at Lake Como and Gunebald's at Pavia.
Among the fourth century saints known to us were Arilda, martyred
in Gloucestershire as well as Grimonia, an Irish maiden whose death
took place at Picardy in Gaul, both dying in defense of their virginity.
A century later Bridget and Maura, virgin daughters of a Scottish
chieftain, were martyred in Picardy while on pilgrimage to Rome. In
addition, we make mention of Marcellus, a Briton, who in c. AD 180
became the first Archbishop of Treves. He died a martyr's death as
had three earlier bishops whom we have already noted as first century
missionary bishops from Britain. We also know of a Briton, Melonius,
who in AD 314 became the First Bishop of Rouen.

A Roster of British Saints before the Coming of the Roman Mission

To this point we have listed the names of many who had roles in the founding of the Early British Church. We have likewise included the names and tasks of some of their successors. Beginning around AD 400, we are helped immeasurably by written record and oral tradition provided by those on the scene. For our purposes, this is basically where our *The Book of Saints* begins.

When Gregory's mission arrived in Canterbury, the Celtic Church had been on the island five hundred sixty years. This included at least four hundred forty years as an Established Church. Even if there had been no invasion by Anglo-Saxons, this Church's rate of growth would have slowed down for the reason that nearly all the population was Christian. But there *was* an invasion, and the Christians of Britain lost more than half their land and a great many of their people. Those who survived were squeezed into the far reaches of Wales, Cornwall and Brittany. Understandably the figures we have shown for those areas–in Table 1 of Chapter 12–reflect the ingress of refugees at the expense of "other British."

Ireland is another story. Though there is record of Christians there as early as AD 61, the Irish Church's real beginning comes with the arrival of Patrick in AD 432. At that point it was one hundred sixty-five years before Rome's Canterbury mission arrived in Britain. Yet as a result of Patrick's presence, when the first thirty of those years had gone by, Ireland was a Christian land.

It is evident from Table 1 that the sixth century marked the largest growth in numbers for both the British and Irish churches. If we consider the two centuries before the start of the Canterbury mission, i.e., the fifth and the sixth, we see that the one hundred fifteen Irish and Scottish saints recorded for those years* are nearly equal in numbers to the one hunded twenty-nine from the remainder of the Celto-British Church. As this volume's primary objective is to demonstrate that the Early British Church *actually existed*, we believe it is important to set down the names of all the fifth and sixth century saints of the British for whom we have an accepted record. Likewise we name the Irish

*Note that we have omitted the twelve entered in Table 1 as "Iona English." Whether they were English, Welsh or Irish, can only be conjectured; they were the "losers" at Whitby whom the Roman Church so admired that they are listed as saints regardless of their default.

and Scottish saints converted before the founding at Canterbury of the papal mission.

British Saints of the Fifth Century

The following abbreviations are used in our listings:

A	abbot	N	nun
B	bishop	P	priest
C	confessor	Q	queen
D	deacon	R	recluse
H	hermit	W	widow
K	king	V	virgin
M	martyr		

Women's names are <u>underlined</u>. Names in caps indicate official canonization in the Roman or Eastern Ortodox Churches as saints:

Aldate, **A**, Briton of the west country, pious and patriotic, who stirred up his countrymen to hold fast against Saxon aggression.
Biblig, a Welsh saint of Carnarvon.
Breaca, **VR**, One of several Irish women who settled in Cornwall.
Brynach, **H**, Irish hermit settled in Wales at Carn Englyi near Nevern.
Cadoc, patron of Llandog Faur in Carmarthen.
Cajan, son or grandson of Brychan; at Tregaidian in Anglesea.
Cannog, **M**, eldest son of Brychan, known in Brittany as Cenneur.
Cledwyn, son of Brychan, patron of Llandledwin (Caermarthen).
Conogan, **B**, successor of Corentin in See of Quimper in Brittany.
Crewenna, companion of Breaca, Irishmaid in Cornwall, near St. Erth.
Cynfran, Welsh, son of Brychan, founder of church in Carnarvonshire
Cynlio, Welsh, several churches took his name.
Digain, son of Constantine, Cornish king; name at Langernw, Denby.
Dingad, **H**, son of Brychan, a hermit in Monmouthshire.
Dogfan, **M**, Welsh martyr; son of Brychan.
Dunawd Fawr, preacher and teacher, father of Deiniol Wyn.

Dwynwen, **V**, family of Brychan. Church name in Wales and Cornwall.

Dyfnan, son of Brychan, founder of church in Anglesey.

Elian ap Erbin. a saint in Welsh calendar about whom little is known.

Erbin, patron saint of several churches in Cornwall.

Feock, **V**, patroness of Cornish church thought to be from Ireland.

Fingar, *Piala* & others, **MM**, brother and sister, children of Irish king, murdered with companions at Hayle near Penzance in Cornwall.

Fragan & *Gwen*, refugees from Britain to Brittany, parents to SS Jacut, Wenwaloe and Guithern.

Germanus, **BM**, Scot disciple of Germanus of Auxerre, missionary bishop martyred in Normandy c. AD 460.

Germanus of Auxerre, **Bp** with Bp Lupus of Troyes denounced *Pelagianism*, led British to Alleluia Victory over Saxons, d. AD 448.

Gildas the Elder, **H**, associated with Cadoc, lived as hermit.

Gildas the Wise, disciple of Illtyd, first British historian, moved to Brittany, founded monastery at Rhys, d. AD 570.

Gladys, **W**, daughter of Brychan, mother of Cadoc.

Gowan, **Q**, wife of Glamorgan's King Tewrig, her name to Llangoven.

Gunthiern, **H**, Welsh prince, a hermit in Brittany.

Gwen, **W**, sister of Non, aunt of David, mother of Cuby and Cadfan.

Gwen, **VM**, of family of Brychan, died at hands of Saxons 492.

Hydrock, patron saint of Llanhydrock, Cornwall.

Ia, **VM**, Irish princess, sister to Ercus, murdered at Hayle in Cornwall, her name given to town of St. Ives.

Illtyd, **A**, pupil of Cadoc. Founded abbey of Llan-Illtut, d. Brittany AD 470.

Kennera, **VM**, companion of Ursula, escaped that massacre only to die later in a martyr's death.

Kingsmark, Scottish chief in Wales, wed granddaughter of Brychan.

Lewina, **VM**, Briton killed by Saxons, venerated at Seaford in Sussex.

Lupus of Troyes, **B**, saved British from Pelagius, Troyes from Huns.

Madrun, Welsh or Cornish, to whom Cornish churches dedicated.

Melorius, **M**, died in Cornwall, venerated in Amesbury and Brittany.

Menefrida, of Brychan family, patron of Menver in Cornwall.

Merewenna, **V**, Brychan daughter, patron Marham church near Bude.
Morwenna, **V**, daughter of Brychan, Cornish churches named for her.
Nennoc, **V**, child of Brychan, abbess of monastic house in Armorica.
Ninian, **B**, Briton of Whithorn, Apostle to Cumberland & Picts d. AD 432.
Palladius, first **B** to the Scots, d. 450. Buried at Fordun nr. Aberdeen.
Paulinus, **A**, of Whitland, pupil of Illtyd, teacher of David & Teilo.
Primael, Briton to whom churches dedicated in Quimper, Brittany.
Ravennus & Rasyphus, **MM**, in Normandy by governor of Neustria.
Ruan, Irish **B**, consecrated by Patrick, served in Cornwall and Brittany.
Sanasus, Irish patron of Plou Sane in Brittany, d. AD 485.
Servan, Scot **B**, consecrated by Palladius as Apostle to the Orkneys.
Tathi, **H**, Irish monk or hermit, a holy life at Llantathan in Wales.
Teath, **V**, daughter of Brychan, name taken by Cornish churches.
Tegla, patron of Llandegla in Denbighshire. (date uncertain), possibly a *Thecla* by tradition associated with St. Paul.
Ternan, **A**, Scot of Culross in Fife, cons. by Palladius as Bp to Picts.
Tudinus, **A**, Breton of monastic house, fellow worker with Corentin.
Tudy, **V**, daughter of Brychan, name to Llanbydie in Carmarthenshire
Tudy, disciple of St. Mawes in Cornwall, venerated in Brittany.
Tybie, **VM**, Welsh maiden memorialized in Llandybie.
Tydfil, Matron and martyr, many murdered by Saxons and Picts at place to which she is patron, Merthyr Tydfil near Brecon.
Ursula & her companions VVMM.
Ust or Just, a popular saint in Brittany, Wales and Cornwall described as of 5th-6th century, yet not known just what he was.

British Saints of the Sixth Century

Aaron, **AB**, British founder-abbot of monastery at St. Malo in Brittany.
Afan, Welsh **B** of Cunedda family, Llanafan Church in Brechnock.
Agnes, **VM**, British maiden martyred near Cologne.
Albinus (Aubin), Breton **B** of Angers in Brittany, d. AD 529 buried at Lyons.

Almedha, **VM**, Brychan's daughter or granddaughter, murdered near her home.

Amaethlu, **C**, founded a church so named in Anglesey, Llanfaethlu.

Aneurin & Gwinoc, **CC**, Welsh monks, father and son, latter a poet.

Armagillus, **C**, Cornishman in Brittany. Piou-Ermel bears his name.

Asaph, pupil of Kentigern, 1st **B** of St. Asaph's, **A** to 1,000 monks.

Bitheus & Genocus, **CC**, British monks who went with Finnian of Clonard to Ireland, lived and died there in great sanctity.

Brannock, **A**, Welsh founded monastery at Braunton in Devon.

Brenach, **H**, hermit of Pembrokeshire, his cell near Milford.

Briach, **A**, Irish born, a monk in Wales, abbot of monastery in Brittany.

Brioc, Welsh disciple Germanus of Auxerre, **B** in Wales, **A** in Brittany.

Brothen & Gwynnin, brothers & church patrons in Carnarvonshire.

Buithe, a Scot returned from abroad, evangelized the Picts, d. AD 521.

<u>*Buriana*</u>, **VR**, one of many Irish solitaries living in Cornwall.

Cadfan, Breton to Wales, **A** of Bardsey, named Llangadfan Montgomery.

Cadfarch, disciple of Illtyd, name to churches at Penegos and Aberick.

Cadoc, **BM**, founder of Llancarvan monastery in Glamorgan, took charge of Britons in eastern counties, martyred by Saxons AD 580.

Cawrdaf, chief of Brecknock & Hereford, became monk under Illtyd.

Ceitho, one of five brothers Cunedda, his name to LLangeith near Cardigan, Church at Pumpsaint dedicated to all five.

Cewydd, Welsh saint flourishing in Anglesey.

Cian, Welsh soldier who became a hermit in Carnarvonshire.

Clether, descendant of Brychan, disciple of Brynach d. AD 520.

Clydog, Welsh **M**, died in Herefordshire AD 482.

Colman, **B**, disciple of Columba, founded monastery at Clonenagh.

Colman, **DA** of minster on Lambay Island built by Columba.

Columba, **PA**, Apostle to Caledonia, founder 100 monasteries, d. AD 597.

Constantine, Cornish King, repenting evil life, died a martyr.

Cuby, cousin of David, **B** near Tregony, founded minster near Holyhead.

Cumgar (*Cyngar*) **A**, son of Devon prince Geraint, founded monasteries in Somerset and Glamorgan. Gave name to Congresbury.

Curig, **B** of Llanbadarn in Wales, churches there given his name.

Cynwl, brother of Deiniol, man of austere life, churches in his name.

David (*Dewi*), Archbishop of Menevia, Patron saint of Wales, d. 601.

Deifer, founder of Bodfari in Flintshire, Wales.

Deiniol Wyn, **B**, founder of Abbey Bangor Fawr, 1st Bishop of Bangor, his name to cathedral and parish churches.

Deiniol, **A**, son of Deiniol Wyn, Abbot of Bangor Fawr.

Derfel-Gadarn, **H**, Welsh soldier become hermit at Llanderfel, Merion.

Devinicus, Scottish **B** assoc. with Columba, evangelized Caithness.

Dotto, **A**, Abbot of monastery in Orkney Islands.

Drillo, Breton monk at Bardsey, patron at Denbeigh and Merioneth.

Dubricius (*Dyfrig*) **B** of Llandaff, David's predecessor as Archbishop of Caerleon, leading light Brynach family of saints, buried at Bardsey.

Edeyrn, **H**, associated with King Arthur, with age hermit in Brittany.

Efflam, **A**, son of a British prince, founded monastery in Brittany.

Eigrad, pupil of Illtyd, Sampson's brother, founder, church in Anglesey.

Eingan, member of Cunedda family from Cumberland in North Wales.

Elaeth the King, Briton driven to Wales by Picts, monk under Seiriol.

Elerius, **A** of monastery in North Wales.

Elian, Cornish or Breton, in a family of many saints. Author of hymns.

Elwyn, one of holy men going with <u>Briaca</u> from Ireland to Cornwall.

Enoder, **A**, grandson of Brychan, church name in Cornwall, Hereford.

Enodoch, **V**, from Brychan family, possibly Gwendydd, his daughter.

Finian, Ninian's disciple at Strathclyde, to Ireland as **B** & **A** of Maghbile.

Gallgo, Welsh founder of Llanalgo in Anglesey.

Germoc, Irish, brother of <u>Briaca</u>, settled in Cornwall near Mount's Bay.

Gerontius, **KM**, King of Devon died in battle with Saxons, AD 508.

Gistillian, monk of Menevia, uncle of St. David.

Gluvias, brother of Cadoc of Llancarvan, built monastery in Cornwall.

Goezenoveus, Cornish brother of Maughan, **B** of Leon in Brittany.

Goneri, exile from Britain to Brittany.

Goran, contemporary and friend of St. Petrock.

Guainerth, patron of a chapel in Herefordshire.

Guenhael, Breton noble's son pupil of Wenwaloe, following him as **A**.

Guevrock, **A**, British pupil of Tugduald in Brettany, aided Paul de Leon.

Gundleus, **H**, husband of Gladys, father of Cadoc, in old age a hermit.

Hernan, **H**, British refugee in Brittany; hermit at Loc-Harn.

Herve, blind Welsh singer in Brittany, loved as teacher and minstrel.

Joavon, **B**, born in Ireland, educated in Britain, succeeded Paul de Leon in Brittany, d. AD 540.

Justinian, **HM**, Breton hermit martyred in South Wales.

Kanten, Welsh founder of Llangenten Abbey in Brecknock.

Kea (Kay), Briton's name to Landkey in Devon, St. Quay in Brittany.

Kecsag, prince of Cashel, missionary bishop to Scotland, d. AD 521.

Kenneth, Welsh hermit, his cell on Gower peninsula, Atlantic coast.

Kessog, Irish prince, missionary **B** of Lennox and elsewhere in Scotland.

Keverne, Cornish friend of Kieran of Ireland.

Kewe, **V**, Welsh saint venerated in Monmouthshire.

Keyna, **V**, Brechan's daughter, recluse, returned from Somerset to die.

Kybi, **B**, Apostle to Anglesey, son of Salomon King of Brittany.

Lawdog, Welsh saint giving name to four churches in St. David's.

Leonorius, Breton King Hoel's son, pupil of Illtyd, consecrated by Dyfrig, as **A**; founded monastery in Brittany.

Levan, Irish saint come to Cornwall, his name taken by church there.

Libio, patron of Llanlibio, Anglesey, with brothers said to have been at Dunawd's Bangor-ap-Dee.

Llendad (Laudatus), **A** of Bardsey, accompanied Cadfan to Brittany.

Llewellyn & Gwenerth, Welsh monks at Welshpool, later at Bardsey.

Louthiern, Irish **B**, patron St. Ludgran Cornwall, possibly the same as

Luchtigern, **A** of Innistymon associated with St. Ita.

Mabenna, daughter of Brychan of Brecknock.

Mabyn & Mabon, associated in Cornwall and Wales with St. Teilo.

Maden (*Madern*), Breton saint from Cornwall, name to holy well.

Mael, **H**, came with Cadfan from Brittany to Wales, hermit on Bardsey.

Maelrhys, saint of Bardsey, born Brittany, venerated in North Wales.

Maethlin, saint of Anglesey, his name given to Llanfaethlin.

Maglorious, from Wales to Brittany with Samson, **A** of Lanmeur and, in retirement, of Jersey.

Maidoc, **B** or **A** of Llanmadog in Glamorganshire.

Manakus, Welsh **A** Holyhead, with Cybi at Manaccan, Cornwall.

Mawes, **H**, Cornish hermit near Falmouth, also known in Brittany.

Melangell, **V**, recluse in Montgomery, name at Pennant-Melangell.

Melanius, Breton **B** of Rennes, friend of King Clovis, d. AD 530.

Merinus, disciple of Dunawd of Bangor, churches in Wales and Brittany.

Meugant, **H**, disciple of Illtyd, **H** in Wales, Cornwall, finally at Bardsey.

Moloc, Irish disciple of Brendan, **B** in Scotland and Hebrides. d. 592.

Nectan, **M**, descendant of Brychan, patron of Hartland in Devon.

Nonnita or *Non*, mother of St. David of Wales.

Noyala, **VM**, Briton greatly venerated in Armorica.

Odhram, Irish or Scottish **A** of Iona and Meath. Name to Oronsay.

Oudaceus, Breton reared by Teilo, following him as **B** of Llandaff.

Pabo, **A**, border Scot, founded Llanbabon Minster in Anglesey.

Paternus (*Padarn*), Breton, educated in Ireland, hermit in Wales, became **B** of Avranches in Normandy, d. AD 550.

Paul de Leon, educated at School and Monastery of St. Illtyd, crossed to Brittany with 12 followers. As **B** of Leon, St. Pol and Quimper, founded a number of dioceses and monastic abbeys.

Petrock, Welsh **A**, educated in Ireland, founded monasteries at Padstow and Bodmin in Cornwall, known in Brittany as St. Perreux.

Piran, **H**, Cornish hermit, cell near Padstow, patron saint of miners.

Sadwen, brother of Illtyd, disciple of Cadfan.

Salomon, Prince of Cornwall, husband of Gwen, father of Cadfan & Cybi, David's uncle, refugee ruler in Brittany till martyrdom AD 550.

Sampson, Welsh, disciple of Illtyd, **A** of Lantwit, **B** of Dol as refugee in Brittany, assisted at Council of Paris in AD 557.

Sawyl, Welsh, father of St. Asaph.

Seiriol, Welsh saint, his name associated with Ynys-Seiriol.

Sezin, British **B**, assisted Patrick in Ireland, founded Breton monastery.

Sidwell, **VM**, Briton killed by Saxons, her name to churches in Devon.

Silin, prince of North Wales, hermit near Anglesey, to Brittany as missionary.

Teilo, **B** of Llandaff, successor to Dyfrig and David as Archbishop of Wales.

Tremorus, youthful pupil of Gildas, murdered in monastery at Rhys by father, miracles at tomb, he and mother invoked in 7th c. litanies.

Triphina, mother of Tremorus, holiness of years in Breton convent.

Tudno, Welsh saint after whom Llandudno (Carnarvon) is named.

Tugdual, like Lenorius his brother, prince of Brittany; Bishop of Treguier.

Tydecho, Welsh, brother to Cadfan, churches in Merion bear his name.

Tyssilo, Welsh, of Cunedda family whence David, Teilo & others.

Uni, like his sister, *Briaca*; from Ireland to Cornwall; is patron saint of churches in Lelant and Redruth.

Veep, **V**, daughter of Caw in North Britain, sister of St. Samson of York, Pict-driven patron of St. Veep's church in Cornwall.

Vivian, Scottish bishop, abbot of monastery in Fife.

Vorech, Irish **P** from Armagh, hermit in Cornwall, patron of Llanlivery.

Vougas, Irish hermit who settled in Brittany near Lesneven.

Winnow, Mancus & Myrbad, Irish saints who lived in Cornwall and had churches named in their honor.

Wynnin, Scottish saint and missionary bishop.

Yarcard, Scottish bishop, ordained by St. Ternan and, like him, a missionary among the Picts.

St. Patrick, Apostle to the Irish

As a sixteen year old Briton, Patrick was kidnapped by Irish pirates and held captive for six years in that land. His origin seems to have been at Kilpatrick near Dumbarton, the capital of British Strathclyde, where his father, Calpurnius, was a deacon and magistrate, and his grandfather Potitus a priest. Ninian is thought to have grown up there as well, and several bits of tradition support what we have already been told. One is that Ninian's father, Gorthol, was a prince of the Strathclyde Britons. Another is that Ninian, while building Whithorn Abbey, made visitations to Strathclyde. While still at Whithorn, he assigned Strathclyde to his disciple, Finian, who later became Bishop of Moyville in northern Ireland. In support of the above is a remarkable coincidence involving St. Caranoc the Pict, who remained at Whithorn when Ninian extended his ministry to Ireland. Two ancient Irish manuscripts, the *Book of Ballymote* and the *Book of Lecan*, tell us that Patrick was baptized while still an Irish captive, by Caranoc when Caranoc was visiting a small Christian settlement at Nendrun in Strangford Lough in easternmost Ireland not far from Belfast. In later years, Patrick would begin his missionary work at the same Strangford Lough in Ninian's final year.

Both Apostles appear to have received training from their kinsman, Martin of Tours. Ninian was the more scholarly and, with his aptness for Scripture, manuscripts and their adornment, set a high standard for later Irish scholars. Patrick was almost unlettered, yet by his persistency and devotion set an example that may never have been surpassed. After study at Lerins in the south of Gaul, he was ordained priest by St. Germanus of Auxerre, later consecrated as Bishop to the Scots (Irish) by Amandus, archbishop of Bordeaux. Patrick's ministry in Ireland, begun in AD 432, continued until his retirement in AD 460, when he and Benignus went to Avalon and converted the Arimathean Joseph's foundation of anchorites to what would become England's greatest abbey. During his apostolate in Ireland Patrick is said to have built three hundred sixty churches, baptized ten thousand converts and ordained enough men to Holy Order to provide for the conversion and pastoral care of all Ireland and the Isle of Man.

Saints in Ireland: Patrick's Family and Friends

Darerca, **W**, Patrick's sister had many sons, some of them bishops.
Loman, **B**, St. Patrick's nephew, first bishop of Trim.
Mel, **BA**, Patrick's nephew, abbot and first bishop of Ardagh.
Neachtain, Kinsman of Patrick, died in his presence.
Mun, **BH**, Patrick's nephew, Bishop of Longford, hermit in Lough Ree.
Patrick, **A**, a later saint thought to be a kinsman of the Apostle.
Seachnall, **B**, Nephew of Patrick, became Bishop of Dunsaghlin.

A Few Preceding Patrick or on Hand when He Came

Albeus, 1st **B** of Emly-Cashel, patron saint of Munster.
Iberius, an evangelist briefly in Leinster and Meath.
Kieran, 1st **B** of Ossory, in old age known in Brittany as St. Piran.

Irish Saints Directly Associated with or Converted by St. Patrick

Abban, **A**, founded Kill-Abban Abbey in Leinster.
Asicus, **B**, disiple of Patrick, First Bishop of Elphin, lived to great age.
Auxilius, Iserninus, Secundinus, Bishops who were missionary co-workers with St. Patrick.
Attracta, **V**, founded monastery in Sligo, famed for charitable works.
Benignus, **B**, Patrick's successor at Armagh, again at Glastonbury.
Bridget, aka *Bride*, **V**, Patroness of Ireland, founded Kildare, d. AD 523.
Bron, **B**, disciple of Patrick, Bishop of Cassel-Irra, d. AD 511.
Cettin, **B**, assistant to Patrick for apostolic work.
Cinnea, **V**, Princess of Ulster, veiled by Patrick, won many converts.

Colman, disciple of Patrick, who buried him at end of holy life.

Crummine, **B**, placed by Patrick over Church of Leccuine.

Dichu, Patrick's first convert in Ulster, a swineherd.

Fiace, Irish **B**, friend and disciple of St. Patrick.

Fiech, **AB**, bard baptized by Patrick, abbot and bishop for Leinster.

Fortchern, early convert of Patrick, devoted to Apostle's service.

Guassacht, **B** son of Patrick's boyhood captor, Bishop of Longford.

Ethenia & Fidelmia, **VV**, early converts. daughters of high king, to whom death came after adoption of the religious life, AD 533.

Jarlath, **B**, disciple of Patrick, succeeded Benignus as Archbishop of Armagh.

Jarman, **B**, sent by Patrick as First Bishop of Isle of Man.

Kinnia, **V**, holy maid baptized & veiled by Patrick, venerated in Louth.

Loarn, a holy man converted by St. Patrick.

Macaille, **B**, disciple of Patrick, Bishop of Croghan, King's County, d AD 489.

Macanisius, baptized by Patrick, First Bishop of Connor.

Macartin, **B**, disciple of Patrick, First Bishop of Clogher, d. AD 506.

Machai, **A**, disciple of Patrick, founded monastery in Isle of Bute.

Maughold, **B**, Patrick's convert, sent as 3rd Bishop of Isle of Man.

Moeliai, **A**, baptised by Patrick, Abbot of Nendrum with Finian & Colman.

Monessa, **V**, converted by Patrick, died at moment of baptism.

Muredach, **BH**, disciple of Patrick, 1st Bishop of Killala, in old age a hermit.

Nissen, **A**, convert of Patrick, Abbot over monasteries in Wexford.

Odhran, **M**, Patrick's driver, gave life in his behalf.

Rioche, **B**, convert of Patrick, made Bishop but left & founded monastery.

Romulus, Cointrus, Bishops sent by Patrick to Isle of Man.

Tassach, **B**, of Raholp (Down), Patrick converted him and in turn was ministered to by him when at the point of death.

Trea, convert of Patrick, a lifelong recluse at Ardtree (Derry).

Trien, **A**, disciple of St. Patrick, Abbot of Killelga.

Missionaries Brought to Ireland from the British Church

Carantog, Welsh evangelist leaving name at Llangrannog in Cardigan.
Cairnach, 5th century Welsh prince used by St. Patrick as a missioner.
Kenan, **B**, also disciple of St. Martin of Tours, Bishop of Damleag in Meath.
Mochteus, **B**, a Briton consecrated by Patrick as 1st Bishop of Louth.
Olcanus, **B**, a Briton, consecrated by Patrick Bishop of Derkin in Antrim.
Modomnock, **H**, disciple of St. David of Wales, hermit in Kilkenny.
Sanctan, **B**, son of St. Salomon, Briton to Ireland as bishop near Dublin.
Schotin, disciple of St. David of Wales, anchorite/schoolmaster in Kilkenny.

We must appreciate that *The Book of Saints* shows hundreds of additional Irish saints for later centuries. The same is true with the Gallican and British, as it will be with the English now appearing on the scene. With regard to the saints listed above from the Irish Church, we should note that these few have one thing in common which is that Patrick was their shepherd and created the fold they dwelled in. As for the others, we have scarcely begun to touch upon those great saints of Ireland and Britain whose lives and scholarly legacy have so greatly shaped man's concept of God, Church, Scripture and the holy life. With the introduction of the Gregorian Mission in the closing years of the sixth century, we are given occasion to examine and sort out the threads from all four churches that, by God's grace, may provide a heavenly garment for the Bride.

ᆼ Chapter 14 ᆼ

Triumphs of the Welsh:
The Age of Patrick and Arthur

I f R.W. Morgan's account is correct–that the year AD 86 saw the final failure of Rome's invasion[1]–we must hold that there never was a Roman Britain and that the notion of a mini Pax Romana lasting several centuries is in contradiction of the facts. From AD 43 to AD 86 Rome was Britain's mortal enemy, dominating her territory with active opposition of council, crown and people. From AD 86 to AD 116 Rome was an enemy expelled and debarred from re-entry, with a state of war continuing in force. In AD 120, after four years of negotiation, a Roman presence was allowed in Britain but limited to the restrictions of a treaty signed by both rulers. Britain, while now Rome's ally, continued to be an independent kingdom as it had been for nearly two thousand years. Its concession to Rome allowed a measure of protection against Pictish and Irish invaders as well as such aggressors as might attempt a crossing of North Sea or Channel. As for those decades of stalemate, the Encyclopedia Britannica's Eleventh Edition*. seems to be our best authority, "What frontier was adopted after Agricola's departure... is unknown. For thirty years (AD 85-115) the military history of Britain is a blank. When we recover knowledge we are in an altered world."

*published in 1911, but substantively the most thoroughly detailed on ancient history.

The record then goes on to describe what later led to the legions' withdrawal and the arrival of Germanic invaders–Jutes, Saxons and Angles. Their initial coming was by invitation of the traitor-king Vortigern, whose active years were AD 425-459. Borrowing from Rome's expedients, he persuaded Saxon adventurers to join him in forcing the Picts back to their homeland. Those same Saxons, judging that with little effort they could make Britain their own, in later years returned in such mounting force as to drive the Britons from most of what henceforth would be known as Angle-land or England. The invasion, including time to arrive at some semblance of order, took a century and a half to accomplish.

Vortigern is described in the Triads as one of Three Arrant Traitors of Britain. Already suspect with his people, he allowed the Saxons to massacre 480 British noblemen invited to a feast at Stonehenge celebrating peace and unity between the peoples. On that shameful "Night of the Long Knives," only three Britons escaped with their lives. The second turncoat, Avarwy–aka Mandubracius, "the black traitor"– had persuaded the war council to allow Julius Caesar's 54 BC landing to be unopposed at the beaches. A year earlier the British had prevented Caesar's landing in large part by wading into the surf and attacking the Romans when they were most vulnerable–jumping into the water and unlimbering their weapons, fearful of being cut down by chariots should they gain the beaches. Mandubracius persuaded the war council that it would be more manly to allow the Romans to land their legions unimpeded, so that Britons could meet them in open battle. The British losses as a result of that decision were great, and it was later learned that Caesar had bribed him to make that proposal. (Mandubracius' daughter took after her father; as queen she betrayed Caradoc.) The third traitor, Medrawd or Modred, was Arthur's nephew, who in the king's absence betrayed his trust, seized his queen and throne and conspired with Arthur's enemies to take his life.

Germanus and Lupus: Soldiers of Christ, Godly Teachers

It would appear that Pelagianism got its start in the thought patterns of the British. Not only was Pelagius, at Rome, a well known

British scholar and on respectful terms even with his opponents, he is said to have been the twentieth abbot of the great Monastery of Bangor-ap-Dee supposedly founded by St. Paul. If so, the heresy could have originated with the Druids as an ethical teaching, for the British by circumstance and national character have been more inclined than Continentals to look with optimism on the human condition. Nevertheless, when British lay folk and clergy learned they were being called Pelagian, they asked the Gallic bishops to send scholars who could demonstrate the errors in that teaching. Responding to their plea, the Gallicans sent Germanus and Lupus, respectively the bishops of Auxerre and Troyes. During a few months of preaching and debate these two drew vast crowds of hearers. Everywhere they were able successfully to refute those who held that Christians, relying on their human resources, could live in obedience to God's Law. It became widely evident that the Pelagian teaching represented a false understanding of life in the Spirit, for it showed no regard for the need of God's help in overcoming sin. So eager were the Britons to be doctrinally at one with churchmen elsewhere that they gave their judgment in what amounted to a national consensus.

The Alleluia Victory, an Appeal *to* the British and *for* the Irish

That unity of mind and will was soon put to the test. At the beginning of Lent in AD 430 Germanus and Lupus delayed their departure to work with a now-forming British army, many of whose members were unbaptized and few of whom were equipped with arms. After the Easter Feast, the men, now being of one faith, learned that a large force of Picts and Saxons was nearby and heading their way. Since Germanus had, before his conversion, held high military rank, he took the lead, preparing an ambush along the wooded hills on either side of the valley through which the enemy was expected to pass. His signal for action was to be the Easter antiphon. When the enemy were within the glen of ambuscade, the bishops proclaimed, "Alleluia, Alleluia, Alleluia," their cry echoing and re-echoing among the hills. Now there came a response of electrifying nearness; it was as the roar of a mighty army, "Alleluia, Alleluia, Alleluia!" Unnerved, the Picts and Saxons fled in haste, casting away their arms and whatever else might impede their flight. Many were drowned in the River Dee, swollen by spring rains.

This Alleluia Victory was the first engagement of what would be a long and terrible conflict. Here was a British army, a Christian force that, by the grace of God, had made an impact on its foes. Here was a Gaulish general—a Celt like themselves—who, taken unawares, not only followed Gideon's tactic with the Midianites but in godly fashion refrained from pursuit and reprisal. Yet the lesson was lost on the Saxons so long as Britons lacked the manpower to defend themselves and the readiness to share the faith of Christ with a people whose will was their destruction. What the victory hinted at by way of promise seems to have gone unfulfilled—unless for an Irish people ripe for Christ and with ears to hear the Gospel.

It is quite possible that Saint Patrick had a part in the Alleluia Victory, for his ministry in Ireland began soon after that event, and it is widely believed that Germanus consecrated Patrick as well as his contemporaries Dyfrig and Illtyd. If Patrick was present at the Alleluia Victory, and especially with Germanus as his mentor, the experience would doubtless have had an immense impact on him personally and on all that he subsequently said and did.

Why Did Bede the Historian Make No Mention of St. Patrick?

It is odd indeed that while Bede tells virtually all that is known of the Alleluia Victory,[2] nowhere in his writings does he refer to Patrick. Other scholars have raised the question without satisfaction as to why Bede failed to write about Patrick, but the following provides possible reasons. Initially, two things come to mind. One is that Bede, whose work was completed in AD 735, may not have been occupied with what Patrick had done three hundred years earlier. In support of this supposition, it may be added that Bede mentions none of the fifty-eight saints earlier described as connected with Patrick's ministry. Bede's concern seems to have been with the Celtic Church as Columba left it. The background setting for Bede's history must then be AD 597, the year of Augustine's arrival at Canterbury and of St. Columba's death.

Another possibility for the oversight is the difficulty Bede might have had in evaluating the man. He himself, though the prime scholar of his generation, could not fail to base his understanding and judgments on the tribal pattern that is ever present for a Church whose self-image is that of a living, organic body. The members of such an entity (whether ecclesial or political) must view themselves as subordinate to the head, with judgment and ordering coming from the head rather than from the body or its members. Bede's sense of ethnicity–undergirded by the organic view–required the understanding that the Roman and the Celtic churches were essentially two bodies rather than one. It was a setting where a judgment on unity might be invited from one held to be Vicar of Christ rather than from Spirit-given consensus or evidence of ultimate design.

Aware of this, we can understand why Bede, ethnically a Saxon and ecclesially Roman, could hold the Celtic Church in contempt. Yet there is considerable ambivalence in what he wrote. Despite his oft-voiced disdain for the Celts, Bede, with remarkable grace and in considerable detail, describes godly qualities in such leaders of the Celtic Church as Ninian, Columba, Adamnan, Aidan, Colman, Hilda, Eata, Tuda, Cedd, Chad and Cuthbert. His admiration was in no way diminished by the knowledge that several had been in sharp conflict with two bishops of the Canterbury Church, Augustine and Wilfrid, whose prickly dispositions and ungracious manners he acknowledges while supporting their position. Even Theodore is described by Bede as falling short of the humility and holiness to be seen in such as Chad or Aidan.

There was one figure, however, in Bede's survey of the Celtic Church who differed greatly from those named above. Moreover he was more typically the Celt, and may well have been so like St. Patrick as to lead Bede to say nothing of Patrick rather than run the risk of mistaken judgment or damning with faint praise. That man was Columbanus, a self-defined individual who did not hesitate to ignore, scold or ridicule synods, emperors and popes when they appeared to be lacking in godliness or wisdom. Columbanus was a powerful leader.

He founded great abbeys in Gaul, Switzerland and Italy, all of which prospered despite their use of Celtic rule, Celtic rite and the Celtic date of Easter. He tried the patience of rulers whether in Church or State. Yet they could not suppress or rid themselves of him short of murder. Even when he was imprisoned or banished, he made his return. Years after his death he was joined with eight of the eleven just referred to by canonization as a saint by the Roman Church–the exceptions being Colman and Eata, bishops of Lindisfarne, and Chad's brother Cedd. Despite the sanctity thus acknowledged, *The Book of Saints* says of Columbanus in conclusion,

> "He was a man of great ability, as his writings show, and rendered many services to the Church, but his mistaken zeal for the Celtic date of Easter and the ill-advised letter he wrote to Pope St. Boniface IV against Pope Vigilius, and upholding the so called "Three Chapters" rejected by the Church has ultimately served as a weapon against her in the hands of Protestants."

Patrick, although he tells little of his own life and experiences, nevertheless reveals much about himself. His energy and achievements were not unlike those of Columbanus. Like that saint, his strength lay in the intensity of an I-Thou relationship with God, and it was the manifestation of that nearness that drew people to him. He makes it evident that his calling came directly from God without the mediation of the Church, and that the fulfilling of his vocation required little out of the ordinary from the Church by way of teaching, testing and ordaining. Once in the field he was not dependent on a hierarchy. Yet missionaries and teachers joined him in great numbers, many of whom he trained and ordained to be bishops or abbots, or set apart as monks or nuns.

Patrick as Founder and Patron of the Church of Ireland

It has been observed that when Patrick died there was none to replace him. A generation or so later, we find a transformed culture. What Patrick had achieved by his energy and charisma had been converted into enclaves that were unique in style yet uniformly alike. Because Ireland was entirely rural, its structures became monastic rather than diocesan in form. They were based on geographic units of clan and family rather than on see cities, towns and villages. The rulers for the most part were abbots rather than bishops. In some places the abbot was a presbyter or lay brother. Columba, for example, was both presbyter and abbot, and so were most who succeeded him at Iona.

Two things stand out by comparison with other Celtic churches. One is that Ireland was won to Christ in a far shorter time than Britain and with no record of martyrdom. Even that in Britain bore the blood of an Aristobulus. The second fact of note is that, so far as apostolic descent is concerned, Patrick's ordering is linked with the Celtic Church into which he was born rather than with the Roman. Moreover, Patrick's Church had its orders perpetuated in what is today the (Anglican) Church of Ireland rather than that of Rome. The first instance where the Church of Ireland's autonomy was overridden came in 1156, when Henry II of England petitioned Adrian IV (the only English pope) to grant Ireland's dominion to the English Crown in accordance with the Donation of Constantine. In the Pope's answering bull, the Crown was granted that privilege, as the prelate put it "to widen the bounds of the Church, *and to extend her jurisdiction where she has none at present* (emphasis ours)." Though the grant was made and until 1440* adhered to, there was no attempt to restructure Ireland's succession of bishops till the Reformation, when Rome set up a separate "Church of Rome in Ireland" having a Spanish-Italian, rather than Celtic, succession. Though in schism from Patrick's own line of patriarchs, the new church possessed apostolic order and is, today, far larger in terms of membership. For this reason—and appropriately if belatedly—the older Church's claim to tithes was discontinued in 1735, and her establishment ended in 1869.

Institutions of Learning in the Welsh and Irish Churches

Charts for the several Celtic churches demonstrate that the Church of Ireland's growth from nothing in the fifth, sixth and seventh centuries was phenomenal. The number of Irish saints added to the

---

*By this date the *Donation of Constantine* was everywhere acknowledged to be a spurious document of 8th or 9th century invention. Prior to that it had been universally accepted and acted upon.

Benedictines' roster in those three hundred years was equal to those provided in the same period by all of Britain and Brittany combined. Even more impressive, the Irish saints of those three centuries were as many as the Roman Mission (i.e., the Church of England) would acquire from its start until the Reformation.

Virtually all of the Christian teachers who, as missionaries, carried the Gospel to Ireland, came from other Celtic churches. In later years, however, the majority of teachers were those Irish who had studied at the monastic schools in Wales or who, still later, had attended the Irish schools that sprung up at home. Of the colleges in the Welsh Church, one, founded by St. Dyfrig at Llandaff, provided for a thousand scholars, among whom had been St. Teilo. Another was that at St. Asaph associated with St. Kentigern where its members numbered 965. A third was the College of St. Illtyd (now Llantwit Major) where the historian St. Gildas had studied and where many of the English nobility would in later years receive their education. In addition was the College of St. Padarn in what is now the Diocese of St. David's. David himself had been trained at Whitland, founded by the Welsh Paulinus in Carmarthenshire. The largest of the Welsh monastic schools was at Bangor-ap-Dee, encompassing twenty-five square miles and containing ten thousand at one period in its monastery and schools. Though there were others, one comes to mind which may have been the earliest of all–St. Cadoc's at Llancarvan.

We turn to the Irish schools, giving attention to the founders and their backgrounds. Nearly all got their training in Wales, though in a few generations their schools exceeded the Welsh both in size and number. One founder was St. Kieran, "the firstborn of the saints in Ireland," who is believed to have preceded Patrick and been consecrated by him as First Bishop of Ossory. In Cornwall the same Kieran is remembered as Piran, where he began his work and is patron saint of miners. Another is St. Kenan, also pre-Patrick, a youthful hostage to King Leoghaire, whose release–negotiated by St. Kieran–led to his studying under St. Martin of Tours for the priesthood. He returned to Ireland as one of Patrick's bishops. St. Finian of Clonard, after training under Cadoc and Gildas in Wales, was consecrated by Patrick as the first Bishop of the Diocese of Meath. He founded the greatest monastic school in Ireland, that of Clonard, and became known as teacher of the "Twelve Apostles of Ireland," of whom the greatest was St. Columba. Still another teacher was St. Brendan the Navigator, a pupil of Finian and Gildas in Wales. Brendan later founded many monasteries, the largest of which was at Clonfert, where three thousand monks studied, prayed and worked. St. Comgall's school in Ireland followed that saint's training and early ministry in Wales and Cornwall. He was consecrated by St. Fintan as Abbot of Ben-Chor (Bangor), where his pupils included Columbanus and Gall as well as Luanus, who himself would found one hundred twenty-nine monasteries in Ireland and Scotland. There was also the school of Canicus, who served as a monk under Finian of Clonard and trained for Holy Order under Cadoc in Wales. He founded churches and monasteries in Scotland and Ireland and is patron saint of Kilkenny. While there were doubtless other teachers and other schools, we may close with Columba, a disciple of Finian of Clonard as well as of Finnian of Moville, who was trained under Ninian's line at Whithorn. Columba founded over a hundred monasteries and is remembered as first Abbot of Iona and Apostle to the Scots.

A Pooling of Resources for Celtic Missions to the North of Europe

There can be little doubt that Ireland got its faith from a British Church that since its beginning had been evangelizing in distant lands. In considering what we know of those Celts named in *The Book of Saints*, we can not only discern the growth patterns of their churches but judge how, when and in what manner these bodies interacted with one another. A study of the saints as individuals enables us to decide whether their activities were initiated and supported by church structures or whether they were acting on their own. The records seem to show that the British Church as a whole had more concern than the Gallican for the evangelizing of distant peoples. It likewise appears that the Irish, despite their Church's later start, had considerably more missionary ardor than the British at that time. In carrying the Gospel to the Irish, however, there is clear evidence that the Welsh, who were nearest, gave strenuously of themselves. A lack of earlier commitment to mission on their part could have been the prevalence of piracy, kidnapping and slavery among the Irish. When Patrick returned to the land of his earlier captivity, Welsh teachers and preachers were quick to join him.

It can be noted that the mission activity of the Welsh, which began in the fifth century, appears to have been terminated in the seventh. Yet that seems inconsistent, considering how heavily and how recently they had been involved with their daughter Irish Church. The claim has been made for these Irish, that from the seventh through the tenth centuries they were providing unimaginable benefits for peoples of the Low Countries, Germany and Gaul–"saving civilization" as it were. If true, all we can reasonably presume is that, as the Saxon threat intensified at home, many Welsh, who in the past had taught Irish scholars and missionaries, would close their schools, pack their books and scrolls and move to Ireland, reopening in that land. In the process they would not only enrich the Irish Church and culture. They would, perhaps without being aware of it, be transferring the heart of the Celtic Church from Britain to Ireland for the remainder of the millenium.

An Event or a Non-Event?

There are three reasons why we can believe the center of Celtic mission had moved from Britain to Ireland. One is that students and teachers need to work in peace. They require sufficient leisure to focus on their studies, following a disciplined routine without which few accomplishments can be made. The record of events early in the seventh century seem to indicate that Britain and Brittany could no longer provide this environment. For several hundred more years Ireland could and would.

We can demonstrate this by recalling Wales' violent history in religious matters as well as wars. In AD 61, there had been the massacre of five thousand Druids at Anglesey. There the Romans had destroyed the center of the Druid cult. The same occurred for Christian Wales in AD 607 when one thousand two hundred fifty monks of Bangor-ap-Dee knelt on a knoll near where an Anglian army of fifty thousand under King Ethelfrith of Northumbria was attacking a smaller British force taken by surprise. The monarch inquired about the nearby men in white garb who carried no weapons and were kneeling there, hands stretched upward. When told they were monks praying to their God he demanded they be killed immediately, since they could only be praying for his defeat. The massacre of one thousand one hundred of these monks was followed, after the battle's end, by the killing of teachers and students at the college and the burning of the buildings in that monastic city. Such an atrocity could hardly fail to lead to a flight to Ireland of most of those remaining in the British Church committed to learning, scholarship and training for Christian mission.

What has been proposed here seems borne out. The missionary activity of those British nearest to Ireland–the Cornish and the Welsh–appears to have ended by the middle of the sixth century. The shift in numbers in those years from Britain to Cornwall and Brittany is simple evidence of migration. It marks the flight of thousands of Christians because of Saxon aggression as well as the appearance in Britain of the first of two epidemics of bubonic plague that would take the lives of half of Europe's population.

One more suggestion in support of this proposal concerns a belief held by some about artistic genius latent among the Celts. It came to mind when archaeologists discovered a treasure-trove of Celtic art near LaTene in Switzerland dating back to 600 B.C. In elegance and craftsmanship, the LaTene ware matched the Church art produced in Ireland during the Dark Ages and Early Medieval years. Because of the connection, Gaelic art is described by some as a classic example of genius gone underground and resurfacing in a later age. Yet to attribute to Irish Gaels the work done at LaTene is a false linkage. It was the Brythonic Celts rather than Goidelic who produced the art of LaTene; the Brythonic settled in Great and Lesser Britain. Those who produced the Book of Kells and the Cross of Monasterboice almost surely were Goidelic. They were descended from the ancients who came to Ireland by way of the Mediterranean and Spain rather than through the Alps.

That being so, the genes involved at Monasterboice and Kells were Gaelic while the requirement of perfection that passed from man to man (whether father to son or monk to monk) was Brythonic, coming from those Welsh teachers. Only they would have brought to bear the techniques and artistry passed from one generation to another and necessary to that Irish work. Because of the "combat fatigue" present in the Welsh, they could have lost the *elan* needed for such creativity. But they provided the necessary linkage. The Irish brought the nature and the Welsh the nurture. Together they created consummate religious art that has been a joy to God and man.

Chivalric Champion for a Darkening World

It is understandable that the greatest age of the Christian Faith would commence after the barbarians had been won to Christ. To reach this we must turn from the sixth Century–when the Darkness settled in–to the Twelfth, when it ended. It was not until then that Celts would recover a long-lost recollection–while Franks and Germans would obtain knowledge of a world they never knew. The means for obtaining that knowledge would be the First Crusade–for whose participants the travel, sights, experiences and adventure were an education for men already-veteran and thirsting for knowledge to take home The Crusaders' contact with Greeks and Arabs enabled them to bring home books, manuscripts, drawings, notes, recall of tools, techniques and invention sufficient for a lifetime of studies and teaching. They brought enough information about the Ancient World for a New World to be built upon the foundations of the Old.

The literature of the Medieval World was steeped in heroic legend. It was clothed in the ideology, custom, manners, dress, weaponry and drama of the period even though the figures they idealized came from a remote and different past. The medieval age summed up man's awareness of things pertaining to a divinely ordered cosmos. Such culture can only exist when the strong are inclined by grace and training to protect the weak–when courtesy, honor and valor become the hallmark of an elite who set examples for all and any others. If there are no paladins of the age, its bards must retrieve from the past the best that have been known. For chivalric perfection among their contemporaries, the Crusaders could find none greater than Saladin. Though he was a princely foe and a Muslim, he served as a kind of blueprint of the type they sought. If none of their own generation bore emulation, the French could look back to a Charlemagne or a Roland, the Germans to a Siegfried.

Fortunately for the British, men everywhere looked to Arthur. His appeal spread so widely that he became—and to this day remains—*the* heroic example for the Age of Chivalry. Yet the man of legend must be one of history as well, and it troubles the intellect that the pages of Arthurian literature while overflowing, are matched by so little that is suitably historic.

The "real Arthur" appears actually to have been two historic persons. Each bore that name and were kings of Britain, one descended from the other. It took romantic imagination to make them one, for they were separated by six generations. The first, who died in AD 388 and was the son of the Uther Pendragon, who is Arthur's father in the legend, was a conqueror of much of western Europe and briefly of Rome. His grandfather was Magnus Maximus, a Briton who for a time was Emperor of the West.

The Arthur of our concern was the greater by far, though his existence is found only in snippets of record and tradition. Taken together they give a dependable picture even if unclear in particulars. What points to him as Heroic Warrior on the enemies' part is a sequence of silent years in the Anglo-Saxon Chronicle, which the chroniclers have labored to explain away. Their failure to speak of Arthur is consistent with the Egyptians' unwillingness to acknowledge Moses—and with those empty pages describing thirty consecutive years of Rome's "military governance" of Britain. With the Saxons' oblique admission added to the records we have, we can judge Arthur's reign to have begun around AD 542 ending with his death in AD 570. Our most reliable source for this is the Church herself, involving figures we have noted in *The Book of Saints*. Arthur was a first cousin of King Brechan of Brecknock (one generation removed). Illtyd was a brother-in-law who, prior to his conversion, had been one of Arthur's knights. Cadoc was his cousin and fearless critic, Samson his nephew, David a cousin of his father, Meurig or Maurice. The historian Gildas writes of having met with Arthur when the king asked to be reconciled with him after killing Gildas' older brother Hueil in a battle brought on by that brother's rebellion. Lastly is Edeyrn, one of Arthur's knights who in old age became a hermit in Brittany.

Historians tell of twelve fierce battles fought by Arthur and his Britons against the Saxons, ranging from Siluria to Edinburgh. The last and fiercest involved three days' hand-to-hand fighting at Mount Badon. There the Saxons sustained such terrible losses that there was no further aggression for a generation following Arthur's death. Only in the Battle at Camlan is there an element of myth, though few question that it happened or that Arthur subsequently died at Glastonbury and was buried there.

There are two reasons why we must deal with the real Arthur. One is his achievement in suppressing the Saxon threat for many years. The other is his link to the British Church and the Isle of Avalon. When, years after Glastonbury Abbey's disastrous fire in 1184, the monks recovered the remains of Arthur and Guinevere from the burial ground, an occasion for disbelief was introduced. The Abbey still needed to be rebuilt. Because the recovery of Arthur's remains could be used as part of a fund-raising drive for that purpose, the monks were—centuries later—accused of exploiting what some believed in any case to be a fiction. Yet it is well known that Henry I ordered the recovery of these remains for the purpose of enshrining them before the high altar of the rebuilt Abbey. The evidence of authenticity is too convincing to be doubted. Centuries earlier, when St. Dunstan was Abbot, the level of the cemetery had been raised by twelve feet, yet the monks knew exactly where to dig. The coffin from which the monarchs' remains were recovered was a hollowed oak trunk buried eighteen feet below the ground level. It was sealed at both ends, and on its top was affixed a leaden plate identifying it as Arthur's. When the skeletons were clothed in silks by King Henry and Queen Eleanor prior to the 1278 dedication, it was noted that Guinevere had been small and delicate, her hair in golden ringlets. Arthur had been an enormous man–perhaps, like Charlemagne, as much as seven feet tall. His skull showed ten severe cranial wounds–nine of which had healed. Since Arthur died from wounds received in combat–and that battle itself an accompaniment of his betrayal–his death is in keeping with that prophesied for "the Celtic Sagittarius who is Arthur," whose horse and rider were, more than five thousand years ago, graven into the landscape of Glaston's ancient Zodiac as part of the Summer Land's terrain.

I am indebted for the following to a son whose word-puzzles trace Welsh roots in the English tongue and suggests there could have been many who, rather than flee, chose to remain on their land and take their chances with the Saxons. (More than likely these would be rural folk, like farmers, herders, woodsmen, miners, fishermen, hermits, recluses as well as some monastics.) We already know that members, all champions, of Arthur's Round Table, would have gone out singly as knights-errant, accompanied by no more than a squire and one or two servants–all noncombatant. Perhaps, as my son suggests, they went out, not primarily as Grail-seekers, but as chivalric combatants ready to lay their lives on the line on behalf of sufferers of injustice. The purpose would be to assure that Britons who remained and peacefully worked their land would be treated fairly and justly by the conquering Saxons.

The thought bears consideration. The concept of a champion is ageless and understood by all. The self-offering of one on behalf of many would be preferable to war-to-the-death of large armies for the settling of small differences where, given the opportunity, peace could be obtained. The idea of one-to-one combat by champions is found in several religions and among most peoples. In the Old Testament it is illustrated in a Goliath overthrown by a David. In the New Testament it is achieved on a cosmic scale with a Satanic Prince of Darkness being set at naught by a Prince of Peace who is an historic figure as well as divine.

Such conflict as existed between Britons (as displaced persons) and Saxons (as uneasy victors) would require that the champion's presence and harmlessness be known to all. Likewise must be known the conditions on which he would be willing to engage in mortal combat in the interests of justice. The responding Saxon combatant must likewise be a man of honor, trusted and acceptable to his people. His life–if he should lose it–could be deemed as requiring surrender of Saxon claims and a willingness to abide by God's will in determining the course of honor and obligation. It would be a matter of honor that the Britons' knight-errant have free passage and freedom from indignity pending combat with chosen champions of neighboring Saxon people.

Two additional observations remain about King Arthur. One is that those Welsh saints noted in connection with him included nearly all the founders of schools from whom the Irish obtained their training in the faith. The second is that Arthur's war against the Saxons– probably coming in the final years of his reign and after some years of "peacekeeping" by means of knight-errantry–meant as much to the Irish as to the Welsh. He kept the Saxons at bay during those years when the Irish were being taught the Christian faith and when Welsh and Irish scholars were preparing for the daughter church to become the base for Celtic scholarship and mission. As to those unknown knights-errant sent out earlier from Arthur's court, it could be said, as in 1940 Winston Churchill said of British fighter-pilots, "Never in the field of human conflict was so much owed by so many to so few." What the knights-errant did in the sixth century set the standard of chivalry for the entire Medieval world.

For those Irish and Anglo-Saxons who owed their conversion and training to British teachers it can be said that the Alleluia Victory was Act I, Scene 1 of their national conversion. Mount Badon and Camlan, followed by Arthur's death and burial, signify the lowering of the curtain. Arthur held the Saxons at bay while the Welsh evangelized the Irish. Almost immediately the Irish, via Iona, evangelized the Germans both in Britain and on the Continent. The English in turn evangelized the Frisians, the Germans, the Danes and the Vikings in their homelands as well as in lives laid down in Britain before the onslaughts of these not-yet-Christian peoples.

ৎ৩   Chapter 15   ৎ৩

Looking Back at Whitby

Our first retrospective is that of British bishops being asked to
meet with Augustine and a few of his monks from Canterbury.
Arriving in AD 597, they were received by the Bretwalda
(High King) of the Jutes and baptized that king, Ethelbert, and many
of his people. Augustine had been consecrated bishop in the following
year and in AD 603 requested a parley with the British bishops who
acknowledged the need, for the Saxon aggression had already forced
the Archbishop of London to make Gloucester his See city, while
Caerleon transferred, first to Llandaff and then to St. David's. They
met on the banks of the Severn later referred to as Augustine's Oak.
Augustine asked that they join him in brotherly relations in the unity
of the Catholic faith and to work together in preaching the Gospel
to the heathen. It was a commendable start, but differences became
apparent and increasingly so, till there seemed little reason to continue.
Augustine proposed to close the meeting by having everyone pray for a
miracle that could be a sign from heaven as to which party had God's
blessing. Bede describes a miracle wrought at that time by Augustine,

the healing of a blind man in his company. The British acknowledged the miracle but could see no way across the impasse between two such differing churches. They did, however, request that the talks be resumed.

At their second meeting seven British bishops were in attendance, with them Abbot Dunawd of Bangor-ap-Dee and several of his monks. While en route, they consulted a hermit known for his wisdom, asking whether they should submit to demands made upon them. The response was, "If he be a man of God, take his advice." But how, they asked, would they know if he were a man of God? The hermit said, "Our Lord says, 'Take my yoke upon you and learn of me, for I am meek and lowly of heart.' Therefore if Augustine is meek and lowly in heart, it shows that he bears the yoke of Christ himself, and offers it to you. But if he is haughty and unbending, then he is not a man of God, and we should not listen to him." To which the bishops replied, "But how can we know even this?" The hermit's suggestion was, "Arrange that he and his followers arrive first at the place appointed for the conference. If he arises courteously as you approach, rest assured that he is the servant of Christ, and do as he asks. But if he ignores you and does not rise, then, since you are in the majority, do not comply with his demands."[1]

When the Britons arrived at the chosen place they found many in attendance. The archbishop was seated and remained so as they approached. While we have no record of the manner of his greeting, the substance of his address is quoted in Bede's *A History of the English Church and People*[2], "In many ways you act contrary to our customs, and indeed to those of the universal Church; yet if you will obey me in these three things—to celebrate Easter at the proper time, to perform the Office of Baptism, in which we are born again to God; according to the custom of the Holy Roman Church, and join with us in preaching the Word of God to the English nation; we will tolerate all your other customs though contrary to our own."

There must have been other demands and disagreements, however, because of the tone of Abbot Dunawd's parting statement* on the bishops' behalf, "Be it known to you, without any ambiguity, that we all and singly are obedient to the Bishop of Rome and to every true and

---

*copied from an ancient British manuscript by Sir Henry Spelman.

devout Christian, to love each in his own order with perfect charity, and to aid them all to become children of God in word and deed. And I know not of any other obedience than this due to him whom ye style Pope, nor that he had a claim and right to be Father of fathers. And the aforesaid obedience we are ready to yield at once to him and to every Christian. Further, we are under the jurisdiction of the Bishop of Caerleon-upon-Usk, appointed to oversee us, and to make us keep the spiritual path."*

Bede ends his account of the meeting by saying, "...the bishops refused [his proposals], nor would they recognize Augustine as their archbishop, saying among themselves that if he would not arise to greet them in the first instance, he would have even less regard for them once they submitted to his authority. Whereupon Augustine, that man of God, is said to have answered with a threat that was also a prophecy; if they refused to accept peace with fellow-Christians, they would be forced to accept war at the hands of enemies; and if they refused to preach to the English the way of life, they would eventually suffer at their hands the penalty of death. *And by divine judgment, all these things happened as Augustine had foretold.*" The emphasis is ours, because in the following paragraph Bede describes the frightful slaughter of Dunawd's monks at the Battle of Chester.[3] He also treats what happened at Chester as God's punishment of the British Church for its bishops' rejection of the papal invitation.[4] The British appear to have viewed the matter in an entirely different light. Morgan, in his *History of Britain*, repeats what apparently was an old accusation,[5] "Augustine found means...to execute his threat. At his persuasions, Ethelbert instigated Edelfrith, the pagan king of Northumbria, to invade the territories of Brochwel, Prince of Powys, who had supported Dunawd and the Bishops in their rejection of the Papal claims." He then describes how Ethelfrith ordered his army to kill the British monks and destroy their monastery.[6] Morgan continues, "Thus was fulfilled, exclaims the pious Bede, the prediction of the blessed Augustine, the prophet being in fact the perpetrator." He goes on to tell how, a short time later, Brochwel's

* It seems not to have occurred to the bishops that they could mention two specifics in the nation's Constitution. One was this, "The nation is above the king," the implication being that the Church can be thought to be above the pope. The other, "There are three things that require the unanimous vote of the nation to effect,–the deposition of the sovereign–the introduction of novelties in religion–suspension of law." A case could have been made that the subordination of the Celtic to the Roman Church would require not only the approval of archbishop and bishops, but the unanimous vote of the nation.

strengthened forces attacked Ethelfrith's army and routed it, wounding the Anglian king and causing the loss of ten thousand of his men. As they returned from their victory, Morgan concludes the sorry saga, "the British army...halted at the scene of devastation at Bangor; the ashes of the noble monastery were still smoking–its libraries, the collection of ages, were consumed–half-ruined walls, gates, and smouldering rubbish were all that remained of its magnificent edifices, and these were everywhere crimsoned with the blood and interspersed with the bodies of priests, students and choristers. The scene left a quenchless desire for further vengeance on the minds of the Kymric soldiery."[7]

If Morgan's charge is indeed a part of the ancient tradition, we are left with a serious problem concerning Augustine. We already know him to be timid enough to have sent word back to Gregory asking permission to return before they got near the Channel. We know him to have been indecisive, asking questions of Gregory both by messenger and in correspondence for whose triviality and lack of gravitas he got a scolding. But we are faced with a British claim that Augustine asked for and obtained the destruction of Dunawd's Abbey and the murder of one thousand one hundred of his monks. It is a shocking and very real possibility. If we can work our way around some curious phrasing in Bede's remarks following Dunawd's summary, we may be able to give Augustine the benefit of the doubt. After describing what may or may not have been meant as a threat, Bede immediately follows with an explanation of how it was fulfilled. In dating the battle and massacre Bede speaks of them as taking place *"some while after"* Augustine made the threat. He ends the paragraph describing the bloodletting by saying, "Thus, *long after his death*, was fulfilled Bishop Augustine's prophecy that the faithless Britons, who had rejected the offer of eternal salvation, would incur the punishment of temporal destruction." I have emphasized two phrases as curious, considering that Augustine is thought to have died within a year of these talks and that the massacre may have taken place soon afterward. There are reasons to discount what Morgan reported and the Britons are said to have believed; they give Augustine, a conscientious priest and bishop, the benefit of the doubt. Augustine's death is dated by no one later than AD 609, while the Battle of Chester is described by many as taking place between AD 613 and AD 617. This tends to relieve Augustine from the charge of planning or encouraging that slaughter. Yet we can point to one error that may have been linked with a desire to moderate the stigma associated with that event. The "battle" at which the massacre took place was nowhere near the city of Chester, from which it received its name, nor could it possibly be called a battle. It occurred at a village four miles beyond the modern Wrexham–still called by its ancient name of Bangor-ap-Dee.

History Retold: a British View of the Gregorian Mission

If we look at the Christian Church in Britain and Ireland, we see no evidence of hierarchical ordering or planning beyond what has been described in this volume. Each became a national Church in the shortest time span we know of, and had its origin in a direct and unmediated act of God involving one or very few who were chosen and called to his service with the Apostolate coming at or near the start. Each was autonomous regarding sacerdotal authority, functioning independently of all others. Each followed a set of rules common to the Holy Catholic Church as to doctrine, discipline, worship, order, ethics and personal behavior. These had been given by God in historic action and preserved in Holy Writ. Except for those in which some variableness could exist (i.e., in discipline and worship) they were in themselves a sufficiency for all times and places. The older British Church was distant from most others but at no distance in essentials. What had been true of the British Church would be as true of the Irish as it was of a Gallican Church founded at the same time and under the same circumstances as the British.

Despite the primacy of this Celtic Church, a branch not native to Britain was planted without the approval of its bishops and in disregard of rules laid down in the first Four General Councils. This alien branch had become nearly defunct when the Council of Whitby was summoned sixty-seven years later. Yet it was chosen by one of seven monarchs of the Saxon Heptarchy to be his kingdom's church.

This is the story of Augustine, whose line died out a few weeks after the Council of Whitby, leaving England without an episcopal presence until the arrival of Theodore of Tarsus four years later. Though the presence of the second mission was as irregular and unlawful as the first, the Saxons remained in Britain as did the Canterbury Church as an affiliate of the Roman. However, since ours is a record of the Celtic Church and since that body has never been without its visible, viable and audible adherents–in its faith and practice a true and ancient branch of the Holy Catholic Church–it is reasonable that the record be published as some parts of it may not have been brought to light before.

Gregory the Great as Bishop, Metropolitan and Pope

We are told that the term "pope" was not applied to the Bishops of Rome till the time of Boniface III, the second successor to Gregory the Great. The title had earlier been offered to Gregory by the Emperor Phocas I, when he was excommunicated by the Eastern Orthodox Church, both being aware that the Patriarch of Constantinople was styling himself in that manner. Gregory, however, declined the title and the authority it implied, writing to fellow Patriarchs in the East advising against the granting of papacy (i.e., supremacy) at any time and for any reason. He begged that the form of the Church's polity be continued as it had existed from the beginning. This polity was one of primacy, under which the bishop holding the highest office would be, as it were, the eldest among brothers. A polity involving papacy would require the chief bishop to be, in effect, a father rather than an elder brother. To accept such a change would invite and confer, a radical enlarging of authority, bestowing supremacy rather than primacy to one Bishop Over All. The duty of other archbishops and bishops would require obedience to this Holy Father rather than respect and deference to a Primate who, to his fellow bishops, remained an older brother.

Despite Gregory's commitment to primacy, he undoubtedly overstepped the bounds of law and custom when he sent a Canterbury Mission without the knowledge and approval of bishops known to be in Britain. He had already expressed himself on the authority of the Four General Councils in force since AD 431,[8] "I acknowledge myself as holding the same reverence for the Four Councils as I do the Four Gospels of the New Testament." Yet this did not hinder him from acting in violation of Canon VIII of the Third General Council held in Ephesus, which declared, "None of the God-beloved Bishops shall assume control of any province which has not heretofore, from the very beginning, been under his own hand or that of his predecessors. If anyone has violently taken and subjected (a Province) he shall give it up."[9] Gregory must have known of the existence of the British Church. Yet he gave to Augustine, while still a priest, authority to place such churches and bishops as he found in Britain under his authority and that of the Roman See.

Termination of the Gregorian Mission

The story of the Gregorian Mission, begun in AD 597, was one of initial success, then flowering, decline and cessation. Its initial acceptance came from King Ethelbert of the Jutes in Kent and from Bertha his Queen, who was a Gallic Christian. The flowering came with the marriage of their daughter Ethelburga to King Edwin of Northumbria, who himself became a Christian and consented for his Queen's chaplain, Paulinus to become Archbishop of York and continued when Augustine ordained one of his Italian band to be bishop of the East Saxons–though he had to be replaced with a Gallican . In later years, when two Gallicans volunteered their services, Canterbury's fifth Archbishop, Honorius, sent one as bishop to the East Anglians and the other to the West Saxons. Their ministry continued with the addition of a Scot[1] as assistant bishop in East Anglia and of two more Gallicans in that capacity in Wessex. Though consecrated in the Roman line, all the Gallicans had been disciples of Columbanus in the Celtic Church.

The decline began when Edwin of Northumbria was killed in a battle with Penda of Mercia, a powerful enemy of the English Church. Edwin's queen returned to Kent with her chaplain the archbishop, the

East Anglians' suffragan who was transferred to France while his Gallic diocesan was yet alive, serving there with distinction. However, those in Wessex failed to hold their own. Both of the Gallican suffragans were expelled, and after their bishop died a falling away ensued. It was the same in East Anglia with that bishop's demise. An anxious flight to the Continent by two who would later be archbishops of Canterbury pointed to the frailty of the Kentish Mission. That people's return to paganism had begun with the disavowal of Christ by Ethelbert's son[1] on his accession to the throne. Fortunately he changed his mind after some years and became a supporter if not an enthusiastic patron.

By AD 660 the reversion to paganism was widespread. Six of the seven kingdoms in the new Heptarchy had been evangelized by the Canterbury Mission. Yet in the entire Roman Province there was only one bishop in good standing, the Archbishop of Canterbury, the last to continue in the Italian line. Several of the kingdoms in the Heptarchy were, at that time, without a Christian king as sponsor for the faith. One of the expelled bishops of Wessex, Wini who, after being driven out by his people, had persuaded the Mercian king to sell him the bishopric of London,* remained in the Canterbury Province, but under charge of simony. During the archbishop's remaining four years no bishops were added to the Canterbury jurisdiction. Of abbots or other clergy, little is known, nor is there record as to whether Archbishop Deusdedit even knew of the Synod of Whitby.

Whitby and its Aftermath

Since the real vitality in Early England's Christian ministry came from the Irish/Scottish branch of the Celtic Church, we may set this fact aside for the moment and attend not only to what happened at the Synod, but what led up to it and what came in its aftermath. While the Celtic and Roman parties were represented, there were only a few whose voice and presence were significant. The principal figures were Oswy of Bernicia, his son Alchfrith King of Deira, and Wilfrid, an intimate of the son and adviser to both. Wilfrid had briefly been a

---

*Little more is known of Wini than his assisting Aidan at Cedd's consecration and years later being a consecrator at Chad's. He may have come from France for the Synod and Chad's consecration, living there to avoid punishment for his misdeeds.

novice at Lindisfarne, but after years of travel and study in Italy and France, had become a zealous protagonist of the Roman Church and its Benedictine order. All three men were ambitious, unscrupulous and occupied with private designs and personal reward. Oswy's father had been the infamous Ethelfrith, who had massacred so many monks at the "Battle of Chester." Ethelfrith was succeeded by his cousin Edwin, who, while monarch of Northumbria, had his capital in Deire at York. Oswy's immediate predecessor was his brother, the holy martyr St. Oswald who while reigning at Bamborough in Bernicia, brought St. Aidan to the nearby Isle of Lindisfarne, creating a second Iona for the conversion of his people. Oswald's reign was short, for after seven years he, like Edwin, was killed in battle with Mercia's Penda. Oswald's heirs divided the rule of Northumbria's double kingdom with Oswy becoming King of Bernicia and his cousin Oswin the King of Deira. Both kingdoms (as well as others nearby) were evangelized by monks of Lindisfarne under its Bishop and Abbot, St. Aidan. After Oswin's death in AD 651, Oswy seized control of Deira, so that like his father Ethelfrith and his brother St. Oswald, he served as King of Northumbria and ruler of both kingdoms.

Three years later, when Oswy's forces defeated Penda's and took that king's life, Oswy became Bretwalda of all England. During the decade leading to Whitby he used his bretwaldaship and patronage of Lindisfarne to encourage and support neighboring kings in the evangelizing of their kingdoms. While Aidan was still at Lindisfarne, he and Oswy persuaded the East Saxons' king and council to ask for Cedd's consecration as their bishop. After Aidan's death his successor Finan joined Oswy in persuading Mercia's King Peada (a convert of Cedd's) to ask for the consecration of Diuma, a Scottish monk of Lindisfarne, as Mercia's bishop. The conversion of England had become Oswy's high purpose and he was uniquely in a position to achieve it.

Unfortunately, Oswy did not have Constantine's character. Nor did his son Alchfrith, nor their counselor St. Wilfrid. When Oswy brought his army to unseat his cousin, Oswin disbanded his small force, sent them home and took private refuge in a place known only to his nearest friend. That man betrayed him and Oswin was put to death by an assassin sent by Oswy. When the scandal had abated, Oswy installed his son Alchfrith on Deira's throne, with his capital in old Roman York where Edwin's had been. As king in his own right, Alchfrith gave Wilfrid the land and buildings for Ripon Abbey. He sent to France for Agilbert, the ex-suffragan of Wessex, and on his arrival had him ordain Wilfrid as priest and Abbot of Ripon.

Bede tells us that twelve days after St. Oswin's assassination Aidan died from age and grief at the death of this king to whom he had been utterly devoted. Since this happened in AD 651, it is unlikely that Wilfrid was in the picture. But the mantle of power that came to Oswy on the death of Penda, and the uses to which saints as well as sinners could be put by one in high authority, seem to point to a Whitby of the flesh rather than a Whitby of the Spirit.

A Racial Attribute of the Celts: Neither to Rule nor be Ruled

Based on earlier evidence, we have already noted the Celts' lack of interest in building empires and ruling other peoples. While the German characteristic of ambition-to-rule (shared with other continental peoples) may be seen in what preceded Whitby and what followed, we should note an important difference–ignored by the Synod and only dealt with later by the Roman Church. It was the way in which the Iona clergy seems to have been taken advantage of by the English Church. In Ireland, the abbots had administered and ruled–with the bishops as necessary-but-subordinate functionaries. In England those bishops asked for and received from Iona continued to be in a subordinate situation, but to kings instead of abbots. There was a big difference here, for while we have no evidence that those bishops were less than holy men, the situation was one for *The Screwtape Letters*. The bishops for at least the remainder of the Augustinian period would be under pressure to be "house bishops" to kings instead of abbots. The exception that failed to improve their rule would continue at least until the coming of a wiser and more pragmatic Theodore. What "worked" earlier between Aidan and Oswald–and did so later between Aidan and Oswin–could hardly have worked between two such different men as

Aidan and Oswy. That fact–in addition to lengthy absences on Aidan's part in Deira and elsewhere–could have exacerbated a jealousy that led to Oswin's murder.

What Happened During and After Whitby

The key figures at Whitby were Oswy, as convener; his son Alchfrith, King of Deira and Wilfrid, the Abbot of Ripon, who was an intimate of Alchfrith and adviser to both. Of the Celts attending, the leader was Bishop Colman of Lindisfarne, who had doubtless been Oswy's house-bishop in succession to Aidan and Finan. With him were Cedd, Chad, Cuthbert, Tuda, the resident Abbess Hilda and well over thirty abbots, bishops and monks. Besides Wilfrid, the only clergy representing the Roman Church were James the Deacon from York; Romanus, a priest of Kent serving as chaplain to Eanfled, (Oswy's queen); and Agatho, another Kentish priest. The sole bishop of Rome's ordering was Agilbert, the exiled suffragan of Winchester brought back from France for the occasion. James, Romanus and Agatho seem to have had no part in discussions. Agilbert, despite his years among the West Saxons, was still unable to speak English. When invited to address the Synod, he asked permission for Wilfrid to do so on his behalf. Although later he was one of Wilfrid's consecrators, here at Whitby he was no more than a useful presence.

As is well known, the Roman cause won the day. Although little progress was made with the divisive matters of the date of Easter and tonsures used by monks and clergy, Oswy next asked for debate and discussion on the real choice before them–which of two churches should be established among the English people. As Bretwalda, the choice would be Osby's, and he chose the Church of Rome even though custom and sentiment were markedly in favor of the Celts. For generations this preference persisted. Yet even with indications of a staged performance, the Whitby Synod became a landmark for the English Church.

Few benefits came, however, to the three who set the stage and guided the performance at Whitby. In a matter of weeks Oswy's son

Alchfrith died of the plague as did Archbishop Deusdedit, whose death brought Augustine's line and the Gregorian Mission to a close; Cedd of Mercia; and Tuda, who, following Colman's resignation and departure, became Bishop of Lindisfarne for a few weeks. It would be four years before Theodore of Tarsus was sent from Rome to install a new regime at Canterbury and even longer for Eata to be installed as Tuda's successor at Lindisfarne.

For Wilfrid the timing seemed right, though a case can be made that his every action was wrong. Unsatisfied with the validity of Celtic ordering, he obtained Oswy's permission to be consecrated by Gallicans in France. Yet there were differences between the two men that must have been unexplored, for their views of the episcopate were in conflict and unresolved. Oswy seems to have anticipated that Wilfrid would be his house-bishop, taking the place of Bishop Colman and under obligation to Oswy (even as in Ireland bishops had been under obedience to their abbots). Wilfrid could hardly be unaware of the difference, for he was in this respect less than observant toward the Roman model. In fact, on several occasions in later years he consecrated house-bishops on the Continent for service to Christian rulers. He seems to have been aware, however, that there could be no consecrations either in the Gallican or the Roman Church without specific naming of the posts for which ordinands were being consecrated. The evidence seems to be that Alchfrith as King of Deira issued a writ of election "to whom (in France) it may concern" asking consecration of Wilfrid as Archbishop of York. It may well be in addition that Oswy as King of Northumbria issued (or thought he was issuing) a writ of election for Wilfrid as Bishop of Lindisfarne. The evidence that this was Oswy's intent can be demonstrated in his having had Chad consecrated Archbishop of York while Wilfrid was still out of the country. It can be demonstrated also in his anger upon learning, on Wilfrid's return, that his candidate for house-bishop had been consecrated Archbishop of York rather than Bishop of Lindisfarne.

We can only guess that this is what created the mixup, for although Oswy died in AD 670, Wilfrid's insistence on being installed at York became a source of trouble for monarchs, archbishops and popes for the next eighteen years, leading on one occasion to lengthy imprisonment. On another it brought such a long banishment that Wilfrid was able single-handedly to convert Sussex, the last of the pagan Saxon kingdoms which had been ignored for more than half a century by the mission at nearby Kent. But Wilfrid finally got his way and was forced on reluctant kings and bishops as the Third Archbishop of York.

Iona's Ministry to the Heptarchy, Requested by its Monarchs

By contrast with the Roman Mission, there had been no lack of growth in Columba's mission at Iona. Initially the mission had been intended for the Picts and newly arriving Scots. After AD 634 Iona provided a ministry to all who sought it—especially to monarchs and councils of the Saxon Heptarchy. Beginning with Oswald's request in that year, the monks of Iona did for the English what for thirty years Canterbury had been unable to attempt. Aidan's Abbey at Lindisfarne became, in short order, the spiritual center of the English Church. By the time of Whitby, thirty more years passed, and nearly all the Saxon clergy had been trained in the Celtic manner. Thus, it took Wilfrid's zealotry and Oswy's ambition for the English Church to emphasize its Roman rather than its Celtic roots. Yet even with Rome as the Western Church's active center, Lindisfarne and its daughter abbey Melrose became the Church of England's heart—the soil where the Church took root and grew. The two strains of churchly existence—the Celtic for holiness of life and the Roman for efficiency of administration—were joined in what would prove for centuries to be a singularly fruitful way.

Considering that five of the seven kingdoms of the Heptarchy had their consecrations from Celtic bishops and their training from the Celtic Church, it may be fair to hold that Aidan of Iona was the Apostle to the Angles and Saxons while Augustine of Canterbury was Apostle to the Jutes. No one but Theodore of Tarsus, by his achievements, could rightly be called Apostle to the English.

It must be remembered too that several of those Celtic saints so admired by Bede were themselves Saxons. All were sorrowful at the outcome of Whitby, including Hilda, Edwin's niece, who conformed to the new rule, yet was hostile to Wilfrid's doings from beginning to end as were Cedd, Chad and Cuthbert. Yet four years later, when Theodore came to Canterbury, all but Cedd (who had died) subordinated themselves to Theodore's obedience. They were shining examples of gracious humility for all to see and note.

Of those Celtic churchmen who returned from Whitby to Iona, at least thirty were Anglian or Saxon, preferring the old form of religion to the new. Colman and Eata went on to Ireland, perhaps in the knowledge that sooner or later Iona must conform to Roman custom. In the west, at Mayo, they founded a training college for English ordinands who wished to be schooled in Celtic faith and order. In its charge they placed a young Saxon whom they had taught and trained. *The Book of Saints* says of this young man, St. Gerald the Abbot, that in the course of his life at Mayo he trained, for the sacred priesthood, more than a hundred English saints. Measuring that against the book's tabulations, Gerald's influence on the English Church must have been enormous, for in the remaining three hundred thirty-five years of the first Christian millennium, there is a record of only one hundred ninety-nine described as English saints.

Waxing Saxon, Waning Celt

The interest people have in things Celtic has never been more evident than today. Bagpipes, ballads, kilts, tartans, torques, shillelaghs, shamrocks, even songs of love and longing, all "belong," as do the honoring of Saint Patrick and wearing of the green. Considering the delight in these things, it may come as a surprise that the Celts are regarded by some demographers as threatened if not endangered. A recent survey suggests that the Celts may have been dwindling in numbers since before the time of Christ.[1] During the first millenium BC they occupied most of northern Europe. By the third century AD their habitation had narrowed to the British Isles, northern Gaul, central Spain and Galatia in Asia Minor. By the end of the Dark Ages they had ceased to predominate anywhere but Ireland, Scotland and Wales. There also remained a Celtiberian populace in parts of Spain.

It is unlikely the Celts are truly threatened. There has been more creativity, vitality and resilience among them than any people we know of save perhaps the Jews. If we reflect on why–or whether–the Celts may have become fewer and weaker, it should be evident in the history we have been considering. The early Christians of Mediterranean lands became an instant minority. Millions were put to death for acknowledging Christ as Lord. Except in Gaul where, at Lyons and under the personal direction of Septimius Severus,[2] "nineteen thousand Christians not counting women and children" were martyred in three days, Celts tended to be spared persecution by their distance from the scene.

Other factors led to the Celts' reduction. First was the determination of Imperial Rome to wipe out the Druids and make Britain a source for marketable slaves. Their invasion took hundreds of thousands of British lives. But the Britons kept their freedom and by the war's end a great many of those still alive had been won to Christ. We may note that, as Rome's aggression brought a readiness to die for God and country, so did a peace won so dearly bring Britons to take the Gospel to peoples not yet in servitude to Rome. The Celts had been famed for their love of freedom. This seems to have been the chief reason why they had no aspiration to rule others. It is noteworthy that so great and proud a nation could find its highest freedom in obedience to the Risen Lord.

We already know that AD 86 through AD 116 were years in which a resurgent Britain, not occupied by the Roman, was free to evangelize—with its sister Church in Gaul—those parts of northern Europe where Christ was still unknown. From records already mentioned, including hundreds of saints described in the Roman Church's own handbook, we are able to show the validity of this claim and the efficacy of those labors. As already pointed out, the British Church's overseas missionary work began in the middle of the first century AD. Long after the Roman legions were withdrawn in AD 410 that missionary fervor was still there and would not be diminished until the Anglians', Saxons' and Jutes' invasions drove Britons off their homelands beginning in AD 430, when the British had their Alleluia Victory over Saxons and Picts, won without force of arms. Yet if the way to the Continent was now blocked by a Saxon presence, the path to the mainland via Ireland was not. In two years St. Patrick would begin his mission among an

Irish people already ripe to the harvest.

As to the coming wars in which the Celts suffered, we must note the difference in character. The sixth century Britons were not called to a patriotic *and* religious war, as was the case when Rome was bent on stamping out Druidism and nascent Christianity. The invading German tribesmen were more bent on seizing Britain's agricultural domain than in killing Britain's people. The chivalrous manner of the Celts' defense and their adjustment to the outcome left their mark on the invaders. If the Celts' new faith enabled those few who clung to their land to live without rancorous disputes with the uninvited neighbors, the simplicity and wholesomeness of their lives helped with the ultimate conversion of Franks, Saxons, Danes and Vikings as well as Normans. All would in time acknowledge the Celtic way of thinking and worship, whether in Gaul or in the British Isles.

There was another benefit from the Celts' missionary endeavors which continued long after the Germanic tribes were converted. The scope and generosity of Celtic missions allowed Christian peoples of distant lands to take their turn in becoming buffer states. With that protection the whole of Western Christendom was set free from the law of vengeance which, from man's beginnings had brought an unceasing dependence on violence and death.

Responding to the love revealed in Christ, Christian peoples and monarchs turned away from vengefulness, inspired by the Celts, who had the largest burden of suffering and forgiving as successive hordes of heathens came their way. The will, for Jesus' sake, to live in peace with one's neighbors was an essential in the leaven of forgiveness and reconciliation. This was hard for the natural man to accept, either in practice or beholding it in others. But it was God's way. Because men found it to be the only path to peace and righteous living, they sought and were given the grace to effect it. The idea of Christian rule on earth–a Christendom whose influence extended throughout the world–came into being. As a theme with variations, it has been sustained for nearly two thousand years.

Social Teachings of the Druids

One feature would distinguish the British and Irish Celts even when usurping kings pressed a foreign Church upon them as replacement for their own. Their social teachings, learned from the Druids, allowed every citizen to be entrusted with personal freedom and responsibility upon proof of his ability to use that freedom in conformity with custom and expectation. As a people, the Celts never forgot the principle, and its usage has long since spread through the English speaking world. But its surrender was, for many years, forced upon the British and Iona-Irish by the circumstances of Whitby and what followed. The Roman Church's accession was concluded with the thinnest of pretexts by a monarch who had licensed the murder of Christian kings and was advised by a turncoat son and a self-important cleric ordained through his own devices. The latter was an ardent Romanizer who would not be bound by the Roman Church's own rules and, until his demise, was an embarrassment to Canterbury's archbishops and perhaps to Rome's.

The Council of Whitby and the steps it traced appear to have been undertaken without knowledge of or endorsement by authorities at Canterbury or Rome. Moreover, it came at a time when the Saxon Church included no more than a small percentage of Britain's total Christian population. Given that the British Church was native to the island and by many centuries the senior body, the Council can be said to have been illicit and its actions unwarranted. Yet it must be acknowledged that, even if irregular and unjust, the Synod was carried off successfully. What authority it lacked at the moment, the Canterbury Mission was at length, with Rome's support and local acquiescence, able to obtain.

Vindication of the Celtic Way

However, if the Divine Law is self-enforcing in spiritual as well as physical contexts, the Celtic Church must have been vindicated over the long run. Though its people acquiesced with mixed grace to hierarchs' and kings' presumptions, they eventually became spiritual masters of those they served. During the centuries when lip-service was paid to unity and obedience, the Celtic agenda continued to be followed for the reason that it was so thoroughly and effectively ingrained. Considering the Celtic Church's reputation for holiness, the motivation is likely also to have been an insistence on truth and rectitude rather than accommodation, ignorance or envy. As an example, the ingraining of the Celts' concern for individual freedom and responsibility–taught from earliest times by Druid preceptors and confirmed by Christian teachers–made so much sense and was so widely practiced that, throughout the life of this monarchy already two thousand years old, it applied to kings as well as subjects. As with the Jews, the Celts' belief had been, "One God, one Law." It was a concept their ancestors had brought from Troy, whose first axiom was, "The country is above the king." Having received an understanding of Divine Law as a mandate that applied to all, the Celtic missionaries to the Continent were clothed with a magisterial authority for those in whose lands they had previously dwelt and to which they were returning with the Gospel. This was as true after Whitby as before.

Based on what has been stated here, the Celtic view of man and of what would one day be called "the social contract" would have been a novel view both for the Roman and the Eastern Churches. That it was not new to history will be shown in a later chapter. For the moment it suffices that we focus on the disordering of the Church in Britain by one of seven Saxon kings whose Christian subjects were–and for many centuries remained–a minority of the whole. The pagan character of his reign and the smaller numbers of Saxon Christians can be deduced from *The Book of Saints*' own records which provide convincing evidence that at no time before the Norman Conquest did the Celtic Church fail to exceed the English in size, even though the larger body was dominated by the smaller.

Though the following figures (Summary of Table 1) reflect only known saints of the three churches, they give a good idea of what these churches' respective proportions must have been. (There is no duplication here. Each who served as abbot *and* bishop is counted as one person.)

Summary of Table 1: Saints through Century of Norman Conquest:

Church	5th	6th	7th	8th	9th	10th	11th	Total
					Century			
British	70	141	65	19	10	5	7	317
Irish	57	107	101	36	7	6	4	318
Celtic	127	248	166	55	17	11	11	635
English Mission			78	76	26	24	17	221

By mid-6th Century, the Iona-Irish Church was present and active in all of Britain. Table 3 (Chapter 12) shows bishops and abbots of the three bodies, including all these years, to have numbered 128 British and 185 Irish, that is, 313 Celtic in all as compared to 95 Saxon-English.

Knowing what we do of the three bodies, and considering that the Synod of Whitby took place well before the end of the seventh century, we may reasonably conclude that, whether we consider respective numbers, scholarship, character of devotion, spirituality, missionary fervor or historic importance, the Celtic Church appears to have been a more significant body than the Saxon by any measurement or assessment and would remain the more significant until the Late Medieval years, by which time a considerable intermingling gave the English Church a character uniquely and distinctly its own.

While still able to make comparisons, let us call to mind the occasion when St. Augustine, after six years in Britain, invited British bishops to meet him with the hope of benefiting their Church. After an unresolved initial meeting, seven British bishops attended a second with Abbot Dunawd (Donald) as their spokesman. To what has been said of that meeting, we may add that the Celtic Church at that time (AD 603) had three archbishops in Britain and one in Ireland. To those in Ireland and the seven above referred to, we must add thirty additional British dioceses and bishops. By comparison, when Augustine left Rome for England he had authority to consecrate twelve bishops. Yet none had been consecrated by the time of this meeting. Before his death he would consecrate two, Mellitus and Justus. Each would in time succeed to the office of archbishop, and both came from Rome.

A Parallel on the Organic Nature of Growth in Unity

Travelers who have flown over the Mississippi River near St. Louis may have noted how the Missouri River flows into it north of the city. Prior to their confluence, the Mississippi's waters have been clear, while the Missouri, after crossing more than two thousand miles of prairie, has earned its name the Big Muddy. For two hundred miles, the two rivers flow side by side without seeming to mingle. Then they are joined by another clear river, the Ohio. Even from this point, for three hundred miles further, all the way to Memphis, Tennessee, the Missouri retains its distinction, hugging the western bank in such a way that its line of demarcation is still noticeable. Not until many miles below Memphis–after dozens of twists and turns, leaving a great many spun-off, landlocked ox-bow lakes–are the rivers visibly united. As "the Father of Waters" they become a vast, turgid flood whose load of prairie soil gives breadth and fertility to the Mississippi delta.

So it was with the Celtic and the Roman churches of the British Isles. The British and the Irish churches were formed at different times, but were one in character. The Roman church was foreign to both (as in "same tree, different branch"). Apart from official definition and sacerdotal validation, the joining of Roman with Celt would have been "in name only" even if Oswy and Alchfrith had been the most Christian of monarchs and Wilfrid and Agilbert the most humble and holy of saints. Our parable of two rivers seems apt in respect to time and natural processes anticipated in each church. The Mississippi's two distinctive waterways are not clearly one until they have traveled more than halfway to the Gulf of Mexico. Likewise the Celtic Church, the native and far larger body, though in a subordinate position at the managerial level was "unsubordinate" (i.e., itself) at the broader and more vital level (that is, for the sanctification of members) until many centuries had gone by. Granted the Celts of Iona adopted Rome's dating of Easter in AD 715. Granted that by AD 772 (108 years after Whitby) they accepted the authority of the Papacy. The conforming of Celtic to Roman–of one whole church to the other–was in most respects glacially slow. It can be held that the Celtic Church was still undigested–and the union therefore incomplete–by the onset of the Reformation. William the Conqueror, a Catholic monarch, refused to grant to the Papacy that which his Catholic predecessors (Celtic, Saxon, Dane and Viking) had not granted.When King John, out of fear for his throne, gave Pope Innocent III in fief the property and wealth of England plus what had been seized in Ireland, his barons demanded and got his signature on a Magna Carta whose first provision required that Ecclesia Anglicana remain forever free. A mark of the icy slowness of the Celtic Church's spiritual and organic unity with Rome–following the Norman Conquest–is the three hundred years it took before a Welsh diocese accepted a Norman as its bishop.

Waxing, Waning, Death, Rebirth

In AD 670 Britain was hit once again by an epidemic known to the Britons as *Dial Duw* and to later generations as the Black Plague. It seems to have been more moderate in Ireland. Its effect in Britain was most deadly south of the Humber. Here it was so virulent that whole counties were left without inhabitants, while many who survived the disease succumbed to famine or despair. Morgan quotes Henry of Huntington as saying that whole companies of men and women, crawling to the edge of cliffs above the sea, would throw themselves, hand in hand, into the waves below.[3] He adds by way of comment, "All distinction between Briton and Saxon was lost in this appalling state of things." It would be twelve years before the epidemic had run its course, and very little would remain. Fortunately the Celts in Ireland and Scotland and the northern counties recovered, maintaining a healthy and vigorous life until well after the Norman Conquest.

The End of the Ancient British Monarchy

The last of the British high kings, Cadwaladr Sanctus, came to the throne in AD 664, the year of Whitby. His father, Cadwallo had been a monarch whose career of violence dated from what, in the index of Morgan's, is styled "Augustine's Massacre of 1,200 British Clergy with destruction of their Books and Colleges." Cadwallo's father, Cadvan, had forced Ethelfrith to surrender the kingdom of Deire to his nephew Edwin, and, in another battle, brought Ethelfrith's defeat and death. As evidenced in the previous chapter, Cadwallo never relinquished his vengeful rage. Succeeding his father, Cadvan, in AD 628, he waged lifelong war against the Saxons. In the Battle of Hatfield Chase he brought death to Edwin and the flower of Anglo-Saxon nobility. Later he defeated the Mercian King Penda, sparing that monarch's life at the intercession of his sister Elditha, whom Cadwallo married after obtaining Penda's oath of lifelong allegiance and promise of the Saxon crown. Together Cadwallo the Celt and Penda the Saxon precipitated a reign of terror, fighting sixteen battles and putting down Anglo-Saxons with as much severity as had Arthur a hundred years earlier. Sorrowfully, they brought death to many of Cadwallo's own British kindred. At one point Cadwallo and Penda were defeated by the Saxon king, St. Oswald of Northumbria. In a later battle they killed him, nailing his body to a tree at a place first known as Oswald's Tree and later as Owestry. When Cadwallo became too old and infirm to fight, Penda continued their attacks on his own and with thirty of his principal leaders was killed in battle by the same Oswy who in the year of the Celt Cadwallo's death would preside at the Synod of Whitby.

Cadwaladr succeeded his father, Cadwallo, as king and Pendragon in that year. In his father's right he was the heir to the throne of Celtic Cambria, and in right of his mother Elditha (through Penda's promise to Cadwallo), he was heir to Saxon Mercia and Wessex. Earlier in life he is said to have desired the monastic life and for his piety was called "Sanctus" by his people. Coming to the monarchy as king equally of Britons and Saxons, Cadwaladr hoped to unite the two peoples in the years given him to reign. Perhaps because Penda's promise had been counter to the Saxon custom, Cadwaladr failed in this purpose. As a result, it was seven generations before the Celts under Howell the Good joined with the Saxons under Alfred the Great in a patriotic war to save their land from the Danes. Yet the worthiness of Cadwaladr's goal could have been seen in the very name ascribed to the plague. To call it *Dial Duw, Vengeance of God*, suggests that Celt and Saxon–along with others of man's sinful race–recognized that God can be the giver of punishment as well as love.

The last battle between Britons and Saxons came in AD 684, when the Britons of Strathclyde overthrew Egfrid of Northumbria in Forfarshire, leaving fifty thousand Anglian dead.[01] By that time Cadwaladr Sanctus had abdicated his throne* and retired to Rome, where his death in AD 689 brought the line of Cymric high kings to an end. Meanwhile the kingdoms of the Strathclyde Britons, the British Picts and the Scots of Ireland united as the Kingdom of Scotland. The highlands remained as before, occupied by the ancient British clans, who did not incorporate with the rest of Britain until 1745. Writing in AD 729, the Venerable Bede informed us that no further attempt had been made against the liberties of the Britons and that the Picts had recovered their territories while the power of the Angles continued to retrograde.

With this, Morgan's narrative comes to a close as anticipated by his title, *History of Britain from the Flood to AD 700*. But why that date? We know the (Celtic) Church of Ireland was still intact until 1565 when the Roman Church, in response to England's Reformation, instituted a line of bishops to replace that of Patrick. This action was taken after centuries of Norman-English domination of Ireland's Church and State. For their persistence, in 1921 the Irish got their Free State. In 1937 its name was changed to Eire.

In Scotland the record was altogether different. The Scots, as a Celtic people, had retained their Church and Celtic line of kings (collateral descendants of St. Columba). Malcolm III's queen was Margaret, a Saxon descended from Alfred the Great, who had been raised in the household of her uncle, the English King St. Edward the Confessor. Margaret, though by her subjects acknowledged in her lifetime to be a saint, was devoutly Roman Catholic. Because her husband predeceased her, she, in Celtic fashion, became the Sovereign.** Yet St. Margaret's three-day reign was so brief she could hardly be said to have given

*Cadwaladr's son Edwal Ewrch, hearing that the plague had ended, returned from self-exile in Brittany, claiming his father's right to British as well as Saxon thrones. But on arrival he found another such claimant already consecrated for what in future would be the English throne. The Celtic line of royalty returned to that throne only with the Tudor monarchs, beginning with Henry VII and ending with Elizabeth I.

** St. Margaret became Sovereign with her husband's death in battle. But she died of grief three days later, mourning the King as well as their eldest son, who also had died there.

the kingdom a matrimonial as well as Catholic lineage; still, that is what eventuated. One daughter became England's queen. Three sons in turn served as king, and by the death of the youngest, King David I, Scotland had become a daughter of the Roman Church. Though the substance remained Celtic, the form was Roman. What King and nobles, Archbishop and bishops were, that the people would be. If we may place the date for change as that of St. Margaret's accession as Sovereign (though death precluded her consecration) the end of Scotland's Celtic form of Church came in 1079.

Yet since the British Church had been the Celts' mother church, we may wonder why Morgan brings his *History of Britain* to an end in AD 700. He does not spell it out, but we can deduce the answer. It was not that Welsh Christianity had come to an end, for it had not, nor did the Welsh Church ever cease to be. What ended was the *continuity of establishment* of a British Church under a British monarch in its native land. The line of Cymric Kings of Britain had its start around 1,800 BC with the coming of Hu Isaacson Gadarn. The culture in time became Druidic, yet as one Body under one Head. Britain's conversion to Christ was synchronized in graceful fashion. The old Establishment converted to what, from the beginning, it had meant to be and thought it was. In coming to Christ, it kept its ancient form and customs. Its Kings and Pendragons remained the same. With its conversion, the Archdruids became the Establishment's Archbishops and its Druids the Christian priests. With the people baptized and confirmed in Christ, an Apostolic Establishment of *episcopoi, presbuteroi and laoi*, a priestly people, was given new life and grafted onto Christ. The Establishment was Celtic, Christian, Catholic and Apostolic. It came to an end, as an establishment, when there remained no Celtic British King or Crown.

The (Saxon) Church of England

The first generally accepted monarch of the Saxon people was Cerdic, king of the West Saxons, i.e. Wessex. Cerdic, who died in AD 535, is held to be ancestor of all the kings of a united England except for its dynasty of Danes. Cerdic, whose name is Celtic rather than Saxon as is that of his grandson, Cynric, is believed to have fought on several occasions against King Arthur including the decisive, three-day Battle of Badon. A curiosity concerning Cerdic is that his name has the same meaning and virtually the same pronunciation as Caradoc. There is further mystery in that a line of Anglo-Saxon kings, not related to Cerdic's (so far as we know) had become Christian, joined in marriage with the British royal line from a very early date. Through this line the House of Windsor is descended not only from King Arthur, but from Joseph of Arimathea. The Arimathean Joseph's son and daughter–Josephes and Anna–followed him to Britain, marrying into the royal line that one day would be the House of Tudor. Through these two (who were cousins of St. Mary the Virgin) the British monarchy can trace its line to the great King David, who, according to Jeremiah's prophecy (33:17) "shall never want a man to sit upon the throne of the House of Israel." It is believed that the English and Spanish Crowns continue as recipients of that promise. Both monarchs are descended from that Davidic line and, as shortly will be shown, appear to be entitled to consideration as bearing rule, in their generation, over the Israel of God.

Regardless of Cerdic's eminence as the Saxons' founding father, it is likely that Cadwaladr Sanctus–of the Tudor line we have referred to–was the first who joined the kingly bloodlines of both races. Cadwaladr was the King of Cambrian Britain by right of his father Cadwallo. He inherited the title of King of Wessex and Mercia through his mother Elditha, as the means by which her brother Penda's oath to Cadwallo could be fulfilled. Seven generations later the incumbent of Cadwaladr's line, Howell the Good, could bring his people, the British Celts, to join with Alfred's Saxons in war against the Danes. Though they remained as distinctly different peoples, by frequent royal intermarriage and the need for common defense (in this case against the Danes), they were in process of becoming one.

A Precis: Transition from Ancient British to Early English Church

Since our study is that of the Celtic Churches, and especially the Ancient British, the transition from British to English requires no more than a few observations based on the tables in Chapter 12. The decline in the number of British saints from the sixth century's one hundred forty-one to the seventh century's sixty-five, may be traced to three factors that need not be thought of as "negative." One is the way in which the Black Death reduced Britain's Celtic population. Another is the flight of many Britons to Brittany to avoid the plague, taking the same precaution as did Prince Edwal. This had happened also in the sixth century when Saints Brioch, Cadoc, Illtyd, Gildas, Kay, Paul de Leon, Teilo and Samson, along with many others, fled to Brittany. (Some, but not all, returned when that earlier plague had ended.) There came too the transfer of teachers and scholars from Wales to Ireland, described in Chapter 14. These saints were survivors, active in their labors but living elsewhere in their later years.

Notable in Table 4 of Chapter 12 is the Celtic churches' dedication–followed by the English Church's like devotion–to foreign missions which no amount of violence by invaders could quench. From the first century to the fifth, Christ's Great Commission was followed by the British and Gallican churches. As discerned in *The Book of Saints*, the growth in those years seems to have come at a modest rate, i.e., "arithmetically." Beginning with the fifth century, however, the churches of the British and Irish Celts and to a lesser degree though for a longer period the English, grew "exponentially." A surge of commitment to mission came in each church, the emphasis of which depended on the timing of peoples' conversion, their dedication and opportunities for service.

One notable fact is the large number of native-born saints in the Gallican areas of Europe, in large part a result of the British, Irish and English missions to the continent. Yet of 460 saints in those lands ranging from the Channel to the Baltic shores, 363 were found in the Gallican areas of France alone. We acknowledge the difficulty of determining who were Gallican Celts by birth and culture, as compared with Franks. If, however, our estimates are realistic, they may point to an hypothesis if not a conclusion that the Celts were not only the first to be converted to Christ, but appear to have been (if numbers count) a New Testament people whose relationship with God was comparable

*This proposal is offered only as a bit of speculation–grist for thought and discussion. The author has made no similar studies of other peoples whether in the Western or Eastern Churches, and will go no further than to point to the possibilities of unique purpose that God may have had for Celtic peoples–and may continue to have for the future.

with the Old Testament relationship between Yahweh and the Jews: "To whom much is given, of the same shall much be required."*

Table 8: Celtic Saints, 5th through 13th centuries; Saints of Celtic Mission lands: Switzerland, Low Countries, Germany, Scandinavia:

	British	Irish	Gallican	Non-Celtic North European peoples
Saints	311	328	363	97

A Witness to "The Truth Against the World"

It must be evident that in this story of the ancient Celtic Church, I have relied for facts and interpretation chiefly upon two men. The first, J.W. Taylor, was an English physician who, for many years, studied the Gallican Church and its introduction to Christ at the hands of his disciples. The second, R.W. Morgan, was a 19th century Welsh priest whose knowledge of the ancient Gallican Celts may have been unsurpassed, though his narrative ends at the point where their Crown passes from Celtic to Saxon hands. We are fortunate in the timing of his work for a summation of the British Church's oral history and tradition. Considering our culture's disrespect for history and tradition and the blizzard of material heaped before us by our Information Age, Morgan may be the last to have had access to the faint and receding voices of oral learning. Unlike the careful and methodical Taylor, Morgan is the protagonist—impulsive, loyal and bluff, like Simon Peter. We are fortunate for the diligence, honesty and devotion of both men. We end this chapter with a few excerpts from Morgan's introduction to the book he calls *A British View of British History*, written in 1857,

"Had no other monument of Kymric antiquity but the Code of British Laws of Molmutius (600 BC), which still forms the basis of our common or unwritten law, descended to us, we could not doubt that we were handling the index of a very high order. In such a code we possess not only the most splendid relic of pre-Roman Europe, but the key to all our British, as contradistinguished from Continental institutions. After perusing it, we stand amazed at the blindness which wanders groping for the origin of British rights and liberties in the swamps of the mother-land of feudal serfdom–Germany....We may safely contend that no part of the Continent could supply Britain with what it never possessed itself. British spirit and freedom are wholly of native British origin... The Continent is an aggregate of nations ruled on the despotic principle."

Morgan closes with a bit of patriotic pride and wry and humble humor,

"There must be something worth studying in the constitution and spirit of a race whom forty centuries have failed to destroy or demoralize...whose peasantry are now as distinguished for their freedom from crime as they were in past ages for their unbought patriotism and valor."

The Waxing/Waning Celt

It is insufferable that Queen Victoria's Prime Minister, Benjamin Disraeli, could refer to the Irish as "the last Stone Age people in Europe." We find sorrow in that Morgan could describe the Scottish, Cornish, Manx and Welsh–not only in other English-speaking lands but in their homelands–as "serfs, no, peasants, yes." The sign, "No Irish need apply," has been rewritten for other Celts in a Diaspora that has often been the land of their fathers. Yet the Celts were the first to come to Christ. They may have been the first to discover the need for freedom and responsibility in human institutions. In moral and spiritual realms, they taught the private accountability of each soul to God as well as the accountability on Earth of leaders to the led. Our coming chapters may depend on Celtic wisdom and experience while we look for unity in Christ's Church, in human families and in the soul of man.

꿍   Chapter 17   꿍

Celts, English, and the Church of Rome

With the possible exception of the Ethiopian Copts, the earliest of all peoples to become Christian—and in great numbers—were the Celts. Their conversion began in AD 37 when the Gospel came to Gaul and Britain. In a matter of months, Jesus' Death, Resurrection and Ascension were proclaimed in Provence, the Rhone Valley, the trade routes through Brittany to the Channel and the south and west of Britain. Those who came to Christ were evangelized by some of his nearest friends and kindred. Of the fifteen or sixteen who landed in Provence, most would bring fruit to God as castaways in Gaul. For historians the most convincing evidence of this earliest of Christian missions would be the fruits borne to those who continued to Britain in that year. Several of their converts carried the Word to peoples of Gaul, Germany, Switzerland and the Low Countries. Most died as martyrs before the First Century AD had ended. In Trier alone are the tombs of Germany's first three bishops—Maternus, Eucharius and Valerius. All three came from Britain, were martyred by AD 96 and are entombed in or near the cathedral Constantine built abutting the palace of his mother St. Helena, Empress of royal Caradoc's lineage.

From that point and through the Age of the Universal Councils there would be two very different Churches in the West. One was the smallest and the other the largest of seven patriarchates in the Holy Catholic Church. Rome's was more powerful than any in the East, where most of the Empire's population lived, where all seven Councils were held and where Jerusalem, Alexandria, Antioch, Constantinople and Athens became the seats of patriarchates headed by metropolitan bishops of equal rank with Rome's. The Celtic Churches were chiefly noted for scholarship and holiness of life–to which may be added an admirable lack of interest in power or high position.

Ultimately every branch of the Celtic Church was subsumed, for a time at least, into that of Rome. The joining of the Gallican Church with the Roman took place quite early, so that the Celtic Church could be seen only within the Gallic as lending a distinctive flavor. In the years after the Norman Conquest, the Breton and Irish Churches linked with Rome as well, still so to the present day. In the case of the Scottish, Welsh, Cornish and Manx Churches the linkage came gradually and indirectly, lasting only until the Reformation. At that time all four were withdrawn from Rome, with their younger half-sister–at its beginning a Roman Mission and later the Church of England–taking them under her wing and "doing the honors" on their behalf.

It is plainly understood that the British Church came to its end when the 2,400-year-old dynasty founded by Hu Gadarn was supplanted by an English Crown. Yet it remained. That is to say, the British Church was no more undone by a change of names than a bride would by surrendering her maiden name for her husband's. When the Britons' Church was given that name change in AD 664 by England's Chief of State, their Church did not cease to be but was linked in an unwilling, irregular and morganatic marriage by a Bretwalda–high king of the north Saxons–who had the authority to require it. By the same token, Henry VIII, who has been accused of *starting* the Church of England, was actually *ending* that body's standing as England's Established Church when he broke the tie with Rome that the regicidal Oswy had solicited and a Pope had sealed. As Head of that Church throughout his reign, Henry had the same obligation as every Catholic monarch to deal with a papacy that not only bore spiritual authority but was at the same time a *de facto* foreign power with secular and temporal interests inimical to those of his realm. Henry's position was strengthened by the fact that among England's ranking families the Tudors were the sole remnant of the royal Celts. Things remained that way, for by breaking with Rome and re-establishing the ancient *British* Church as the Reformed (and still Catholic) Church of *England*, the monarch was regularizing a marriage that he, as Head of both Churches, had authority to do.

In terms of the divine standard, we can hold that the two were one and seamless from the start. Given eyes to see, we can believe that those "genes" within the English Church that originated in the Jerusalem Church were so dominant as to give the Church of England, even to the latest generation, the traits of social and spiritual character found in those of Jesus' disciples who won the Celts to Christ. Even so, their unique pattern of social identity could hardly have been imparted in a single generation. Its presence at the time of their conversion must hinge on the fact that, many centuries earlier, the Celts had come to share the same sense of personhood the Jews already had. This was a social pattern that by the Reformation years would characterize virtually all of northern Europe. The remaining peoples of the early Church–including those of East as well as West–appear to have been unable or unwilling to consider the validity of anything but the corporal (i.e., the tribal) identity that characterizes primitive peoples and those cultures still in a process of individuation. We know that the Greeks had become inner-directed by the time of their Golden Age. Yet their social character had long since reverted to the tribal mentality that, from the beginnings of our race, had occupied all but the Jews, Israelites and Celts.* Since the differences between the tribal and individual formats are not germane to our immediate concern or that of this work, let it be said that the individuating form of character found from the early Renaissance and onward in what would become the Protestants' portion of Europe cannot be considered as heretical, for it had characterized the Jews more than two thousand years before

---

*As mentioned elsewhere, this format may have included Phoenicians and Arabs.

the Reformation. Moreover, the change in format (given around 600 BC) came by divine command to Jeremiah and Ezekiel. (The fact of that change and an analysis of its significance has been featured in an earlier work of the author.*) What must now be noted is that the Celts, in a way we can only guess at, had developed an individuated character of their own.

Celts' Cross-Grain Connection with the Roman Church

Paradoxically, most Celts today may be members of the Roman Catholic Church. Among those living on the Continent, this is because their forebears lived there all along. Those in northern Spain and Gaul, like others in the Roman Church, were subject to a gradual enlargement of doctrine and discipline from the time of Leo the Great and Gregory the Great, a change that in later years developed in a way that was disparaged in advance by these Popes (the only "Greats") and was never accepted or followed by any other church of the Catholic and Apostolic Tradition. Generally the Roman Church's Celtic members have "gone along with" its enlargement of claims regarding faith and order as well as the papacy itself. They make good and loyal followers, and may have accepted Rome's additions to dogma by simplicity of heart and sense of obligation. Yet despite their willingness to do so, we have no reason to regard those Celts in France, Spain and the transalpine lands as "less the Celt" because of their having accepted what Protestants might regard as a narrowing of the individual's freedom.

The Bad Hand Dealt the Irish

The question of the Irish Catholics is an altogether different matter. Here are a people more purely Celt than others in Britain *or* on the Continent. Why would they, valuing personal freedom and independence, continue as Roman Catholics—and as faithful and devout as any to be found? Any worldly answer must include resentment for centuries of mistreatment by the Norman English. The "tip of the iceberg" bespeaks an enormous weight beneath the surface—a bulk that

---

*Harvey, Robert C., *The Restless Heart: Breaking the Cycle of Social Identity*, William B. Eerdmans Co., Grand Rapids, 1973, 216 pp.

would take centuries to melt. The fateful action dates from a generation or so after the Norman Conquest when the first and only English Pope found reason to strengthen the hand of England's ruler, Henry II. That Pope, Hadrian IV, sought an alignment with the English *vis a vis* the Continental monarchs, between whom there could be little trust and in the face of open hatred for his person by the commune that dominated Rome's unruly people.

To further his objectives, the Pope conferred upon King Henry the privilege of incorporating all of Ireland as a feudal fief held by the English Crown. This arrangement allowed a Norman gentry to be imposed upon the Irish as governors of the people and as stewards having complete control of land use. When this took place, England was still recovering from a civil war that came after the Conqueror's death because of enmity among his sons and conflicts of loyalty among barons of his Realm. Pope Hadrian could not know that the king's intent had been to dominate the Church and hold the papacy at a distance. Henry II was the king whose disappointment with Thomas Becket in later years would lead to the Archbishop's assassination. Still later came such terrible misrule by his sons that a Magna Carta would be drafted to provide a limit on kingly and papal power. But to wish and hope, for the Irish, what would take many centuries for the middle and lower classes of England to win for themselves, was futile. What came to the Irish as a consequece of this betrayal is one of history's great tragedies. The Catholic religion held the Irish together, but their co-religionists took advantage of their weakness. The tribal Law of Retaliation returned to the fore when injustice and exploitation had become part of the daily scene.

Brythonic Celts–Gallicans and Britons

Despite their later ties with the Roman Church, the distinctly Celtic portions of that Church have been a breed apart. We have earlier noted the affinity of the British for the Pelagianism that appears to have been an outgrowth of Druidic teachings on human freedom. It is likely that Janssenist views–emphasizing the mercy of God as against the severity found in such as Augustine, Calvin and the Spanish Inquisition–had sufficient appeal for Celtic elements in the Gallican Church to lead, one day, to their withdrawal from Rome. One such parting took place in the 19th century with the breaking away of the Old Catholics centered in Utrecht. A similar departure came later with the excommunication of Latin-rite Catholics along with their Archbishop, the late Rene Lefebvre. They may have been conscious of the absolutes implied in the Druids' motto, "The Truth against the world." They may have recalled, too, the slogan of the Trojan Celts, "The Country is above the King." For such a mentality, Holy Reason would seem to require that a Church having Jesus' guarantee of protection must be above its human leaders. All men are sinners. None is above the Law.

Searching for a Celtic Pope

The election of John Paul II as the 267th Patriarch of Rome in the succession of Peter and Paul was an agreeable surprise to many. He was the first Slav to reach the papal office and the first non-Italian since Hadrian VI. With one notable exception, this Hadrian may have been the first and only Celt. It can hardly fail to disappoint those who have a love of Celtic history and tradition that this earliest of peoples to come to Christ has had scant representation in the papal office. Not only have no Irish "made it," there may have been no *Celts* except for Lleyn [Linus], the Welshman who served as Bishop of Rome. He is remembered as the son of Caradoc, brother-in-law of St. Paul's half-brother Pudens and immediate successor to the Apostles Peter and Paul. None of the eighteen French popes appear to have been Celts nor were the two Spanish popes. The one Celtic possibility besides St. Linus is the pope just referred to–Hadrian VI, the son of a carpenter in Utrecht and, after his father's death, cared for by the Brethren of the Common Life, a community associated with the inner life of the Spirit and the New Learning. Prior to his election to the papacy, he served as Cardinal Bishop of Utrecht. Yet his earlier service had made him Inquisitor for Aragon, Navarre, Castile and Leon in Spain. He was among the first to condemn Martin Luther's teachings, yet during his two years as Pope was utterly helpless in dealing with the crisis before his Church. It is quite possible that a pragmatic majority in the College of Cardinals held before themselves the example of this pope's ineptitude–while having also in mind the other extreme, the ebullient Columbanus, a zealot among saints, openly critical of popes and ever an advocate of reform. Behind the scenes may have been an unvoiced consensus that it was better that Celtic Christians serve as parish priests, monks, nuns and lay folk in the pews.

Celts' Infusion of Social Traits into English Church and People

If our concern is for lasting influence, we can find satisfaction in the extent to which English Christianity was influenced by the Celts' teaching and by their manner of life and thought. By growing to cultural and spiritual maturity in a land steeped in the Celtic mindset, the English became–and have remained–a very different people than their Saxon counterparts on the Continent. The ingraining goes back to England's earliest centuries and distinguishes the Anglo-Saxon British from peoples on the Continent whether Catholic, Protestant or "post-Christian." An explanation may not be hard to find.

In an introductory essay to *Anglicanism*, (Society for Promoting Christian Knowledge, 1962) co-edited with Frank Leslie Cross, Paul Elmer More points to one feature that distinguishes Anglican (or English) religion from that of the Catholic and Protestant Churches of Western Europe. A feature they share with Orthodox Christians of the East, the Anglicans have, in their religious life, been concerned primarily with *observance*, whereas the concern of other Western churches has been with *doctrine*.* Rather than theorize, we may cite what seems to be a widespread consensus that acknowledges a notable difference in thought and decision as between the English Reformers and Continental theologians on either side of the great 16th Century Divide. The thought and scholarship of Continental scholars tended to be cerebral and very carefully and logically stated. This was true of their best and finest–the Italians' Thomas Aquinas, France's Calvin, the Germans' Luther and Melancthon and the Swiss' Zwingli. To

---

* *Nota bene*: this has nothing to do with the issue of *faith* versus *works*.

people such as these and those they wrote for, the English scholars, like their people, were hard to fathom. They seemed averse to making clear distinctions. In this they were like the Jews, who as is well known, never gave thought to the subject of theology until driven to it by Christian theologians. Yet the century itself had been one of intellectual ferment, and people on both sides of the Channel were familiar with the issues involved in the Reformation. Even so, despite the issues and the intensity of interest, there was little of quality or character coming from the pens of English theologians, and few could even say who those men might be, much less describe their thinking. The likeliest would be Richard Hooker, a comparatively obscure parish priest. But even Hooker only theologized in one corner of the arena. His work on ecclesiastical polity dealt with an important, but only one, part of the Church's doctrine of salvation.

There is one simple explanation for this estimate of the English and of Anglican religion. As members of a nationally established Church, they were not eager to be drawn into the niceties of definition. What they needed were definitions broad enough to allow a *catholicity* that could accommodate in One Church all who accepted Jesus Christ as Lord. What they sought, in the matter of doctrine *and* observance, was to hold fast to all that had been believed and practiced during the years when the Church was undivided, including those years when the Holy Spirit, working through the General Councils, could be counted on to guide his Church into what was right, good and true. In addition, the English churchmen offered a concession to those non-conformists at home as well as to Continental Protestants whose conversion and learning had come at the hands of Celtic missionaries from Britain and Ireland. This concession was to require, as personally necessary to salvation, no more than what was stated in the Creeds and proven in the canonical Scriptures of the Old and New Testaments.

By comparison with this position, the 16th Century Churches of the Continent, whether Catholic or Protestant, became "confessing" or "confessional" bodies. They fenced themselves in with definitions as the Spirit seemed to be guiding *each one*. This included careful statements as to what they believed *and* what they did *not* believe. In so doing they made themselves exclusive rather than inclusive and particularist rather than universal. Protestants gave no credence to what the Romans called Tradition, instead requiring that nothing be taught or believed except what could be demonstrated in the Bible. The Romans not only gave equal authority to Church *and* Bible, but also extended the authority of Tradition to include the findings of Councils called by the Roman Church for its own members. All of this followed the last of the General Councils in AD 787, and most came after Rome's break with the Eastern Churches in AD 1054. What this signifies is that, unlike other churches at the time, the Roman Church possessed a Doctrine of Development to which it alone was privy. Its implications could only be that the Holy Spirit's guidance of the Church has included a great deal of Revelation in addition to what had been made known in Christ and summed up in Law and Gospel. Other branches of the Church Universal have held, since early times, that the *data* of Revelation included all of God's Mighty Acts ending with Jesus' Ascension and the Pentecost that followed, with one brief exception. This involved a period of waiting until the Jews could decide officially whether to accept Jesus as their Messiah. (They had to be given the benefit of the doubt.) The period ended with visions given by the Risen Lord to Peter, Paul and other disciples–and authenticated at the Council of Jerusalem. There it was accepted and proclaimed that the Church's mission was to bring all men to Christ–Jews as well as Gentiles.

At this point the Churches other than Rome's held that Christ's Vicar on earth was God the Holy Spirit. They accepted that the content of Revelation was limited to what God had given to the first generation of the Church plus those in the second generation who had been disciples of the first and could certify to their witness. The Books were finally closed with the establishing of a Canon of New Testament Scripture. The Spirit's guidance would lead to the surest understanding of what had been revealed in Christ and likewise would provide for grace to live in accordance with that Word. Those other Churches, however, had grave reservations about Rome's Doctrine of Development because of the implications of what Jesus said of the Holy Spirit in John 16:13, "(He) shall not speak of (i.e., from) himself, but whatsoever he shall hear that shall he speak, and he will (show) you things to come." That "hearing" could only come from consultation with the Father and the Son. It would appear that as Jesus humbled himself to take the form of a Servant, the Spirit likewise humbles himself to keep our attention focused away from him and on the Lord and Master who continues to be the Way, the Life and the Truth–and who alone can lead us to the Father.

The Nature of Jews' Influence on the Celts

Two points remain to be made about the Celts' contribution to the character and spirituality of the English Church. One is to note the abstraction that is a necessary concomitant to the theologizing of the Continental churches. The Old Testament Scriptures given by God and preserved by the Jews were anything but abstract. Neither did the Celts find delight in abstraction. Both peoples–the Celts and the Jews–had been given instincts, language and a capacity for worship and creative artistry that was richly productive, vibrant and alive. Along with the Eastern Christians, they internalized–by their *observance* in worship the living, breathing words of Scripture.

The second point has to do with the individualism we have noted in the Celtic character. Bede's description of the Celts were a classic statement of the fact, and of its linkage with what–a thousand years later–would be called evangelical Christianity. Celtic religion was not so much sacramental as mystical. Its focus was on the Bible rather than on a hierarchical Church. As is the case with an already-individuated people, the Celts whom Bede observed had found that the Scriptures are sufficient in themselves for the attainment of self-knowledge and identification with a community of faith. A brief quote from More's introduction to *Anglicanism* imputes to the English a grace that seems almost certainly to have been an attribute observed in their Celtic teachers:

"(If) there is any outstanding note of the English temper, it is a humility of awe before the divine mysteries of faith and a recognition of the incompetence of language to define the ultimate paradox of experience."

Concerning what has been summed up here, there can be no question of the catholicity of Celtic religion. We must admit to its attention to the mystical–as compared with the sacramental–and its focus on the individual rather than tribal which points to a "Protestant" outlook as compared to a "Catholic." Yet we cannot jump to conclusions, for these seeming opposites–mystical/sacramental, Protestant/Catholic and individual/tribal are concomitants of one another. They are as intimately related as the two sides of a coin. In the case of what More calls a "humility of awe," what is it but *holy fear*, quite properly one of the Spirit's sevenfold gifts?

The Search for Links between Celts, Jews and Ten Lost Tribes

Several related questions come eagerly to mind. How could the Celts have obtained an individualist social character if not from the Jews? On what occasions in ancient times could they have been in contact with–and learned from–Jews, Israelites, even members of the Ten Lost Tribes? Considering that a connection between Jews and Celts has been one of our concerns from the first, I can only say that throughout the months and years required for the current task, the question has gone unanswered. How did the Celts come to know so much about Jewish religion–and so early? It would have been an enormous factor in their readiness for the Gospel when it came. Aside from the few clues here reported–such as the coming of Jeremiah to Ireland and traditions associated with the Stone of Scone–I have found nothing whatsoever. Actually, it could be described as "less than nothing," for recent research on the Ten Lost Tribes indicates that traces of nine tribes have been found scattered across the Asian Continent from Persia to China. These tribal remnants are few and remote. They consist of little more than names of ancient memory and a few habits of family observance. Otherwise there has been an assimilation with neighbors. Only the tribe of Asher is unheard from.

Yet, putting pieces together of things already known, I have found one piece so compelling that it can be treated as *the* answer until something more convincing comes our way. We know that after their arrival in Britain, and for some centuries before their conversion, the Druids conducted their studies in Greek. During those years they arrived at a theology so adaptable to that proclaimed by the Jerusalem Church that the peoples of Britain and Ireland came to Christ in an almost bloodless conversion. I am ready to believe that the Celts' preparation for the Gospel may have taken place with no contact with Jews except for a few chance meetings that made the Greek Septuagint available to Druidic scholars. This could have happened as early as 300 BC, the date ascribed to its translation from the Hebrew by seventy-two rabbis at Alexandria. In those years there were Druids in many parts of the Mediterranean basin as well as the Near East. Likewise we know there were Jewish scholars and synagogues in those same times and places. In such a setting, Druidic scholars could have made their own copies of a Septuagint that achieved its final form around 125 BC. Making an "educated guess," the recipient could have been the famous Abaris who was welcomed throughout the Mediterranean world and, because of his facility with language and philosophy, invited to speak in many cities. He became legendary for the colorful trousers and tartans he wore, the bow and arrows slung at all times at his side, and above all for the compass needle by which he guided himself in his travels. However the Septuagint may have arrived in Britain, there is no question as to availability, and it would account for the Druids' understanding of God, of their acceptance of the Hebrews' understanding of sin and redemption and the promise of salvation yet to come.

We may rightly ask how Scripture alone—without the benefit of a mediating and teaching cult—could have contributed to the Celts' transformation from a tribal mentality to the individualism we have found to be present at their time of conversion. Druidism *was* their cult. The Greek Old Testament—or even their knowledge of it by recitation—became their sourcebook. The knowledge of the Law and Prophets and such of the Writings as were available became a basis for their study, meditation and worship. Their form of worship could have been that practiced by the Jews since their Babylonian Captivity and used in Synagogues wherever Jews could be found. The inner-direction that went with their individualism came with their use of the form of worship that in Christianity is called the Divine Office—whether in its Sevenfold Monastic Form or in a congregation's twofold use as Morning and Evening Prayer. The inner-direction would have come when the tribal *shame culture* changed to a *guilt culture* by the implanting in individuals of a conscience whereby each person could guide his conduct based on a personal, one-to-One relationship with the God revealed in Holy Scripture. The promise given to Jeremiah (Chapter 31:33,34) may be sufficient explanation for the moment:

> "This shall be the covenant that I will make with the house of Israel; After those days, saith the Lord, I will put my Law in their inward parts, and write it in their hearts; and will be their God and they shall be my people. And they shall teach no more every man his neighbor, saying, Know the Lord ; for they shall all know me, from the least of them unto the greatest of them, saith the Lord; for I will forgive their iniquity, and I will remember their sin no more."

What is implied here is the startling promise that those who participate in the synagogue worship or the Daily (or weekly) Office will learn enough *from* God *about* God to have that knowledge become the substance of the inner conscience he consults. If we appreciate that the Roman Church's tribal model of identity was kept intact by keeping the laity from having knowledge of the Bible, we can understand not only *why* the privatizing model was discouraged, but *how*. The proof of the connection between Bible-reading and personal identity has become evident throughout the Roman Church in the years since Vatican II. It seems simplistic to say this, and even prejudicial (though I deny such intent), but if the lay person is unable to know what God's will is by reading it in Scripture, he must hear it from a priest at Mass, a nun at school or a parent in the home. The failure to become inner-directed will result in the individual's governing of self mainly through fear of public shame rather than of private guilt.

While the purpose of our closing chapters is to speak of Celtic influence during the Medieval and Reformation years, I must tell of a special recognition accorded the British Church prior to the Reformation. Fifty years into the Avignon Exile, three emergency councils were called in short succession–at Pisa in 1421, at Constance in 1423 and at Siena in 1427. Their purpose was to end the disruptive papal schism and restore the proper papal line–which finally they did. In the process, however, an old jealousy surfaced. The French and Spanish Churches were larger than the British, and their bishops were offended that because the British Church was senior to all others its bishops had been entitled to privileges and courtesies not accorded any others. Three times this protocol was challenged by the French and Spanish, both of whom insisted that their churches had been the first. The challenge came with the convening at each of the three councils, and on each occasion the protocol was reconsidered and upheld by a vote of all the bishops. Their declaration was the same each time that "the British Church took precedence of all other Churches, being founded by Joseph of Arimathea immediately after the Passion of Christ." After the third such occasion the challenge was never raised again.

Yet regrettably, since the British Church broke with Rome that claim has never ceased to be raised by people in some way connected with the Roman cause and using tactics that will not stand the light of day. Fortunately Rome's finest historians have long since accorded the historical precedence to the British Church. These include Cardinals Baronius and Alford, Fr. Parsons and Cressy, Polydore Virgil and Pope Pius XI–all prominent in the years since Britain's break with their Church. Yet while these men spoke truly and rightly, they tend to be forgotten. The revisionists, by comparison, repeat their claims so often that many people assume falsehoods to be true. Fortunately a fine and scholarly work was published by Little, Brown (New York) in 1969. *The Secret Archives of the Vatican*, by Luisa Ambrosini, a prominent Italian lawyer, who was given a free range of inquiry, and the book is without imprimaturs. In an eleven page chapter on Gregory I she devoted five pages to Joseph of Arimathaea, Glastonbury traditions and the Early

British Church. We are grateful to the Vatican for allowing this good work—and thankful that Roman Catholics can have their Celtic roots thus recognized by their Church.

❧ Notes ❧

Chapter 1: Traditions of the Early British Church

1. Bede, *A History of the English Church & People*, I-4, V-24, Penguin, (New York, 1956).
2. Richard W. Morgan, *St. Paul in Britain*, Covenant, (London, 1860), p. 108ff.
3. George F. Jowett, *The Drama of the Lost Disciples*, Covenant, (London, 1980), p. 174 ff.
4. Jowett, p. 192 ff.
5. Jowett, p. 168 ff.
6. Jowett, p. 158-9.
7. Lionel S. Lewis, *St. Joseph of Arimathea at Glastonbury*, James Clarke, (Cambridge, 1922), pp. 129- 141.
8. Jowett, p. 82.
9. Lewis, p. 127.
10. Lewis, p. 127.
11. Lewis, p. 128.
12. John W. Taylor, *The Coming of the Saints*, Covenant, (London, 1969), pp. 61-62, 158.
13. Lewis, p. 128.
14. Taylor, pp. 121-2.
15. Lewis, pp. 92-111.
16. Lewis, pp. 92-111.
17. Lewis, Chapters 1 & 2.
18. Taylor, p. 143 ff.
19. Lewis, pp. 66-67.
20. Lewis, quoting *Epistolae ad Gregorium Papam*, p. 23.

21. E. Raymond Capt, *The Traditions of Glastonbury*, Artisan Publishers, (Muskogee, OK, 1983), p. 55.
22. George F. Jowett, *The Drama of the Lost Disciples*, Covenant, (London, 1980), p. 76.
23. Jowett, p. 76.
24. Lewis, pp. 45-66.

Chapter 3: Burgeoning Skills, Natural Religion

1. *National Geographic Magazine*, Vol. 172, No. 6, December, 1987.
2. Tim Severin, *The Brendan Voyage*, McGraw-Hill, (New York, 1978).
3. Walter Seaman, *Far Above the Stars*, CHREST Foundation, (Bexhill), pp. 45-52.
4. N. S. Hecht, *The Great Pyramid*, Covenant, (London, 1950).
5. Thomas Foster, *Great Pyramid Power*, Acacia, (Blackburn, Australia, 1988), p. 28.
6. David Davidson, *The Great Pyramid: Its Divine Message*, Williams & Norgate, (London,1976).
7. Janet & Colin Bord, *Mysterious Britain*, Grenada, (London, 1974), p. 182 ff.
8. Gerhard Herm, *The Celts*, St. Martin's Press, (New York, 1976), p. 35.
9. John Matthews, *A Glastonbury Reader*, Aquarian Press, (London, 1991), p. 128.
10. Matthews, pp. 117-143.
11. Matthews, p. 130.
12. R. James Montague, *The Apocryphal New Testament*, Oxford, 1924, p. 48, (Book of James).
13. Elizabeth C. Prophet, *The Lost Years of Jesus*, Summit University Press, (Livingston, MT, 1984), p.401.

Chapter 4: The Readying of the Soil

1. Dom Gregory Dix, *Jew and Greek,* Dacre Press, 1955.

Chapter 5: The Firming of the Celts

1. Martin Gilbert, *The Atlas of Jewish History*, Dorset Press, (New York, 1976), pp. 25, 26.

2. Gerhard Herm, *The Celts*, St. Martin's Press, (New York, 1976), pp. 85-91.
3. Herm, p. 93.
4. Herm, pp. 92-98.
5. Sargon II's black obelisk boasting of commerce with Britain.
6. Rodney Castleden, *The Stonehenge People*, Routledge, (Oxford, 1987), p. 131.
7. Castleden, p.119.
8. Herm, pp. 86, 88-89.
9. Herm, p. 97.
10 Herm, p. 98.
11. Rev. W. M. N. Milner, *The Royal House of Britain: An Enduring Dynasty*, Covenant, (London, 1964), Part I.
12. Thomas Foster, *Britain's Royal Throne*, Covenant, (London, 1993), pp. 54-56.

Chapter 6: Druidic Learning and Religion

1. Isabel H. Elder, *Celt, Druid and Culdee*, Covenant, (London, 1962), p. 58.
2. Richard W. Morgan, *St. Paul in Britain*, Covenant, (London, 1860), p. 23.
3. Morgan, *St. Paul in Britain*, p. 25.
4. Morgan, *St. Paul in Britain*, pp. 24, 26.
5. Richard W. Morgan, *History of Britain from the Flood to AD 700*, Covenant, (London, 1857), pp. 107, 129-131.
6. Morgan, *St. Paul in Britain*, p. 25.
7. Morgan, *St. Paul in Britain*, pp. 23-24.
8. Elder, pp. 66-68.
9. Elder, p. 61.
10. William Butler Yeats, *The Second Coming*, found in *Michael Robartes and the Dancer*, Irish University Press, 1970.
11. Eusebius, *The History of the Church: From Christ to Constantine*, Penguin, (New York, 1990), Book I, Chapter 4 (paraphrase).
12. Morgan, *St. Paul in Britain*, p. 22.
13. W. A. Salmon, *Churches and Royal Patronage*, D. Brown & Sons, 1983, p. 64.
14. John St. Aubin, *St. Michael's Mount*, Guidebook, 1978, pp. 4 & 5.

Chapter 7: The Jerusalem Church in Gaul

1. Herbert Danby, *The Mishnah*, Oxford University Press, 1933, App. III, pp. 799, 800.
2. Frederic Mistral, *Mirèio: A Provençal Poem*, published 1859, citing Cardinal Cesar Baronius.
3. Lionel S. Lewis, *St. Joseph of Arimathea at Glastonbury*, James Clarke, (Cambridge, 1922), pp. 23-35.
4. E. Raymond Capt, *The Traditions of Glastonbury*, Artisan Publishers, (Muskogee, OK, 1983), p. 41.
5. Richard W, Morgan, *St. Paul in Britain*, Covenant, (London, 1860), p. 76.
6. John W. Taylor, *The Coming of the Saints*, Covenant, (London, 1969), p. 140.
7. Taylor, p. 89.
8. Taylor, pp. 204, 205.
9   Zacchaeus' as Bishop of Caesarea or Antioch.
10. Many others in Chapter 8 chronicled in Taylor's *The Coming of the Saints*.
11. Taylor, pp. 80-101.
12. Taylor, p. 240.
13. Taylor, p. 239.
14. Taylor, p. 88.
15. Taylor, p. 98.

Chapter 8: The Jerusalem Missionary Church

1. John W. Taylor, *The Coming of the Saints*, Covenant, (London, 1969), p. 84.
2. Taylor, p. 85.
3. Taylor, p. 83.
4. Taylor, pp. 83, 84.
5. Taylor, p. 2, 19.
6   Taylor, p. 91.
7. Taylor, pp. 89-91.
8. Taylor, pp. 95, 99, 100.
9. Taylor, pp. 185, 186.
10. Taylor, p. 187.

11. Taylor, pp. 61, 62, 207, 209.
12. George F. Jowett, *The Drama of the Lost Disciples*, Covenant, (London, 1980), p. 218.
13. Taylor, p. 208.
14. Bede, *The Book of Saints*, Third Edition, MacMillan, NYC, 1934, p. 260.
15. Lionel S. Lewis, *St. Joseph of Arimathea at Glastonbury*, James Clarke, (Cambridge, 1922), p. 128.

Chapter 9: Saints in Caesar's Household

1. Henry Bettenson, *Documents of the Christian Church*, Oxford University Press, 1947, p. 3.
2. Furneaux, Tacitus' *Annales* ad. loc., cited in Bettenson *Documents* above.
3. Richard W. Morgan, *St. Paul in Britain*, Covenant, (London, 1860).
4. Lionel S. Lewis, *St. Joseph of Arimathea at Glastonbury*, James Clarke, (Cambridge, 1922).
5. C.C. Dobson, *The Face of Christ*, Centenary Press, (London, 1933).
6. Morgan, p. 61.
7. Lewis, p. 119.
8. Lewis, p. 118.
9. Cardinal Baronius on Pudens' home.
10. Richard Parsons on same.
11 Bettenson, p. 97.
12. Clement on Linus.
13. Apostolic Constitution on Peter, Paul, etc., of Asia.
14. Paul entombed with Lear in the Pudens' family plot.
15. Morgan, p. 49,50.
16. Morgan, p. 48.
17. Morgan, p. 49.
18. Morgan, p. 49.

Chapter 10: British and Gallican Churches, the Early Years

1. John W. Taylor, *The Coming of the Saints*, Covenant, (London, 1969).
2. Lionel S. Lewis, *St. Joseph of Arimathea at Glastonbury*, James Clarke, (Cambridge, 1922).

3. Gladys Taylor, *Our Neglected Heritage*, Volume 1, Covenant, (London, 1969).
4. Lewis, *St. Joseph of Arimathea at Glastonbury*.
5. E. Raymond Capt, *The Traditions of Glastonbury*, Artisan Publishers, (Muskogee, OK, 1983).

Chapter 11: British and Gallican Churches, the Early Years (continued)

1. William Henry Black, F.S.A, *Observations on the Hitherto Unnoticed Expedition of the Emperor Augustus into Britain*, February 9, 1871.
2. Dio Cassius, *Roman History*, Loeb Classical Library, 1925.
3. Dio Cassius, *Roman History*.
4. Publius Cornelius Tacitus, *The Life of Agricola,* Ginn and Co., (New York, 1900).
5. Richard W, Morgan, *St. Paul in Britain*, Covenant, (London, 1860).
6. Tacitus, *The Life of Agricola*.
7. Tacitus, *The Life of Agricola*.
8. Tacitus, *The Life of Agricola*.
9. *Encyclopedia Britannica*, 11th Edition, Encyclopedia Britannica Company, 1911.
10. Tacitus, *The Life of Agricola*.
11. Morgan, *St. Paul in Britain*.
12. Morgan, *St. Paul in Britain*.
13. Morgan, *St. Paul in Britain*.
14. Bede, *A History of the English Church & People*, I-4, V-24, Penguin, (New York, 1956).
15. Gildas Badonicus, *On the Ruin of Britain*, Phillimore, 1978.
16. Morgan, *St. Paul in Britain*.
17. John W. Taylor, *The Coming of the Saints*, Covenant, (London, 1969), pp. 168, 169.
18. Gildas Badonicus, *On the Ruin of Britain*, Phillimore, 1978.

Chapter 12: A Cloud of Witnesses

1. Andrew Louth, *Early Christian Writings: The Apostolic Fathers*, Penguin, (New York, 1987).
2. Louth, *Early Christian Writings*.
3. Louth, *Early Christian Writings*.

4. Eusebius, *The History of the Church: From Christ to Constantine*, Penguin, (New York, 1990).

5. Eusebius, *The History.*

6. Athanasius, *Early Christian Lives*, Penguin, (New York, 1987).

7. Athanasius, *Early Christian Lives.*

8. Athanasius, *Early Christian Lives.*

9. Athanasius, *Early Christian Lives.*

10. Robert Payne, *The Fathers of the Western Church*, Viking Press, (New York, 1951).

11 Payne, *The Fathers of the Western Church.*

12. Payne, *The Fathers of the Western Church.*

13. Payne, *The Fathers of the Western Church.*

14. Payne, *The Fathers of the Western Church.*

15. Payne, *The Fathers of the Western Church.*

16. Louth, *Early Christian Writings.*

17. Hermias Sozomen, *Ecclesiastical History*, Kessinger Publishing.

18. Theodoret, *The Ecclesiastical History of Theodoret*, Kessinger Publishing.

19. Palladius of Helenopolis, *The Lausiac History of Palladius*, 1967.

20. William Bright, *Chapters of Early English Church History*, Kessinger Publications, 1986.

21. Bright, *Chapters of Early English Church History.*

22. Gildas Badonicus, *On the Ruin of Britain*, Phillimore, 1978.

23. Badonicus, *On the Ruin of Britain.*

24. Michael Alford, *Fides Regia Britannica sive Annales Ecclesiae Britannicae*, Luttich, 1663.

25. Caesare Baronius, *Annales Ecclesiastici*, Barri-Ducis, 1869.

26. Baronius.

27. Baronius.

28. Baronius.

29. Baronius.

30. Lionel S. Lewis, *St. Joseph of Arimathea at Glastonbury*, James Clarke, (Cambridge, 1922).

31. Lewis, *St. Joseph of Arimathea.*

32. Lewis, *St. Joseph of Arimathea.*

33. Lewis, *St. Joseph of Arimathea.*

34. Lewis, *St. Joseph of Arimathea.*

35. Lewis, *St. Joseph of Arimathea.*

36. Lewis, *St. Joseph of Arimathea.*

37. Lewis, *St. Joseph of Arimathea.*
38. Lewis, *St. Joseph of Arimathea.*
39. Lewis, *St. Joseph of Arimathea.*
40. Bede, *The Book of Saints,* Third Edition, MacMillan, NYC, 1934, p. 260.
41. Lewis, *St. Joseph of Arimathea.*
42. Lewis, *St. Joseph of Arimathea.*
43. Lewis, *St. Joseph of Arimathea.*
44. Lewis, *St. Joseph of Arimathea.*
45. Lewis, *St. Joseph of Arimathea.*
46. Lewis, *St. Joseph of Arimathea.*
47. Lewis, *St. Joseph of Arimathea.*

Chapter 14: Triumphs of the Welsh: The Age of Patrick and Arthur

1. Richard W. Morgan, *St. Paul in Britain,* Covenant, (London, 1860).
2. Bede, *A History of the English Church & People,* I-4, V-24, Penguin, (New York, 1956).

Chapter 15: What Happened at Whitby

1. Bede, *A History of the English Church & People,* I-4, V-24, Penguin, (New York, 1956).
2. Bede.
3. Bede.
4. Bede.
5. Richard W. Morgan *History of Britain from the Flood to AD 700,* Covenant, (London, 1857).
6. Morgan, *History of Britain.*
7. Morgan, *History of Britain.*
8. Morgan, *History of Britain.*
9. Morgan, *History of Britain.*

Chapter 16: Waxing Saxon, Waning Celt

1. Richard Overy, *The "Times" History of the World: The Ultimate Work of Historical Reference*, Hammond's Chart (insert), Harper Collins, (London, 1999).
2. Eusebius, *The History of the Church: From Christ to Constantine*, Penguin, (New York, 1990).
3. Richard W. Morgan, *History of Britain from the Flood to AD 700*, Covenant, (London, 1857).

⌘ Index ⌘

BRITAIN

Colchester

WALES

St. David's

St. Alban's

Caerleon

London

St. Donat's

Canterbury

Glastonbury

Chichester

CORNWALL

ENGLISH CHANNEL

River Seine

Paris

Morlais

Ste. Anne-la-Palue

River Loire

Tours

Poitiers

GAUL

ATLANTIC OCEAN

Rocamadour

Bordeaux

River Garonne

Toulouse

PYRENEES

River A...

Carcassone

Narbon...